The structure of this book and its relationship to developmental stages

5 yrs | 9 yrs | 13 yrs

1. The importance of language
- Language, learning, experience, and development. Language and relationships
- The role of the teacher

2. The early years in school
- Children with difficulties. Motivation. Use of questions. Sequencing & recording

3. The growth of language and reading
- The language—experience approach. Readiness and reading ability. Skill development. Choice

4. The organization of the infant classroom
- Organization. Working outdoors. Daily routines. Structuring workcards

5. Developing talk
- The importance of talk. Language of learning. Practical applications

6. Talk into writing
- Listening and auditory skills
- Interview techniques and assignments
- Rough drafts and fair copies

7. Writing
- Style and position. Stages of children's writing
- Writing in the infant years
- Writing in the junior and middle years

Handwriting
- Handwriting in the junior years

Communication
- Modes of writing
- Marking and spelling. Techniques. Writing for others

8. Study skills

Extended reading skills

Comprehension skills

Dictionary and library skills. Reading rates

9. Thematic work

Consideration of a balanced curriculum. Using books and collating information

10. Organization of the junior classroom

Organization of areas and children. The use of exercises. Class discussion

11. Recording progress in literacy

Needs and purposes of record-keeping. Main headings for an individual record. Class records. Children's recording

12. Drama

Directed drama. Drama as a means of learning. Stages in the drama lesson

13. Children's literature

Literature in learning; for empathy; as confirmation of experience; for emotional experience; for pleasure; for life. Response to literature. The read-aloud programme

14. Towards a school book policy

Introducing a book policy. Book provision and selection. Organization and development of books. Use of books. Readability

15. Building a school language policy

Checklist to help in planning a language policy. Checklist for a reading policy

Early reading

Reading and language in general beyond the early years

5 years        9 years        13 years

# Making Language Work

A practical approach to literacy for teachers of
5- to 13-year-old children

McGRAW-HILL series for Serving Teachers (INSET)

*Consulting Editor:*
Peter Taylor,
*School of Education, Bristol University*

**Henderson and Perry:** Change and Development in Schools
**Holt:** Schools and Curriculum Change
**Hopson and Scally:** Lifeskills Teaching
**Hutchcroft:** Making Language Work
**Saunders:** Class Control and Behaviour Problems

# Making Language Work

A practical approach to literacy for teachers of
5- to 13-year-old children

Diana M. R. Hutchcroft

Iain G. Ball
Maude G. Brown
James J. Fairbairn
Ralph Lavender
Brian R. Watkins

## McGRAW-HILL BOOK COMPANY

**London** . New York . St Louis . San Francisco . Auckland
Bogotá . Guatemala . Hamburg . Lisbon . Madrid
Mexico . Montreal . New Delhi . Panama . Paris
San Juan . São Paulo . Singapore . Tokyo . Toronto

Published by
McGRAW-HILL Book Company (UK) Limited
MAIDENHEAD · BERKSHIRE · ENGLAND

---

British Library Cataloguing in Publication Data

---

Making language work. (McGraw-Hill series for serving teachers).
1. Language arts (elementary)—Great Britain
I. Hutchcroft, Diana
372.6'044'0941

LB1576

80–40924

ISBN 0–07–084119–5

89RH88

Printed and bound in Great Britain by
Robert Hartnoll (1985) Ltd., Bodmin, Cornwall

*The authors*

Diana M. R. Hutchcroft, OBE
*Headteacher, Saltford Primary School, Bristol*

Iain G. Ball
*Senior Adviser, English, Drama and Multicultural Education*

Maude G. Brown
*Senior Adviser, Nursery and Infant Education*

James J. Fairbairn
*Director of Teacher Training, College of Ripon and York St John*

Ralph Lavender
*Senior Inspector for Primary Schools*

Brian R. Watkins
*Head of Postgraduate Training, City of Birmingham Polytechnic Centre of Teacher Education and Training*

# Contents

# Foreword

Diana Hutchcroft and James Fairbairn were both members of the committee of enquiry into the teaching of reading of which I was fortunate to be chairman from 1972 to 1974. Reading the book that they and their colleagues have produced has brought back vividly the many days we spent together in the large room at the top of Elizabeth House, looking out over the maze of railway lines that run into Waterloo Station.

The two-and-a-half years during which I was occupied with the work of the committee opened my eyes to the complexity and importance in the arts of language. I have to confess that this came as a surprise to me. The experience that I brought to the committee was that of a chairman, not of a teacher or even a student of language. I knew when I accepted the invitation that literacy was a controversial subject—the first paper I asked the Secretary to write for me was on the politics of literacy—but I had no idea of how far the study of the uses of language could be carried as the foundation of the individual's intellectual development. For me the evidence and discussion were a privileged form of 'continuing education' which I found exciting, particularly when the practical experience and theoretical grasp that the membership of the committee brought together illuminated each other. No one, indeed, has learned more from the so-called Bullock Report than the chairman himself.

This same combination is characteristic of the present book. Every page bears witness to the seasoned experience that Mrs Hutchcroft and her colleagues have of teaching the uses of language at many different levels; but they rightly lay no less stress on the importance for teachers of keeping in touch with the course of theoretical discussion and the new practices to which it can lead.

In the five years since the Bullock Report, *A Language for Life*, was published it has been gratifying to learn of the influence that it has come to have on the education and practice of teachers. *Making Language Work* starts from the recommendations of the Report and sets out to explore and extend them further. It does so, in my opinion, with marked success. Like the Report, it is addressed to teachers and to the discussion of the problems they encounter in the classroom. I cannot believe that anyone interested in the role of language in education will fail to find it of value, and I recommend the book to others with an enthusiasm that reflects the interest I have myself found in reading it.

St Catherine's College                                        Alan Bullock
Oxford
11 January 1980

# Preface

It is not easy to make language work, and sometimes it is even more difficult to persuade ourselves that it is necessary to be aware of the crucial importance of language in our teaching and learning. This book sets out to demonstrate the belief that, without an understanding of how to interpret that knowledge in a practical manner in the classroom, teachers will be handicapped in their basic role and the children in their care will suffer accordingly.

The views expressed are those that are shared by all who have collaborated in the preparation of this book. We wish to emphasize the collective nature of our experience and the enjoyment we have shared in pooling this experience and refining it so that the suggestions made for classroom practice stem from our considered views.

Diana Hutchcroft and James Fairbairn were members of the Bullock Committee, and obviously a great deal of the work dealt with here will reflect many of the recommendations contained in the report, *A Language for Life*. All of us share the enthusiasm for language development that the Report envisaged as essential in the curriculum, although the practical suggestions are based on development in schools, and with teachers, since its publication.

We have been very concerned with the problems teachers face when attempting to develop classroom practice in relation to recent language development. It is often difficult for teachers to find material that relates theory to practice, but we hope that this book will demonstrate that it is relatively easy to consider these issues. In addition we have attempted to provide plenty of practical examples to enable teachers to achieve success in this field. Some of the language development discussed in this book is already widely known but we hope that by presenting it in conjunction with classroom expertise it will provide a useful framework.

We share the belief that, unless all teachers in all classrooms remain alert to the new theoretical issues and new practices, education will become moribund. We also believe in the professional role of the teachers and the important part they have to play. We regard this as something that can be discharged effectively only by teachers who are prepared constantly to question and reappraise their work in the classroom.

Talking, reading, writing, and listening form the literacy skills, and in the chapters that follow we attempt to trace both the theoretical development and its direct application in the classroom in each of these four areas.

The structure of the book and its relationship to children's developmental stages is shown in a flow diagram presented on page ii–iii. We hope that this diagram will enable readers to follow the related aspects of literacy as they turn from chapter to chapter.

We have attempted to make it readable. It is a book to browse in, a guide for the classroom, a reference book at home, an aid to evaluation and good practice. We also hope that it will prove to be challenging as well as offering practical help. Above all, we hope that it will lead our readers to find new inspiration and purpose in their own language work in their classroom.

Diana Hutchcroft
Iain Ball
Maude Brown
James Fairbairn
Ralph Lavender
Brian Watkins

## Discrimination between the sexes

In a book on this subject, it is impracticable to eliminate completely the use of genders and retain a fluent and readable text. The reader is therefore asked to accept that no deliberate distinction between the sexes is implied.

# Acknowledgements

The authors wish to thank: the staff and children of Saltford Primary School, Avon; Mr F. Hutchcroft; Mrs M. Thornton; Mrs H. M. Ball; Mrs D. M. Reynolds; Mrs A. A. Williams; Mrs L. Godrich and the children of Bournville Infants' School, Weston-Super-Mare; Sister Bernardette and Sister Elizabeth and the children of Corpus Christi RC J.M. & I. School, Weston-Super-Mare; Miss M. Small and the children of Eastville J.M. School, Bristol. They are indebted to Mrs J. Dubberley for the production of the original typescript.

The authors and publishers wish to thank the following for permission to reproduce copyright material:

CHAPTER 1: from Lev Semonvich Vygotsky, *Thought and Language*, Massachusetts Institute of Technology Press, 1962; Joan and Elizabeth Newson, *Four Years Old in an Urban Community*, Pelican, 1976; Marie Clay, *The Patterning of Complex Behaviour*, Heinemann Educational, 1976; Jessie Reid and Joan Low, *The Written Word*, rev. edn., Holmes McDougall, 1977.

CHAPTER 2: from J. Piaget, *The Child's Conception of the World*, Routledge & Kegan Paul, 1929, and (USA) Humanities Press; M. D. Gall, 'The use of questions in teaching', *Review of Education Research*, no. 40, V, pp. 707–20, 1970; A. F. Watts, *The Language and Mental Development of Children*, Harrap.

CHAPTER 3: from W. S. Gray, *Promoting Personal and Social Development Through Reading*, University of Chicago Press.

CHAPTER 5: from Dylan Thomas, *Quite Early One Morning*, Aldine (paperback 1967, J. M. Dent); *A Language for Life* (the Bullock Report), HMSO, 1975.

CHAPTER 6: from M. E. Wilt, *Journal of Education Research*, Heldref Publications.

CHAPTER 7: from J. Britton et al., *The Development of Writing Abilities (11–18)* (Schools Council Research Studies), Macmillan, 1974; *A Language for Life* (the Bullock Report), HMSO, 1975.

CHAPTER 8: from *A Language for Life* (the Bullock Report), HMSO, 1975; *Primary Education in England, A Survey by HM Inspectors of Schools*, HMSO, 1978; F. B. David, 'Research comprehension in reading', *Reading Research Quarterly*, Summer 1968, pp. 511–12; E. A. Lunzer and W. K. Gardner, *The Effective Use of Reading* (Schools Council Research Project), Heinemann, 1979; Sec. 1.2 in

ACKNOWLEDGEMENTS

'Reading skills', *The Reading Curriculum*, eds. A. Melnik and J. Merritt, Open University Press, 1972.

CHAPTER 9: from *A Language for Life* (the Bullock Report), HMSO, 1975.

CHAPTER 10: from *Primary Education in England, A Survey by HM Inspectors of Schools*, HMSO, 1978; Dennis Lawrence, *Improving Reading Through Counselling*, Ward Lock Educational.

CHAPTER 11: from *A Language for Life* (the Bullock Report), HMSO, 1975; J. Britton *et al.*, *The Development of Writing Abilities (11–18)* (Schools Council Research Studies), Macmillan, 1974; *Primary Education in England, A Survey by HM Inspectors of Schools*, HMSO, 1978.

CHAPTER 13: from Miriam Morton, translator of *From Two to Five* by Kornei Chukovsky, University of California Press, Los Angeles, 1963; Maurice Sendax, *Where the Wild Things Are*, Bodley Head, 1967; Odette Thomas, *Rain Falling, Sun Shining*, Bogle L'Ouverture Publications, 1975; Connie and Harold Rosen, *The Language of Primary School Children*, Penguin Education for the Schools Council, 1973, p. 195; Ted Hughes, *The Iron Man*, Faber and Faber, 1968.

CHAPTER 14: from Russell Stanffer, *Teaching Reading as a Thinking Process*, Harper and Row, 1969.

# 1. The importance of language

For most practical purposes language development and intellectual development go hand in hand. It is through a child's capacity to use language in a wide variety of ways that his ability to think, to reason, and to store and re-use his experiences develops. It is through his capacity to use language that he is able to make sense of what happens around him and absorb and consolidate any knowledge he has acquired. Furthermore, this capacity to use language is the means by which most of his learning in school takes place.

Language seems essential to most thinking. Vygotsky wrote: 'thought is not merely expressed in words, it comes into existence through them'.[1] We can all think 'through our finger tips' in purely practical situations, and if we need to repair a fuse we can pick up the screwdriver in one hand and the plug in the other and insert the sharp end of the screwdriver into the nick in the screw without language entering into the thinking behind the actions. But as soon as thinking distances itself from action, as soon as it requires an element of abstraction or generalization, then, unless we have the language to label and describe, to recall past experience, and to express the relationships we have observed, we are denied much of the means of thinking. It is language that gives our thoughts form and substance.

The operative words are 'for most practical purposes'. Words are the main but not the only way in which we symbolize and express relationships; both mathematics and music have their own sets of symbols, and sometimes we may need to think in colour or shapes. Even in these examples words will help us to formulate and clarify our thoughts and intentions, although they will not replace these other ways of thinking.

Man stands apart from other animals. It seems likely that some alterations in the patterning of his genes in man's early development caused him to be born with a predisposition to language and that this was decisive to his future development. Animals make their meaning clear by signals; if a lion roars, a dog bristles, or a bird calls, its message is usually clear—but a signal is transitory, of the present. Man can also signal by a shout or a gesture, but he can do much more—he is able to use symbols in the form of words to express his meanings. Thus he can store all his past

1

experiences, condensed and codified in words. He can also, by recall, re-use these stored experiences to plan his future actions. Language makes it possible for him to have a past and a future as well as a present.

## 1.1 Language and experience

With young children the opportunity to talk about everyday happenings encourages them to formulate and remember these happenings and to become adept at putting their experiences into words. It has another important effect: the process of formulating their experiences helps children to make sense of this experience and to relate it to a previous experience. This is part of the process by which they consolidate any knowledge they have acquired or any learning that is taking place.

A young child learns through his senses. Indeed, these are exceptionally well developed. The new-born infant has the full complement of adult nerves leading to the surface of the skin but much more closely placed than they will be later. He feels things with great acuteness. His sensory input, whether from seeing, hearing, or touching, is channelled into his intellectual development by language. Language is thus a decisive factor in the development of his thinking, the formation of his concepts, and in the release of his potential intelligence.

Andrew Wilkinson writes: 'We no longer need regard intelligence as a fixed quantity; within limits we may speak of the capacity to acquire intelligence; and the major means of doing this is through language.'[2]

## 1.2 Language, learning, pre-school experience

Once the child enters school, language takes on an added significance. It becomes the principal means by which he learns. It can be argued that too much early learning in school takes place through the medium of words unrelated to experience, and that for children whose capacity to use language is not well developed the excessive use of language as a means of learning is one of the greatest hindrances to learning taking place. Nevertheless, language remains the means, whether through listening, talking, reading, or writing, by which most learning in school is channelled. It becomes at once the key and the greatest barrier to a child's capacity to learn.

The importance of the development of language to a child's intellectual progress seems established, but two important aspects of language development need to be emphasized. If children are born with a predisposition to language, which is a part of their genetic heritage, then all children have a potential for language that is inherent and that develops even in comparatively unfavourable circumstances. We can no longer say of a child from a non-supportive home, 'He has no language'; all we can say is, 'His home seems to have done little to release his language potential and we in school haven't yet found a way.' Or we may say, 'His home has developed for him a language which while effective in the home does not meet the requirements of the school and may even be in conflict with them.' The child's home provides the opportunities for the development of language, and in the case of a supportive home the child will readily use language for a wide range of purposes easily and habitually—to explain what he is doing, to describe something he wants to do and why he wants to do it, to ask questions, to recall a past experience, to explain how and why things happen, to persuade adults to agree to his wishes, to plan ahead.

A child from a less supportive home will have developed a range of uses of language but he is likely to use many of these rarely and reluctantly and only when circumstances force him to do so. It is not that he lacks language, that he has a deficit, but that he habitually uses a narrower range in a less explicit way.

A four-year-old boy was in a nursery school taking part in a language project. He was singled out because of his general reluctance to talk, whether in contact with other children or adults. It would have been easy to assume that his ability to use language was very limited. He was told a story which he enjoyed and asked if he would like to paint a picture about it. He agreed and helped to get paper, paints, and easel ready. He was then asked if he would like to choose a friend to help him with the picture; again he agreed and fetched a friend. 'Oh dear,' said the adult, 'your friend doesn't know the story. You tell him the story and then I'll come and help you get started.' A recording was made of the boy telling the story: he told it sometimes hesitatingly, sometimes making mistakes, but showing a range of complex uses of language at his command.

The difference, then, between children from different types of home is likely to be in the ease and readiness with which they use a range of language functions to make their meaning clear, rather than a lack of capacity to use complex language structures when a situation demands such use.

## 1.3 Opportunities for development

To say that we need to build on the language that a child already possesses when he comes to school contains an important implication. If he is from a restricted background he is likely to be in possession of a much wider range of uses of language than the teacher may suspect. We need to provide opportunities for him to talk freely and easily and to accept his dialect and accent; this is the starting point to encourage a wider range of use as well as greater fluency.

These opportunities may have to be closely linked to practical activities. A child who has not had his capacity to talk developed usually talks with greater ease when he is involved in some activity that both provides a pretext for talk and diminishes his self-consciousness when he is talking.

## 1.4 Early development

A wide range of uses of language develops very early. At about 14 months a child produces his first words out of a range of sounds in babbling. He then discovers the principle of naming. Giving a name to something is like giving a child a filing pin on which he can stick his associations and experiences related to that name. By the age of two he can string together two- or three-word utterances in a form of telegraphese, missing out the connecting words. Thus 'Daddy come' can mean, 'Daddy is coming through the door' or 'I want Daddy to come here', depending on its context. This is a remarkable advance within a few months, yet between the ages of two and four a greater advance takes place: most children develop the full adult range of language except for the use of the passive voice during these two years. They use this range of language imperfectly, making omissions and mistakes, but the ability to use language for a very wide range of purposes is clearly established. The child's understanding of this range of uses then may be imperfect, but it is important to recognize that it exists and can be built upon in school.

When we visited an infants' school a six-year-old called Debbie gave an example of this ability to use language for a wide range of purposes. 'Would you like me to show you something?' she asked. 'Yes.' 'Would you like to see our "shiny" display?' 'Yes.' Her subsequent conversation showed how completely she was in charge of the situation both socially and intellectually. She asked if the visitor knew what different exhibits were made of, corrected him when he made mistakes; she named things, describing them succinctly where necessary; she made comparisons between objects, made simple generalizations, recalled who had brought them or where they had come from, answered questions put to her which showed her ability to give explanations, used such indications of reasoning as 'because', 'so that', 'but', and 'although', and explained how the class might use the display as the basis for future activities.

She was six, but the work of the Schools Council Project, 'Communication Skills in Early Childhood', has shown that four-year-olds have often mastered a much longer and more carefully analysed list of uses of language. In their survey of four-year-olds in Nottingham the Newsons wrote:

> The year between one's third and fourth birthdays is characterized by rapid progress in language development, closely allied with an already broadening of the child's conceptual range. This is the period of 'why?' and 'how?' The child's clearer understanding of basic concepts brings him to an awareness of what questions need to be asked: his surer command of words and syntax enables him to ask them.
> It is no longer enough that mechanisms work and events happen. He wants to know *how* things work, *why* they happen. And the fact that he is also becoming more adept at putting a string of connected thoughts into words has the effect of directing the adult's attention away from his earlier endearing idiosyncrasies and verbal mannerisms, and towards the *content* of the ideas which he is trying to communicate. This in turn stimulates the child to express himself more adequately in whole sentences or series of sentences, which often now have an extremely complex grammatical structure. In short, real conversation becomes possible with a child of four. . . .[3]

This early development of language and the ability of children from the age of four to maintain their own rights and interests through language, to direct their own activities and those of others, to report on present and past experience as well as to reason logically; their ability to predict and anticipate possibilities and to project into the experience and feelings of others and to enter into imaginative play through talk make one suspect that young children's abilities with spoken language are seriously under-estimated and that their early potential is often ignored, both at home and at school.

## 1.5 Language and relationships

In our discussion of the importance of language so far we have concentrated on its spoken form. Speech is the primary substance of language, its basic form; and reading and writing are different forms deriving from and underpinned by the spoken form. All children use talk socially to draw attention to themselves and to maintain their rights and interests, and the talk of young children often includes such expressions as 'I want', 'Give me', 'Look at me', 'Let me'. As children begin to play together they use talk as a means of sustaining their relationships as part of their play, though often without much real exchange of meaning taking place. Two three-year-old boys recorded while playing with cars give an example of this:

Stephen 'Where's the tipper? Yes it is—push it over here.'
Mark 'Get this, Stephen get it. You crash it—crash it.'
Stephen 'Crash it with the tipper!'
Mark 'Fetch it on there—look.'

Here the play's the thing and the language is incidental to it.

As children get older they use language to form and explore relationships just as adults sitting next to one another make remarks about the weather, their shopping, the day at work, the family. The talk is the pretext for establishing contact and they can then go on to develop the acquaintanceship. At school social talk is a significant indicator of the atmosphere, of the attitudes and relationships that prevail. It is the lubricator that makes other more precise and exact talk possible. Yet the teacher needs to be aware of the difference between the two. It is not enough that children should talk frequently and fluently, though that may be one of the best starting points: they must also talk to some purpose, using talk to extend their control of their experiences, the precision of their observations, their powers of recall and of logical reasoning, and their ability to speculate and anticipate about 'what might happen if...', 'if we did..., so that... then we might...', or 'We can't do that unless... but then we could do...'.

We are here focusing on a range of fairly clearly defined uses of language which enable the child to make his meanings clear and his purposes explicit. The teacher's awareness of this range of uses and her concern that children should extend their control of language for these purposes is not to deny the importance of developing other ways of using language in exploratory talk, in language that helps children to make sense of, and come to terms with, their everyday experiences or in language that creates a world of the imagination.

*The Language of Primary School Children*, by Connie and Harold Rosen,[4] is a valuable book because it catches the variety and spontaneity and range of language in children of primary school age. It shows that knowledge and analysis are not, in themselves, enough; that the relationships, attitudes and beliefs, the organization of experiences, the interchange arising from discussion, create the sort of classroom community within which a rich variety of language is likely to develop.

## 1.6 The role of the teacher

Yet knowledge must be there, and it is the lack of knowledge about language that is one of the chief limiting factors in the work of many teachers. The reading list at the end of this chapter is short, yet it gives an essential foundation of knowledge for developing professional awareness and professional skills.

How then does this recognition of the importance of language development affect the teacher? First, it shows the teacher what a very complex and flexible instrument the child enters school with. If it affects the teacher's need for knowledge about language it also affects her in other ways, first as an organizer of learning experiences, second as a skilled listener and analyser of language, and third as a sympathetic adult who is able to develop a child's ability to use language by knowing how, if, and when to intervene.

In good primary schools the easy access to materials and books, the ease with which the local environment can be explored, and the flexibility of the timetable ensure that opportunities for language development are abundant. Yet however interesting the activity, however stimlating the environment, language will not necessarily develop from it. It is the teacher's task to see that it does.

If we take a well-organized first school classroom as our example we may find a display or collection, arranged and labelled with books related to the objects at hand. There will be a book corner with a range of books likely to encourage the least able and stretch the most able, books of stories, legends, rhymes and poems, information books and simple reference books and perhaps the *Thorndike Junior Dictionary* to encourage those with a taste for words. The reading books, from a number of schemes, will be well organized and they will offer different pathways to meet different individual needs. The making, painting, drawing, and modelling materials will be organized so that they are easily accessible and easily returned: the mathematics/science materials will be clearly labelled and easy to borrow, while materials for writing and for making booklets will be laid out. Materials for other activities will have a clearly defined space.

Already we have objects and materials in plenty which will extend the range found at home; they will provide an enormous number of names and describing words—of colour, shape, texture—just as the actions related to the objects and the activities related to the materials will provide verbs and adverbs, whether from exploring the possibilities of the colour red or from a deliberate act of measuring. The opportunities for naming, describing, recalling related experiences, comparing and seeing similarities and differences, the asking of questions and the 'ifs', 'buts', 'mights', 'coulds', and 'I thinks' that may follow, and the imaginings that may arise, are apparent.

## 1.7 Language, observation and experience

The strength of this 'language-in-use' is that it arises from firsthand observation of the subject, material, or action in hand. The senses are at work, seeing, feeling, manipulating, and giving meaning and substance to the words that are used and the expressions that are formulated. These simple, basic opportunities for talk lead on to more complex, more imaginative ones, but in each case many opportunities arise from firsthand observation and experience.

They will be extended by those opportunities for discussion that arise when children are read to, and characters and situations from literature are discussed. Other points of view can be explored—is the 'goody' always good, are stepmothers always bad—and children can be encouraged to try to imagine themselves into another person's point of view.

If we move into a good junior school we shall find the same opportunities present at a more sophisticated level. The materials may be assigned to art and craft; mathematics and science may be separated; books may be more centralized; but the opportunities for language from firsthand observation directly related to experience will still exist.

This emphasis on firsthand observation from organized experience as the basis for much valuable development is especially important for children who are not tuned into the use of language to express the particular functions that arise from such opportunities. Whatever competence they may possess has not been given the opportunity and encouragement to manifest itself in fluent and explicit use; words wash over such children without seeming to communicate. One observes children in school who seem to retreat into a cocoon of detachment before the rain of words pouring over and around them. Words are often the worst starting point for learning with children who have regularly failed with words.

We see this with all ages of children in school, and it is significant that many children of secondary age show a greater interest in those subjects with a strongly applied element, such as science, art and craft, home economics, and different forms of human movement; it is in such subjects that many of the best pretexts for developing language skills occur.

The organization of materials, and the opportunities for talk arising from their use, is a starting point. The teacher now needs to bring her knowledge of children and her knowledge of language together in a special way. First she needs to acquire the skill of listening carefully to children talk. She is not listening in order to judge correctness but for the range and variety of use.

1. In what way does the child use language?
2. Can he describe things with significant detail?
3. Can he give reasons and justification for his actions?
4. Can he make comparisons?
5. In what important ways is he failing to use language?
6. Can he plan ahead, see alternative solutions?
7. Can he explain how he made or did something?
8. What special opportunities and encouragement does he need?

## 1.8 Listening and analysis

The skills of listening and analysis are not easily acquired: but even when acquired we may organize the right opportunities and ask the right questions but nevertheless prevent the child from taking the significant step forward in language and thinking. One of the occupational hazards of teachers is that, while they are doing the talking, they find it difficult to believe that learning may not be taking place. The reverse may be nearer the truth. In a nursery school the teacher had provided a good range of materials and had realized the importance of encouraging the child to observe a simple happening and then say what happened.

> Teacher: 'Denise, choose your favourite colour and watch carefully what happens.'
> Denise chooses red.
> 'Now watch, Denise, when I put a drop of red into this bowl of water. Watch, Denise, and tell me what happens.'
> Teacher and child watch as a bead of colour drops into the bowl and the water goes slightly pink.

> Teacher: 'Now, Denise, what has happened? Yes, it's gone pale
> pink, hasn't it?'
> 'Now watch again and tell me what happens.'
> Denise watches and opens her mouth to reply but teacher says:
> 'Now look, it's gone a bit more pink.'

Teacher creates the opportunity but in each case does the answering for Denise without realizing that, though willing to reply, Denise is prevented by the teacher from doing so. On the final repeat of the question she does let Denise answer.

It is difficult in the middle of classroom pressures to be aware of one's own actual performance, or to listen intently to what children say. A tape-recorder with a long lead and a pin-on microphone, or a portable tape-recorder with a directional microphone, enables the teacher to take samples of talk of those children she has a special concern for at a particular time. The recordings can then be listened in peace and brief notes made.

One teacher used a tape to record a conversation with a group of six-year-olds. She noted: 'Children use phrases with the following frequency:

> Philip: 'I think' (7), 'because' (4), 'it could be' (3), 'if' (4),
> 'perhaps' (1).
> Neil: 'Because' (2), 'I think' (2).

This was a very simple starting point for further observations and analysis.

*Listening to Children Talking*,[5] prepared by the Schools Council Communication Skills Project and described at the end of the chapter, gives the necessary guidance for listening to and recording children's spoken language.

Once the teacher is able to listen to children's talk and spot its chief uses, she needs to develop her skills in being able both to initiate and to sustain children's talk. Here she will soon realize that sympathetic listening is not enough and that she needs a range of cues and questions which both encourage and support the child without doing the thinking for him. Talking through one's impressions, sorting out one's thoughts in words, or formulating a cause and effect is part of the process of learning to think effectively.

Certain kinds of questions require a very limited response from the child. These are close-ended questions which expect a predetermined answer such as a name, a fact, or a 'yes' or 'no' response. Such questions are a useful check on memory but their contribution to a child's ability to use language is negligible.

Questions that are 'open' encourage a range of responses and a child may give a longer description or a personal reaction, explore alternatives, or follow a thought process, which enables him to form some sort of conclusion. While the child is teasing out his reply in talk he may need encouragement and props to support and help him to clarify the next step in his thinking. *Talking and Learning*,[6] from the Schools Council Communication Skills Project, gives help in developing this form of dialogue between teacher and child.

This emphasis on talk is an emphasis on the foundation of all language and on the basis for the development of related skills. It affects skill in listening because knowing what to say next means knowing what to expect next when someone else is talking. Similarly, knowing what to say next means knowing what probably comes next in reading and enables one to predict what the rest of the sentence is likely to be. Thus skills in expectation, prediction, and probability, in knowing what is likely to follow whenever language is used, are acquired when a child acquires fluency in talk.

## 1.9 Talking, reading, and writing

This means that talk is linked to the early stages of reading and writing. Meaning is there from the start, because what a child has seen, touched, heard, or made provides the basis for his talk, which can be written down for him and read back for him, with him, or by him. The meaning springs from his own sensory perception, is formulated in his own words, put into written form by the adult and read back, and thus the skills of speaking, reading, and writing relate to one another from the start. The best language on which to begin to learn to read is language that is as near a child's own spoken form as possible. It thus has the natural rhythms, the vocabulary, the syntactic patterns, and the predictability of his own talk. It can either be his own written words or a specially composed text, but in both cases, 'All language cues the child is skilled in using in his spoken language should be present in the text, and difficulties that arise from complex aspects of the English language (which he does not yet use) should be avoided' (Marie Clay).[7] It follows from the above argument that unnaturally stilted and restricted forms should also be avoided. One boy, whose father was a lorry driver, failed on a reading scheme notorious for its tightly controlled vocabulary but was able to read back a story of his own making which included such words as 'lorry driver', 'axle', 'gearbox', 'diesel', 'articulated', 'differential', and 'bypass'. This is an example of the importance both of interest and of using a reading vocabulary and structures close to the child's own spoken language.

A stress on the importance of using a child's own language as a basis for early reading and for choosing texts that reflect the vocabulary, word order, structures, and idiomatic usage of his talk does not diminish the importance of knowing sounds. It does, however, put sounds in their place as part of a much wider process. In using talk as the basis for early reading many sounds will be acquired; some won't be learned in this incidental way, and checklists are needed to see where the omissions lie. The point of the checklist is that it checks the teacher's observations, record-keeping, and sense of system just as much as it checks the child's weakness.

## 1.10 Sounds and symbols

There is no simple relationship between sound and symbol. Letters vary in the sound they represent according to their context, just as words vary in meaning according to *their* context. It is context that gives a letter its sound and a word its specific meaning. So often sounds have been taught as if their relationship with letters were simple instead of complex and much un-learning has to take place. Young children need to acquire early an expectancy that the letter 'o' may have a variety of sounds depending on its setting. It will have a different sound in one, home, come, women, of, or, to, and do.

A sound may be spelt in different ways, and thus the sound 'i' will have a different spelling in eye, height, ice, island, buy, and guide. Marie Clay writes: 'The child who learns a set for diversity is a more efficient performer when faced with diversity than the child who learns a set for constant relationships.' This seems specially apposite when one considers the teaching of sounds.

The above does not mean that no 'rules' should be taught, but that 'rules' that have a reasonably general application are few and that too much teaching of rules builds false expectations of a regularity that does not exist. At some stage, by using part of a reading scheme or schemes, by games as well as by incidental instruction during individual reading time, a systematic coverage of sounds will be necessary. This coverage should be not in isolation, an end in itself, but part of a much wider view of language. It should be related wherever possible to finding and matching sounds in the child's own writing and in stories he is enjoying. Discussion of possibilities and 'near misses' should be part of this learning wherever this is possible. This approach ensures that understanding is present from the start and that reading is seen as a thinking and not a mechanical process. Through such an approach a child absorbs and internalizes many rules without needing to make them explicit.

If language close to a child's own spoken language is the best written language for beginning reading, we must remember that beyond this early stage the printed and the spoken forms of language are different. At some stage this difference must be bridged.

If children have been read to regularly from a wide variety of books, literary patterns of language will be familiar to them. However, specific features of the written form will have to be introduced and discussed with them as part of the process of teaching them to read. They will need to recognize the difference between narrative, writing giving information, and a poem; between the past sense used in most stories and the 'timeless present' used in so many information books; as well as to understand the handling of direct speech and questions. The work of Jessie Reid is particularly valuable in giving insights into these aspects of the teaching of reading, and the teachers' manual, *The Written Word*,[8] which she and Joan Low wrote for their scheme 'Link-Up' contains a discussion of them which makes valuable reading. It also provides useful book lists and references.

## 1.11 Listening

The regular reading to children of stories is valuable not only for its exploration of the imagination, for its extension of the child's own experience, for the opportunities for understanding other points of view, and for projecting oneself into other people's feelings: it has a more precise and limited function in connection with learning to read in that it lets the child hear written forms of language, offering a wide range of models. This is equally true of factual accounts as of imaginative writing.

Some of these forms may be close to the spoken forms of story telling, but the range should be such that a child meets a variety of written forms. He learns that print 'speaks' differently from talk in its precision, its economy, and its need to be explicit.

The first school usually recognizes the value of a 'listening time', whereas the junior and middle schools all too frequently do not. Short daily readings may well be one of the necessary 'tuning-in' experiences for many children and especially for those whose home has not provided such experiences. Learning to read is not the mastering of a linear process in the sense that computation or music are linear. It is not a succession of small steps leading inevitably onwards. There are broad sequences of development but many pathways from one level to another. Different children need different pathways depending on ability, stage of development, motivation, and background. Thus there is no one recipe for reading, no scheme or prescription that is likely to suit all children.

We see this if we compare the needs of two children—a girl of six whose father is a rising executive and mother a teacher, and a boy of the same age whose father is an unemployed labourer and whose mother, though quick of understanding, disliked school herself and has a suspicion of it. The girl is an only child and the boy the fourth in a family of five.

The learning needs of these two children require manifestly different approaches. The girl is probably already tuned into the language of the school; her knowledge of print and expectations about it are established. So are such fundamentals as the left-to-right flow of print, the separateness of printed words as compared with the flow of speech, and the realization that print means message. She will know the names of letters and such terms as 'word', 'sound', 'capital letter', 'small letter', and 'sentence', and can match some sounds before she even started school. Her knowledge of language and her capacity to predict what is likely to come next in both listening and reading will give her a 'behind-the-eyeball' knowledge which makes decoding a comparatively simple process to grasp. Whatever the scheme used and whatever the approach she is likely to succeed, though she will develop her capacity to use print to a much greater degree if the books available extend her interests and she is encouraged to read for a range of purposes, to make booklets of her own and to read to others.

What of the boy? His stage of verbal development at the first school stage is likely to be behind that of the girl. His vocabulary is likely to be more limited and his habitual use of language much narrower. Being fourth in a family can make as much as fifteen months' difference in reading development as compared with an only or eldest child, and we know that his motivation from stories is likely to be less strong than his motivation when language is related to his actions, interests, and 'awareness of the world around'. Attitudes to school from his home are likely to be less supportive, opportunities to explain things and give reasons infrequent, and the need for such exploration felt to be unnecessary. A fundamental principle such as that 'print means message' may be lacking. Any approach to his learning to read should build on his existing language, relate opportunities for talk and reading to his interests and activities, carefully build up his confidence to use language, and ensure that reading material is carefully selected for its relevance and interest.

No one method could meet the needs of such different children, and no one reading scheme could meet their diversity of background. What then are the implications for the teacher?

First, there should be a clear understanding of the alternative pathways or approaches likely to meet the needs of such different children. Perhaps each school needs to identify and talk through three or four such choices, incorporating them into reading policy. Second, the materials to provide for such approaches will need to be made available and appropriately organized. Finally there must be a discussion of what provision is available for those exceptional children at both ends of the scale who will not be provided for by such a varied and carefully discussed range of alternatives. These three points seem fundamental to any reading policy that recognizes individual needs and differences, the implications of different rates of language development, and the enormous variations in environmental influence.

An appreciation of the exceptionally important place of language in education has general implications for a teacher.

1. She needs a knowledge about language, its functions, how children acquire it, and how it relates to learning. The book list at the end of this chapter provides a beginning for this working knowledge.

2. This knowledge leads to a recognition of spoken language as the basic form. The child's own language, developed out of school, will provide the basis for extending his range of spoken usage, and this will, in turn, lead into reading and written language (further references in Chapters 2 and 3).

3. In order to achieve this development in children the teacher will need to develop her own skills, by becoming a better listener and analyser of language (Joan Tough, *Listening to Children Talking*).

4. One of the essential conditions for a secure development of language skills seems to be interaction with a knowledgeable adult, who not only listens but encourages the child to formulate his experiences, ideas, and questions and provides the

stimulus and support so that the child can develop his thinking (Joan Tough, *Talking and Learning*). For school purposes, this requires a much greater understanding of the use of questions and other cues.

5. The complexity of the reading process needs to be appreciated so that an oversimplified view of the matching of sounds is prevented and the need for alternative pathways to meet individual requirements is understood. Reading should be seen as a thinking process where the understanding of what is read and the use to be made of it forms essential parts of its development. Chapter 6 of *A Language for Life* (the Bullock Report) provides a basis for understanding this complexity (further reference in Chapter 7).

6. The forms of talking, listening, reading, and writing are all aspects of language, their development interacting one upon the other, thus writing will develop as an extension of the spoken form and be closely linked to reading. A key to the development of writing will be the teacher's understanding of its range of purposes and of the need to give written work value and appreciation (further reference in Chapters 5, 6, and 7).

An increased knowledge of language and added expertise in the related teaching skills is likely to improve standards not only in talk and the formal skills of reading and writing, but also in the general effectiveness of a child's learning and thinking.

These implications seem to us to be true for all ages and levels of ability and to be fundamental to the purpose of this book.

## References

1. VYGOTSKY, L. S., *Thought and Language*, MIT Press, 1962.
2. WILKINSON, ANDREW, *The Foundations of Language*, Oxford University Press, 1971.
3. NEWSON, JOHN and ELIZABETH, *Four Years Old in an Urban Community*, Allen and Unwin, 1968.
4. ROSEN, CONNIE and HAROLD, *The Language of Primary School Children*, Schools Council/Penguin, 1973.
5. TOUGH, JOAN, *Listening to Children Talking*, Schools Council/Ward Lock Educational, 1976.
6. TOUGH, JOAN, *Talking and Learning*, Schools Council/Ward Lock Educational, 1977.
7. CLAY, MARIE, *Reading: The Patterning of Complex Behaviour*, Heinemann Educational, 1976.

8. REID, JESSIE and LOW, JOAN, *The Written Word*, Holmes McDougall, 1977.

## Suggested reading

*A Language for Life* (The Bullock Report), HMSO, 1975, Chs 4, 5, 6, and 10.

WILKINSON, ANDREW, *The Foundations of Language*, Oxford University Press, 1971. A short readable introduction to language: see Ch. 3 on the acquisition of language; Ch. 7 on the development of oracy.

TOUGH, JOAN, *Listening to Children Talking*, Ward Lock Educational, 1976. Ch. 8 gives a list of children's uses of language, from which a personal check list can be made.

TOUGH, JOAN, *Talking and Learning*, Ward Lock Educational, 1977. Chs 4 and 5 analyse the teacher's use of strategies when talking with children.

ROSEN, CONNIE and HAROLD, *The Language of Primary School Children*, Penguin, 1973. A discussion of children's language based on examples collected in schools.

# 2. The early years in school

It has been suggested that starting school is the most traumatic event in life apart from birth and death. A child's introduction to school nowadays is usually a carefully planned gradual process and the teacher keeps a watchful eye to ensure that upsets are avoided or speedily overcome.

## 2.1 The importance of the early days in school

In the early days pleasurable activities are provided and the child who is confident will want to try them all, particularly things such as sand, water, paint, and clay, which may not be so readily available at home. Children who are not emotionally secure will usually pursue familiar activities and may indulge in solitary or spectator play for most of the time until self-confidence develops. It is in these initial stages that the teacher's observations are crucial, for they will provide her with much background information which will help her to arrange the child's learning in ways appropriate to him as an individual. This period is also a critical one in forming the child's basic attitudes towards school.

From a child's first day, the skilful teacher will observe his play, listen to his talk, and engineer situations that challenge him to talk and think. By observing his activities she will learn not only about his ability to use language, but also how far his pre-school experiences have enabled him to co-operate with others in many different social situations. His attitudes towards different occupations and towards adults and other children will also be apparent, and his ability to use language in social situations will affect his ability to profit from many classroom happenings.

Michael and Jane had built a fire station and some houses from Lego bricks and were playing imaginatively. One of the houses was on fire, the people had escaped, and the fire engine was on the scene.

    M  All the house has burned.

    J  Yes and all the furniture—the clothes—the food—it's all burned up.

The teacher joined in at this point and said, 'I wonder what the people will do now?'

    M  They'll have to live in another house.

    T  What about furniture?

M   They'll have to buy some more.

T   I wonder where they will get the money to buy it?

J   From the bank—they'll get it from the bank like my daddy.

M   No they won't—you get it from social security.

From this conversation the teacher could see that both children were able to use language to report on present happenings and to construct imaginative situations in co-operation with others. She could also tell that, despite different home backgrounds, they were equally able to state their opinion with confidence drawn from their previous experiences.

## 2.2 Children with difficulties

Sometimes the teacher is faced with a child whose ability to talk is very advanced or with one who does not talk at all, and both these children may be handicapped in their early days in school. Peter had exceptional ability with language which had been fostered by parents who were teachers, and grandma who took a special interest in him. His vocabulary was so advanced for his age that his peers could not understand him, and he tended to play alone or seek the company of adults. After two terms in school he had not made a start with reading, although one might have assumed from his advanced language skill that he would excel at it. At playtime he always endeavoured to walk with the teacher on duty, and one summer day he began to pick the wild flowers on the field, giving each one the Latin name that his grandma had taught him. The flowers were taken into school, pressed, and made into a book using as many basic words as possible plus the long Latin names Peter knew so well. This was his breakthrough into reading, and it helped him to come to terms with the demands of the school, although it was a considerable time before he could communicate effectively with his peers.

Lilian presented quite a different problem: she did not utter a word in school, although her parents assured everyone that she did talk normally at home. Her teacher thought it best not to pressurize her into talking in the hope that, once she had settled into school, she would gradually gain enough confidence to chat. However, Lilian never uttered a word, and everyone accepted the situation. Other children took her by the hand and looked after her but she never joined in any conversations or responded to questions from adults.

At the beginning of her second year she was absent, and on returning to school found that her teacher was new to the school.

No one had informed the teacher that Lilian was an elective mute, so when the child wet herself the teacher asked whether she was unwell, and insisted on an answer, saying 'I can't help if I don't know what is wrong, can I? Now you tell me what the trouble is', Lilian answered, and from then on talked normally to everyone. It was several days before other teachers realized that she was now communicating verbally and asked Lilian's teacher what she had done to her! It was fortunate for Lilian that this teacher *expected* her to talk. Had she known of Lilian's elective mutism she might have accepted the situation and allowed it to continue indefinitely.

In cases like Peter's and Lilian's it is difficult for the teacher to decide on the most appropriate action, and it is often through a chance discovery such as Peter's interest in plants that progress can be made. Teachers need to develop an awareness of children's individual interest so that these can be used as a motivating force in learning. Children's interests should form the basis of activities provided by the teacher for the purpose of extending cognitive development.

These activities should provide opportunities for using a range of language. Observations of children's activities and the language connected with them should be a regular part of each teacher's daily programme. It is through analysis of her observations that the teacher will become aware of the child's present abilities, and this will enable her to plan a programme for further development. It is interesting to note that Corinne Hutt found that during symbolic play children showed much greater competence in language that was evident in their everyday performance.[1] Lilian's predicament perhaps indicates that it is dangerous to accept a child's handicap too readily and that, once he or she has had a reasonable period to become secure in the school environment, the teacher must positively seek a solution to the problem. Children who do not talk to others or to themselves while pursuing activities need special attention from their teachers. Internal speech appears to develop late, and the development of thinking skills may be retarded if infants do not talk aloud or are prevented from doing so.

## 2.3 Motivation

We have all met children who like to make the running and create their own learning situations so that all they require from an adult is acquiescence and occasional participation in an exciting project or imaginary sequence. The teacher seldom needs to motivate such children towards learning: they have a natural bent. All that may be needed is a little influence occasionally to steer them in the precise direction necessary in order to progress in a particular area of the curriculum, and this will mean providing materials and books that will extend their thinking, plus the opportunity and encouragement to use them. In pursuing their interests these children often infect others with their enthusiasm, so that the whole class or even the whole school becomes involved. From time to time it may be necessary to ask questions such as 'How?', 'Why?', or 'What do you think?' in order to extend the interest or to foster deeper thought.

Inevitably, not all children have this zest for learning, and many teachers will say 'No one in my class ever comes up with an interest except me!' It is essential that teachers have a fund of ideas for activities and experiences which will capture the interest of young children and help the teacher to extend vocabulary and increase the children's uses of language by creating the necessity for each child to talk. These experiences will make use of excursions out of school as well as creating a lively, stimulating atmosphere within the school buildings and grounds.

Excursions out of school do not need to be costly. In a social priority junior school one teacher with a class of backward readers arranged weekly visits to the local library, taking half her class on each occasion. This was possible only by arranging for the part-time teacher or the head teacher to work with the remaining children. Through stimulating preparatory work and the co-operation of the library staff the enjoyment of the children was guaranteed. By the end of the term the whole class were 'hooked on books' and were enthusiastically writing and illustrating books for the school library (further reference in Chapter 3).

Quite frequently, the missing motivation is a purpose for the activity expected of the children. Are they asked to involve themselves in something really worth thinking, talking, and writing about, or is their activity simply a time-filler?

In schools in areas where homes do not provide pre-school experiences that enable children to become articulate and to develop the uses of language appropriate within an educational context, teachers will need to supply a great deal of input. Nursery rhymes provide a rich inheritance of language and customs which can be used as starting points for numerous curriculum projects. In addition, much of the preparatory work for basic skills can be accomplished by teaching rhymes: rhythm is needed for accurate counting; singing the tune as correct pitch aids the development of auditory discrimination; and rhyming words aid phonic ability. The two latter abilities are important in early reading skill development. Many illustrations of nursery rhymes provoke discussion about how people lived long ago, and the skilful use of questions by the teacher will encourage the use of higher levels of comprehension by the children. Many children are aided in developing listening skills by the use of a group listening centre with headphones. Sets of pictures to put in a sequence while listening to recorded rhymes may provide the basis for a later discussion with the teacher, and in addition the use of such listening centres in conjunction with various activities lengthens the attention span of children who find concentration difficult.

In one reception class the teacher used nursery rhymes as the starting point for stories invented by the children, who produced 'Another story about Little Boy Blue', 'Another story about Humpty Dumpty', and 'Another story about Bo-Peep'. Children who had begun reading used nursery rhyme cards with matching cards for each line of print and later were able to sequence the separate lines of each rhyme without the aid of the matching baseboard. From the same shared experience resourceful teachers are able to provide different levels of language experience to match the different stages of their children, and it is important to keep careful records of progress so that this can be achieved (further reference in Chapter 14). It is necessary for teachers to realize that success is essential for children to make progress with confidence, and that motivation can be killed by failure. Motivation can also be affected by the context in which an activity takes place, for example whether the child is working alone, with a group, or with the teacher. If a child is working alone, then it is important that he can achieve success. If he is with a group, then together they must be able to cope with the task set for them. If he is with the teacher, then the instruction level will be appropriate and this will mean that the challenge of success can be met with a little help from the teacher. If the child is unable to succeed in any of these situations, then the activity is at frustration level and should either be discontinued or immediately modified to ensure success.

The correct matching of activities to the children's abilities in order to provide the right degree of challenge to ensure progress is crucial in any learning situation. This has been highlighted in the HMI survey of primary education in England (1979),[2] and it appears that the majority of teachers do not 'stretch' the children in their class. In the development of language it is the teacher's skilful use of questions and provision of print materials of sufficient range and variety that provide the necessary challenge.

## 2.4 The teacher's use of questions

'Questions are an expression of curiosity and a demand for information. They are therefore a crucial component of the learning situation and a basic tool for the teacher.'[3] Questions can be explicit or implicit. Although young children frequently ask questions, often to the exasperation of their parents, on many occasions questions are not verbalized at all but are implicit in the children's actions, as for example when taking an object to pieces in order to find out how it fits together. At other times questions are implicit in statements made by young children, and it is necessary for the adult to verbalize the question in order to lead the child on a little further.

An example of this occurred when a teacher was working with a reception class preparing an aquarium for some goldfish. A bag labelled 'Washed Gravel' was emptied into the tank and each child poured in some water. One child observed, 'The water is dirty', and the teacher's question, 'I wonder why?' provided the impetus for an immediate investigation which generated the following questions:

'Where did the water come from?'
'Did the dirt come from the tap?'
'Did it come from the bottles used to measure the water?'
'Did it come from the gravel?'

As each possibility was investigated and eliminated, it gave rise to the next question. The children's conclusion was that whoever had washed the gravel had not done the job properly! It would seem from this that one question can give rise to many others and thus extend the possibilities for learning. Asking a question shows that the problem had been recognized by the person asking the question. Children need to be helped to see the problem and in such situations the teacher's use of 'I wonder why?' can be very useful.

A. F. Watts states, 'The most important kind of question educationally is the self-posed question. Our own peculiar difficulties and needs cannot always be discovered through questions set by someone else.'[4] John Holt, in *How Children Fail*,[5] suggests that children fail to learn because they are afraid. Most of all they are afraid of failing. The type of question used most frequently by teachers is asked in order to test the children's knowledge of facts. Such questions have a negative quality because they pose a threat to the child by raising the possibility of failure. However, the question the child asks himself comes from within and therefore constitutes no threat, allowing a positive search for the answer. Piaget has illustrated the difference between the thinking of a young child and the logical thinking of an adult. It is difficult for an adult to understand the illogical thinking of young children; therefore it is very difficult for an adult to formulate appropriate questions. Piaget incorporated this knowledge into his method of investigation: 'When a particular group of explanations by children is to be investigated the questions we shall ask them will be determined in matter, and in form, by the spontaneous questions actually asked by the children of the same age or younger.'[6]

The Nuffield Project for the teaching of science and mathematics in the primary school[7] placed great emphasis on using children's questions as a starting point for investigations. It was during involvement in the second stage of the project that one expert teacher became aware that the children did not ask the question she had anticipated; they usually made statements about what they had observed. For example, several budgerigars in breeding cages were introduced into the classroom and the teacher had expected some awkward questions when mating occurred. However, the children merely remarked that the birds were 'playing together', and she felt that this was a very appropriate statement for them to make. At a later stage, when they did begin to form questions, they usually had some idea of the answer before the question was asked. This meant that there was a greater chance of their answering the question successfully. As investigations proceeded they gave rise to further questions and this produced a 'snowballing' effect, as in the setting up of the aquarium.

It is vital for teachers to encourage children to form the habit of asking questions, especially during the early years in school. Children will then develop a 'set for curiosity', which is an essential motivating force in learning situations and also a factor in developing the ability to concentrate for long periods. The most successful teachers create in children a desire to know the things that it is essential that they should know so that the child's wants become synonymous with the child's needs.[8]

Skilful teachers make good use of story-telling sessions in order to develop children's language and comprehension skills. It is important for listening skills to be fostered, and the story session is one of the most enjoyable ways to do this. Listening for a purpose can be aided by asking questions on some occasions before telling a story; for example, 'I am going to tell you a story about Rapunzel and when I have finished I want you to tell me who made her a prisoner and how she was rescued.' This gives the children a purpose for listening and will help them at a later stage to define their purpose for reading.

Comprehension at the literal, reorganization, inference, evaluation, and creative levels can be developed if teachers examine their questioning techniques carefully, so that they ensure that over a period they ask questions within each category.

> 'Why did Hansel and Gretel leave home?' (literal)
> 'How do you think Goldilocks felt when she got home?' (if this was not explicitly stated in the story). (inference level)
> 'Do you think Jack was right to exchange the cow for a bag of beans? Why not?' (evaluation level)
> 'Can you think of a different ending to the story of the "Sleeping Beauty"?' (creative level)

From the teacher's viewpoint, questions are an essential diagnostic tool. It is only by posing questions that we can discover the stage of concept development that individual children have reached and thus be able to plan their future activities to accelerate progress or to refine a concept. Whenever we ask a child 'What do you think?' it is essential that we then ask 'Why do you think that?' As has already been mentioned, young children think very differently from adults, and we cannot assume that *we* understand their thinking. Asking 'Why?' will indicate the next step the teacher ought to take. It may be that some activity is needed, and possibly talk with a group or with the teacher will lead to further refinement of a concept by the child.

We would stress the importance of creating an atmosphere in which the child can gain confidence, and with insecure children enabling and sustaining strategies may often be necessary in the initial stages.

## 2.5 The teacher's use of children's questions

Language is the foundation of education, and the uses of language detailed by Joan Tough[9] will be necessary for children to benefit from the opportunities provided for learning in every area of the curriculum and at every stage of education. If the early years at school fail to provide the right foundation for learning, then no amount of special provision at later stages will be able to achieve the full potential of the child in terms of how far his learning will proceed, and how beneficial his attitudes are towards his future life and learning.

As has previously been stated, the teacher's use of questions is a crucial factor in developing language skills, but it is preferable to develop the *children's* skill in asking questions. The starting point for many questions can be found in careful observation of detail which will give rise to questions of 'Why?' and 'How?'

From this an active investigation will frequently arise and an extensive project may develop from one simple question. For example, after hearing the story of 'The twelve dancing princesses' one five-year-old girl was fascinated by the fact that the soldier who kept watch by the princesses' room secured a sponge under his beard to absorb the drugged wine given to him by the eldest princess. The following day she brought a sponge so that a demonstration could be given. This gave rise to a full-scale project on absorption, which led on to evaporation, to streams, rivers, and oceans, to the flow of water from high to low levels and types of soil in river beds; boats sailing with the current and against the current were studied, with the effect of this on speed, the use of the wind through sails, and observations of sailing boats tacking. Then came the development of a musical activity about rowing a boat upstream and downstream by contrasting heavy and slow rhythms with quicker and lighter rhythms; experiments with sections of plastic gutters to investigate the effect of different degrees of slope on the flow of the water; and (later) how water gets to the bathroom upstairs, the water systems in houses, and the electricity systems in the home (see Fig. 2.1). The interaction between the teacher and the children is vital, and it should be noted that the children's questions were used as a *basis for activity* which *the teacher extended* to provide learning situations across the curriculum and to carry the children's thinking to greater depth. All this activity was accompanied by much discussion. Talk was the means by which all the questions and activities were linked and further development ensured. The teacher's careful observation of the children's statements enabled her to turn these statements into questions from which investigations and further questions were developed (see Fig. 2.2).

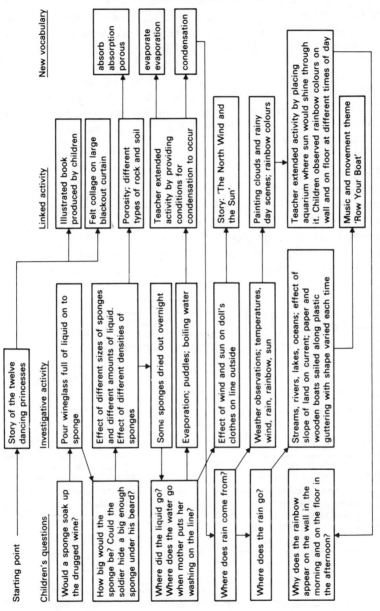

**Fig. 2.1** Children's questions: an example with five-year-olds in the second term in school

## 2.6 Recording the children's investigations

Many children begin to lose interest and develop negative attitudes towards school when it becomes necessary to record the results of their activities. This is frequently because teachers and parents expect too much of children in early stages at school. Their physical development may make it difficult for them to produce acceptable written records, and in addition it is extremely difficult for many children to fuse together the necessary component skills for written recording. Figure 2.3 gives some indication of the complexity of the task.

## 2.7 Sequencing

Sequencing plays a key role in children's recording. Reporting on an activity requires the child to remember details in the order in which they occurred, and sentences describing the activity must be arranged mentally in the right order. The sequencing of words within a sentence is the next step, followed by the sequencing of letters within a word. In the early stages it is helpful if the child

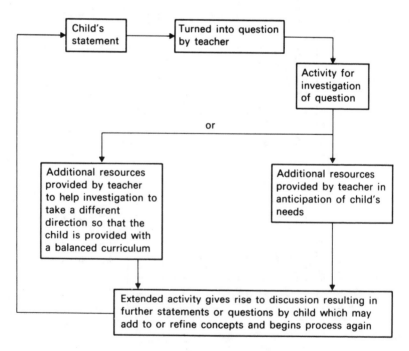

Fig. 2.2 The spiral learning situation

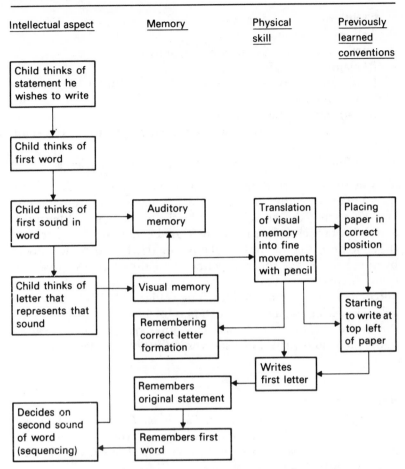

**Fig. 2.3** Skills used in written recording

draws the sequence in picture form or perhaps arranges a sequence of pictures supplied by the teacher. Pictorial activity cards are especially helpful at this stage, and suggestions for suitable apparatus are given at the end of this chapter. When the child can sequence separate pictures correctly, he can be asked to describe the activity, and his description be recorded. This can then be typed on a Jumbo typewriter (or printed with felt-tip pen) and cut into strips to match to the pictures. In this way the child's spoken language is produced in print for him, and this will provide a sound basis for his first attempts at reading. The learning sequence then becomes:

1. Child's question—discussion.
2. Activity—discussion.
3. Further questions, discussion, and activity.
4. Remembering activity.
5. Reporting activity verbally with or without the aid of sequencing pictures.
6. Recording on tape-recorder.
7. Sequencing his sentences which have been printed or typed for him.
8. Reading finished sequence to the teacher and/or friends.

This method of recording children's experiences provides a rich source of early reading material which is developed through using language across the curriculum and is the product of an integrated activity approach to learning. The main benefits are that, because the child produces the content, it is personal to him and understood by him, because the concepts contained within it are the products of his experience. Excitement and motivation are the usual outcome, and the quality of learning is high. The child may also achieve satisfaction if his production is used by other children and the teacher's valuable time saved for other groups. This also adds to the range and variety of resources in the book corner.

## References

1. HUTT, C. (ed. HOWELLS J. G.), *Play in the Under Fives*, Modern Perspectives in the Psychiatry of Infancy, Bruner/Mazel.
2. *Primary Education in England, A Survey by HM Inspectors of Schools*, HMSO, 1978.
3. GALL, M. D., 'The use of questions in teaching', *Review of Education Research*, 40, V, 707–20, 1970.
4. WATTS, A. F., *The Language and Mental Development of Children*, Harrap, 1944.
5. HOLT, J., *How Children Fail*, Penguin, 1965.
6. PIAGET, J., *The Child's Conception of the World*, Routledge & Kegan Paul and Humanities Press, 1929.
7. *Nuffield Mathematics Project Teachers Guides*, Chambers for the Schools Council, 1970.
8. DEARDEN, R. F., *A Philosophy of Primary Education*, University of London Press, 1967.
9. TOUGH, JOAN, *Talking and Learning*, Ward Lock Educational, 1977.

**Suggested reading**

TOUGH, JOAN, *Listening to Children Talking*, Ward Lock Educational, 1976.

TOUGH, JOAN, *Talking and Learning*, Ward Lock Educational, 1977.

**Useful resources**

Sequencing Cards (in graded series), Learning Development Aids.

BURRIDGE, A. and BROWN, M. G., Squeezebox Food Activities, Nelson, 1977.

# 3. The growth of language and reading

It is often difficult to answer the question, 'What is reading?' There are many parents who see 'reading aloud' to the teacher as the only concept of this activity, and a fluent reader who does not read to his teacher during the day or the school week is often thought not to have been actively engaged in reading. In fact, he has probably been engaged in numerous reading activities throughout each day. Reading is, of course, a much more complex activity than just the oral process of reading aloud. Gray's definition of reading is perhaps useful to recall in this connection:

> i A response to graphic signals in terms of the words they represent;
> ii a response to text in terms of the meanings the author intended to set down;
> iii plus: a response to the author's meaning in terms of all relevant previous experience and present judgements of the reader.[1]

Gray does strongly emphasize that reading is not just a decoding process but also a thinking skill. It is of the utmost importance, therefore, in the initial stages of reading to use only those words that are within the child's own language register so that he can recognize the relationship of sound to symbol more readily.

## 3.1 The language experience approach to reading

This approach recapitulates the historical development of writing and reading. Communication first developed through touch and signs, followed by spoken sounds developing into language. The recording of events for future descendants was achieved through pictures, and from pictorial representation writing evolved, followed by reading.

If children are involved in worthwhile exciting activity they will *want* to communicate their achievements to others, and it appears logical to use the stages through which written recording developed. So, to begin with, the children will talk about their activities; later a drawing or painting may capture their enthusiasm, followed by a wish to interpret the printed word which tells of a happening that is personally important to them. This is the basis of the language experience approach to reading.

Some teachers may find it difficult to accept an approach to the teaching of reading that is not dependent upon a 'key word'-controlled vocabulary basis. In fact, the 'controlled vocabulary' element is there. The vocabulary content is limited to words already used by the child. The 'key words' approach, which is based upon words that appear most often in written English, does not include the words that are usually most emotive from the child's viewpoint, so possibly loses some impact.

We have considered the transformations:

activity → discussion → questions → investigations → discussion → pictorial recording → verbal interpretation of pictorial record → printed or typed recording of verbal interpretation.

This provides some meaningful reading material for the child, and at the same time provides practice in the uses of language concerned with reporting and logical reasoning. Part of the investigations and discussions may also involve predicting what might happen during an experiment. However, children also need reading material that stimulates the imagination and introduces them to experiences of other people, experiences at secondhand.

Many teachers find that it is possible to produce their own reading schemes or supplementary readers for the classroom library by producing books invented by the children. One class of backward readers, aged seven to eight years, built a village out of cardboard boxes. They each made a house or shop for the village High Street and invented families to live in them. The teacher then provided a tape-recorder so that the children could dictate stories about their 'families'. The following story was dictated by a seven-year-old boy.

> One sunny day Mr Green was driving his van and he stopped at someone's house to deliver some coal. She said 'I would like two bags please.' While he was waiting for the money, Mr Green slipped inside for a cup of tea and some biscuits.
>
> While he was inside, a naughty boy came along, smoking fags. He chucked the match on to the lorry and it all caught fire. When Mr Green went out, he saw his lorry was on fire. It was all burning and smoke was coming out of the engine. They phoned the policeman and the policeman phoned for the fire engine.
>
> The fire brigade came and Mr Happy was driving the engine in his fire hat and cloak and yellow trousers. Mr Happy got out the hosepipe with the other fireman and connected it to the engine and water came out. They squirted it on the fire and it went out. The police came and looked for fingerprints. They found a fingerprint on the side of the lorry and they looked for the boy. They found him in a field lighting matches to make a fire.

They caught him and took him to the Police Station and asked him questions.

'Where do you live?'

'What is your name?'

'Who are you working for?'

They took him to court and got his mum and dad and fined him two hundred pounds for lighting matches and putting them in a lorry that was worth a lot of money.

Mr Green got his hands burned and Doctor Magpie said 'Is your hand still hurting?' Mr Green said 'No'.

Doctor Magpie gave Mr Green some tablets to take each day.

Many stories were invented and the children were very proud of the books produced. The texts were typed using a Jumbo typewriter and the upper half of each page was used for an illustration beautifully produced with felt-tip pens. Strong cardboard backs were covered with paste papers and decorated labels were fixed on the front covers.

The gains in reading progress were very impressive, and an unexpected result was that these very anti-social children began to co-operate with each other to produce stories, and became mutually supportive.

The teacher found that she had to struggle with herself when she had to type words such as 'fags' and 'chucked', but she had resolved to use the children's language and carried it out with determination. It was noticed that much of the content was concerned with food, which appears to be of universal interest, yet is not mentioned very much in commercial reading schemes.

Projects of this kind give children a real sense of achievement and provide a purpose for writing. In many classrooms the child's writing is usually read only by his teacher and possibly by his parents on an open evening. Even then his work is probably corrected in red ink by the teacher. The Language Experience Approach makes use of the child's creative ability in language and art and presents his skills in such a way that means that other children can benefit from them and show appreciation. When the child has developed his reading to an appropriate standard and has acquired the necessary manual skill, he can progress to writing his own stories.

Above all, the child should enjoy his involvement in talking, writing, and reading. This can be ensured by making the experience personally interesting to him.

Many children will go from strength to strength in their reading achievements, needing little instruction from the teacher and developing their own strategies for decoding the printed word. Other children, however, will need a careful systematic approach which will ensure that they are ready for each new stage in the reading process.

## 3.2 Readiness at all levels

The professional judgement of the teacher is crucial in the reading process, and it is vital that the correct 'match' is achieved when selecting reading material for each individual. Reading tests that give a 'reading age' are of little or no help in achieving this match, and teachers are turning to diagnostic tests as an aid to planning individual learning programmes. The booklet produced by the West Sussex Psychological Service[2] is a good example of tests that help to plan the next step in the teaching programme. Many teachers develop a system within the classroom that enables them to follow a logical plan for the class as a whole, and this requires a wide variety of materials and approaches and may include the development of an informal reading inventory. One such plan for beginning work with a new class in a new school situation is given here. Teachers who are familiar with their school will already have the general information needed.

The plan is set out as a decision-making flow chart (Fig. 3.1), and a list of references is given as a key for ideas that can be developed by the teacher to suit her own class. This plan could be adapted to include the materials already available within the school, so that the teacher has a wide range of materials and approaches from which to select the most suitable for each child.

**Key**
1. J. M. Hughes, *Phonics and the Teaching of Reading*, Evans, 1972.
2. *Classroom Index of Phonic Sources*, NARE, 1980.
3. L. Wenden, *Pictogram*, NARE, 1979.
4. D. H. Stott, *Programmed Reading Kit*, Holmes McDougall, 1971.
5. E. Goodacre, *Pictures and Words*, Blackie, 1971.
6. J. Tough, *Listening to Children Talking*, Ward Lock Educational, 1976.
7. J. Tough, *Talking and Learning*, Ward Lock Educational, 1977.
8. *Assessing Reading Ability*, West Sussex Psychological Service, 1972.
9. C. H. Jones, *Left to Write*, Autobates Learning Systems, 1976.
10. Picture Sequence Cards, Learning Development Aids.
11. J. K. Jones, *Colour Story Reading*, Nelson, 1967.
12. *Concepts: 7–9 Listening with Understanding*, Schools Council, 1972.
13. J. M. Hughes, *Aids to Reading*, Evans, 1970.
14. R. I. Brown and G. E. Bookbinder, Clifton Audio Visual, ESA, 1969.
15. B. Hornsby and F. Shear, *Alpha to Omega*, Heinemann, 1974.

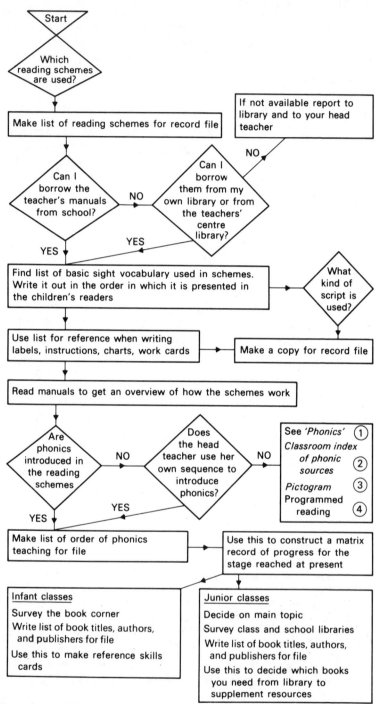

**Fig. 3.1 (a)** Strategy for beginning reading with a new class. General Information

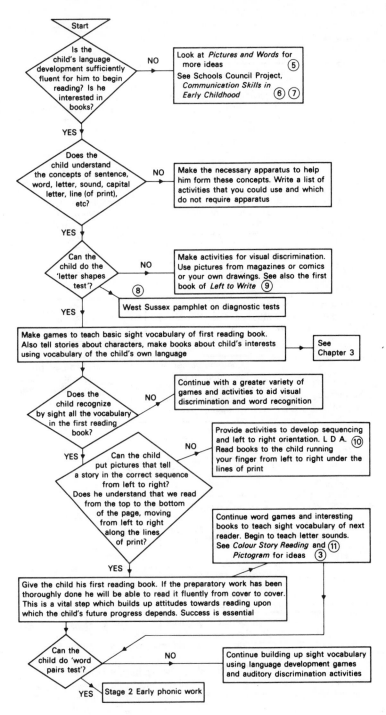

**Fig. 3.1 (b)** Specific information. Stage 1 Introductory

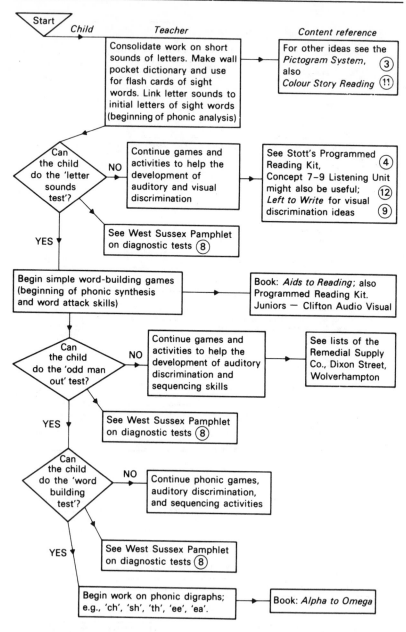

**Fig. 3.1 (c)** Specific information. Stage 2 Early phonic work

## 3.3 Levels of reading ability

It is useful, not only in the infant years but throughout school life, to categorize a child's reading ability with regard to a particular text as at one of the following three levels.

1. *The independent level.* At this level the child can read a text fluently and with understanding, making not more than one error in any 100 words and comprehending at least 90 per cent of his material. Obviously this gives the teacher the clue to the difficulty of the books that the child ought to be using for his own researches and his own pleasure.

2. *The instructional level.* Word recognition at this level should be 95 per cent with comprehension at least 75 per cent. It is this level of text that the teacher should be using when she hears a child read, for at this stage miscues by the reader help in diagnosis of his problems in the actual decoding of the printed word. So, too, at this level the teacher has the opportunity to develop thinking skills and comprehension abilities in the child.

3. *The frustration level.* As its title implies, this is the level that can do great damage. Word recognition is 90 per cent or less, and this trouble with decoding leads to a failure to comprehend even half the subject matter. It is a level of text at which no teacher ought to ask a child to read, for there is no larger obstacle in the path to fluency than failure.

Occasionally when a child is moved from a text that he can just master at the instructional level to one that the teacher thinks will present only slightly more difficulty, he fails. He has obviously not overcome all the problems at his former level and needs more help.

## 3.4 The understanding of the heard text

The comprehension of text that is read aloud can also be considered on these levels and judged when skilled questions, using a language similar in difficulty to the text itself, are posed.

All of this should help the teacher to provide reading material for silent reading and for reading aloud at a suitable level, and not to risk the child's frustration in one area, or an abdication of attention caused by inability to follow oral language in the other. Her ultimate aim, of course is for every child to be able to comprehend fully when he reads for himself, so that there will be no necessity for the teacher to translate the printed word into speech.

## 3.5 Phonic teaching and context cues

In the early stages the child will rely heavily on memory in building up a sight vocabulary through the Language Experience Approach. As his skills in auditory and visual discrimination are refined, he will be able to benefit from phonic teaching which will aid the development of word attack skills.

The key to later success in using flexible reading skills lies in the ability of the teacher to maintain the correct balance in the use of phonic cues and context cues. Too great an emphasis on phonics will result in slow, exact, unimaginative readers. If reading is a thinking activity then children should be encouraged to make sensible guesses by anticipating the text. The opportunity for self-correction will arise if teachers do not correct every word immediately the child makes a mistake, and this will preserve his self-confidence.

## 3.6 Hearing children read

It is important that every school should have an agreed policy about hearing children read. *Hearing Children Read*[3] by Elizabeth Goodacre is useful as a discussion document for staff wishing to develop their skills of miscue analysis. This is a method of diagnosing children's reading difficulties so that suitable activities can be provided to overcome them. Some agreement between staff about the frequency of miscue analysis is needed, and the way in which records of this should be kept will ensure consistency of approach within the school.

Another aspect upon which staff agreement is necessary is the phonic progression to be used. Before choosing a phonic programme care should be taken to ensure that there is a progression. Too often children are expected to decode early words containing phonic digraphs that are taught much later in the programme. This can lead to frustration and failure. Readiness is essential at every stage of the reading programme and the teacher must actively prepare this state of readiness to ensure the child's success.

Many necessary reading skills can be developed through the use of various games and activities and the teacher will need to use professional judgement to decide on the value of particular activities in terms of the needs of individual children.

## 3.7 The development of reading skills through classroom activities

Classroom activities can be evaluated only within the context of the whole reading development programme. A particular activity may have great value in developing reading skills at one particular point in the programme, but be quite useless if used at a different time. The value of an activity is dependent upon a number of factors—the context in which an activity takes place, the expertise of the teacher, the needs of the individual child, the level at which the activity is presented, and the objectives of the whole programme.

The context in which the activity takes place plays a decisive part in estimating its effectiveness. The manner in which the school and the class are organized is important, and various questions need to be considered:

1. How formal or free is the school organization?
2. What type of organization does the class teacher use?
3. Do the children choose their activities or is the decision made by the teacher?
4. If the children choose what they *want* to do, is this also what they *need* to do?[4]
5. Does the teacher make the distinction between 'wants' and 'needs'?
6. If so, how does she do this and what effect does this have on the motivation of the children?

The teacher must know the detailed sequence of stages in any content area in order to provide the optimum conditions for effective learning. Gagné states: 'If learning at any level is to occur with greatest facility, careful attention must be paid to its prerequisites.'[5] In order to know the prerequisites of any task, the teacher's knowledge must be detailed. In addition, her knowledge of the child must be extensive and up to date if she is to provide a suitable programme of activities to ensure steady progress. She needs to know about his background in order to make allowances for his anxieties and to be able to build upon his interests so that he is strongly motivated to develop his abilities. This information needs to be up to date so that she is aware of the stage and level of the child's progress—in Gagné's terms, she knows the prerequisites that have been achieved by the pupil. She can then combine this information with her knowledge of the content of the reading curriculum and decide on the optimum activities for the child's present stage of achievement. The teacher must therefore keep careful records of progress (further reference in Chapter 14).

These records of progress will indicate the stage of development of skills and therefore help the teacher to provide the next step. In the early stages the foundations are laid and activities should be provided to ensure that the later development of higher-order skills is facilitated.

Fig. 3.2 illustrates the opportunities provided for the development of reference skills through a succession of activities spread throughout the primary school.

Many teachers assume that reference skills are developed after children become fluent readers, and some even think that they should be left until the secondary stage; yet we believe that the foundation for these skills begins in the reception class.

The activities are viewed in terms of the 'spiral curriculum', mentioned earlier, which starts from a particular activity—that of finding a specified book—and is returned to and built upon at each successive stage.

The development of reference skills can be started at the pre-reading stage in an incidental manner; the teacher notices that a group of children is particularly interested in the animals in the classroom and suggests that there is a book in the book corner which she will read to them. Some dust jackets have facsimiles of the actual cover of the book. When books are new, these paper jackets can be removed, trimmed and mounted to provide work-cards for practice in early book identification skills, provided that the library books are displayed with their front covers showing, not simply their spines. The teacher can then select the card for the book and ask an individual child to find it. This can be done by simple picture matching which helps to develop visual skills, discrimination between cover illustrations, and sorting and classifying abilities. It also helps to develop the child's ability to scan book shelves for a particular book.

At a later stage the teacher can do the same type of thing in another situation but expect something more of the child, so that after he has found the book he is asked to find a picture. For example, he could be asked to find a picture of a helicopter during a discussion about 'flight'.

When the child has reached the stage of beginning reading and has the ability to match sentences and words, the task becomes more demanding. He can be given a card with the title of a story on it, as well as an illustrated book cover. He then scans the

Activity

| Activity \ Skill development | Scanning bookshelves | Scanning book | Using contents table | Using alphabetical order | Using index | Devising key words | Skimming page | Synthesis of information | Suitability of materials | Using Dewey system | Using card index |
|---|---|---|---|---|---|---|---|---|---|---|---|
| Finding own media for information needed | ✓ | ✓ | ✓ | ✓ | ✓ | ✓ | ✓ | ✓ | ✓ | ✓ | ✓ |
| Finding information from two or more suggested books | ✓ | ✓ | ✓ | ✓ | ✓ | ✓ | ✓ | ✓ | | | |
| Finding information about topic, given book title only | ✓ | ✓ | ✓ | ✓ | ✓ | ✓ | ✓ | | | | |
| Finding information about topic, given book title and key words | ✓ | ✓ | ✓ | ✓ | ✓ | | ✓ | | | | |
| Finding chapter in book when given chapter title | ✓ | ✓ | ✓ | | | | | | | | |
| Finding information in book relevant to present interest, given page number | ✓ | ✓ | | | | | ✓ | | | | |
| Finding story in book (a) picture clues (b) story title matching card (c) given page number | ✓ | ✓ | | | | | | | | | |
| Finding picture in book relevant to present interest | ✓ | ✓ | | | | | | | | | |
| Finding book by matching cover | ✓ | | | | | | | | | | |

Fig. 3.2 The development of reference skills

bookshelves for the book, and scans the book for the story title, developing still further his ability to discriminate.

It is necessary for the teacher to observe how the child goes about his task; she may write out a card for the child indicating the title of the book and the titles of the chapters that he needs to read in order to satisfy his specific purpose. The teacher's objective on this particular occasion may be to create the need for the child to use the contents table in the book, though he could find the chapter by operating at an earlier level (scanning the book to match the chapter title) unless she makes the purpose of the activity clear to him. The opportunities for skill development may be provided by activities, but it is up to the teacher to see that these opportunities are used.

Through the use of classroom activities, many of which can take place in an incidental manner and *at the time when they meet the child's needs*, the teacher is able to lay the foundations for higher-order skills which are necessary at a later stage.

> Discovery methods of learning, to be effective, require certain basic skills of which reading is probably the most important, followed closely by the knowledge of how to use an index, simple dictionaries and reference books. While it is true that young children, even before they have started to read and write, can begin to discover, observe, experiment and compare, their progress is necessarily limited by lack of these skills.[6]

It is important that the teacher discusses the value of each activity with the child so that he is involved in his own progress in skill development. The value of activities cannot be judged in isolation: the same activity used by different teachers will have different values and effects. These effects depend on different school situations, different children, different levels of achievement, and different stages in the curriculum. For this reason it is preferable that the activities should be devised or adapted by the teacher herself in order to meet the varying demands of her class. If this is done, the objectives of reading skill development will be efficiently achieved. This is a dynamic exercise and test of the teacher's skill in adapting to changing situations.

## 3.8 The principles of pleasure and choice

Everyone will pursue an activity that gives him pleasure, and children are no exception. Teachers who give children a choice of activity usually find that children are more committed to their choice than to an activity that is imposed upon them. If the activities for reading can be linked with the interests of the children, then commitment can be sustained and the quality of learning improved. In addition, because the children are interested, there is a greater chance of success, and this builds up positive attitudes towards learning. In the early stages the teacher must be sure to teach, by look-and-say games and activities, all the vocabulary in each book *before* giving it to the child to read. It is important to hear him read his first book from cover to cover so that he has a great sense of achievement, and the teacher must be sure that he can do this with 100 per cent success. This is a crucial step, and an adequate amount of time without interruption should be set aside to do this. Discussion between teacher and child about his first book is another vital factor in establishing desirable attitudes towards reading, and if the content of the book has been dictated and illustrated by the child then his personal interest will be assured. From this talk with the teacher, the child will absorb many things such as how enjoyable it can be to understand the meaning of the printed page; and the way in which the teacher gives him her undivided attention will convey to the child that his progress and enjoyment in reading is important to her. Lots of praise and a shared sense of achievement will enhance his desire to read, and this will be reinforced still further if the book has been made of personal interest to him (see Sec. 3.1 above).

## 3.9 Children's choice

Allowing the child to make choices in a variety of situations has some advantages for the child and also for the teacher. We believe that the use of children's choices is not sufficiently exploited by many teachers. It is fairly common for the children to be allowed a choice of activities and equipment during a 'free-activity' session, but unusual for this to happen in the context of mathematical activities or reading books.

This is probably because teachers feel that they must ensure progression in easy stages in the basic skills, and the most usual way to do this is to adopt set mathematics and reading schemes for a whole school. In this way continuity from class to class is ensured as well as a gradual progression for each individual child. However, this frequently means that when a child has completed one reading book he is presented with the next one by the teacher without having the opportunity to express his own wishes. As adults we would probably feel rather aggrieved if the local librarian chose our books for us, yet we see no reason why we should not choose for children. If only we gave them five or six books to choose from in the early stages many children might develop a strong affinity for books. Engineering this choice would present teachers with the task of grading books at many different levels and ensuring that the child knew the vocabulary necessary for each group of books before asking him to choose from them.

The advantages would be that, because the child *chose* the book, he would be better motivated to read it. The activity of choosing would also help to train his powers of judgement and discrimination. In addition, the child could read six or more books at the same stage of he wished to, thus building up confidence. The teacher could also ensure that children whose progress is slower could stay at the same level until fluency was achieved.

A school policy for children's choice in reading could be organized in stages as follows:

1. Staff meeting to draw up a list of books (i.e., reading schemes and other early books) that members of staff have found popular with children.
2. Ordering of not more than six copies of each book in a large school, less for a small rural school.
3. Rough sorting into stages using any reading scheme books as a framework for grading non-reading scheme books.
4. Setting up a central store with numbered cupboards, e.g., sets of locker cubes in entrance hall or library arranged to form work bays for individuals or groups to use; cupboard number 1 should contain lots of picture books with no written words so that pre-reading skills can be developed from the child's own choice of picture book.
5. Final sorting of vocabulary analysis so that a list of the vocabulary and phonic blends needed for each cupboard can be provided for each member of staff.
6. Each teacher to ensure that the child is taught through games and activities the vocabulary and phonic blends listed *before* he is allowed to choose from a particular cupboard.

The organization of such a method of working is a time-consuming task in the early stages, but it is very easily built upon once the main framework is established.

The initial stage could be spread over two years if necessary or speeded up if interested parents help by listing the vocabulary content of books. One school found that, because no two children had to use the same progression of books, an unexpected bonus was the elimination of competition among parents by comparing one child with another. Progress was seen not only in the difficulty level of books but also by the number of books listed on the child's reading record.

It is important that children are not expected to progress at too fast a pace, and this type of book organization makes it possible for the teacher to say to a child, 'Today you can choose from cupboard number 5 or 6.' If the child chooses a book from cupboard number 5, he will be extending his interest in books and operating at the independent level of reading, thus consolidating skills already learnt and developing fluency. All too often these aspects of reading are not developed when one or two reading schemes are followed slavishly.

As children produce their own story books, these can be slotted into the book organization, thus providing further resources as well as a purpose for children's writing.

### 3.10 Points to consider when choosing a reading scheme

1. The context in which a scheme will be used
   - (a) Will it be the main scheme for the school or used in conjunction with other reading schemes?
   - (b) If so, will it be compatible with the other schemes in terms of vocabulary content, style of language, type of print, content, phonic progression, and size of print?
   - (c) Is it suitable for the type of children and their background of experience?
   - (d) Is it near to the children's natural speech rhythms?
   - (e) Does the vocabulary match the active and passive vocabulary of the children?
   - (f) Are the illustrations meaningful for the children?
   - (g) Which age groups will it suit?
   - (h) Is the construction of the book suitable; e.g., are the covers strong enough and are the books stitched or stapled?
   - (i) Is the paper strength and quality suitable?
   - (j) Does the cost fit in sensibly with your budget requirements? Is it value for money in *your* school?
2. Progression
   - (a) Does the teacher's manual give clear guidance on progression?
   - (b) Is there a suitably planned pre-reading stage?
   - (c) At what pace are new words introduced?
   - (d) Is there a balanced rate of vocabulary repetition (i.e.,

frequent enough to consolidate learning but not so frequent as to develop boredom)?

(e) Are the illustrations complementary to the text and graded in complexity?

(f) Is there a sensible phonic progression and is it acceptable to you?

(g) At what pace are new sounds or phonic rules introduced?

(h) Does the sentence construction encourage contextual guessing right from the early stages? Is this structure for the use of context cues developed gradually to ensure the use of complex context cues at later stages?

(i) Is there a suitable progression in the length of stories and in the development of story plots?

(j) Does the record card indicate clear progression in reading skills?

3. Content

(a) Do the illustrations attract interest?

(b) Do the stories appeal to you?

(c) If there are supplementary readers are they also attractive and interesting?

(d) Is there sufficient variety of content?

(e) What bias do you detect in the content (e.g., is there a sex bias or a bias towards middle class or working class experience)? If so what do you feel about this?

(f) Are there work books? If so, do they help the development of readng skills, or merely test memory at a literal level, or just provide a time filler? Are they varied in format and content? If so, will this be an advantage or a disadvantage?

4. Format

(a) Is there a varied approach? If so does it create interest through different sizes and shapes of books and different styles of illustration or is it likely to develop insecurity through lack of consistency?

(b) Is the print large for early readers and reducing sensibly for readers at later stages of development?

(c) Are the words and lines of print suitably spaced to aid vision?

(d) Are the breaks at the end of a line of print made at points where this is an aid to comprehension?

It should be remembered that structure comes from the teacher's knowledge of the process of reading which leads to alternative pathways to success. This develops from the sensible sequencing of activities and materials, combined with the effective use of records of progress to diagnose weaknesses in reading skill development. Structure does not come from the narrow limits of a reading scheme, although this may provide a rough guideline in the initial stages of development of the comprehensive resources for reading.

### 3.11 The use of play

The importance of activity has already been stressed, and many language and reading opportunities will arise from children's play. From careful observation the teacher will learn when to intervene in order to carry the children's play a stage further, perhaps to develop oral language or to engineer the necessity for the children to write and to read. Guidelines for using children's play in learning situations is provided in *Structuring Play in the Early Years* by K. Manning and A. Sharp.[7] Children choose to play because it gives them pleasure, and many teachers find that using play as a motivating force for learning basic skills facilitates their task. Useful ideas for sand and water play can be found in E. J. Arnold's 'Sand and Water',[8] and one box can provide resource material for a whole school. Other useful material can be found in *Language for Learning* which is produced by the Inner London Media Resources Centre.[9]

Young children learn a great deal through their senses, and for this reason it is wise to use real objects in learning situations rather than substitutes. For example, if plastic fruit is used in the home corner or the classroom shop this will not provide the right experiences for the development of concepts related to weight and texture. The quality of provision for children's play is very important, and skilful teachers will ensure that high-quality materials are provided so that a multi-sensory approach can be used. Descriptive language will arise from questions such as 'What does it feel like?' and 'What does it taste like?' It is the development of oral language concerned with personal sensory experience that will release the flow of written language at a later stage.

### References

1. GRAY, W. S., *Promoting Personal and Social Development Through Reading*, University of Chicago Press.
2. LABON, D., *Assessing Reading Ability*, West Sussex County Council, 1972.

3. GOODACRE, E., *Hearing Children Read,* University of Reading School of Education, 1972.
4. DEARDEN, R. F., *A Philosophy of Primary Education,* University of London Press, 1967.
5. GAGNE, R. M., *Conditions of Learning,* Holt, Rinehart & Winston, 1977.
6. SOUTHGATE, V., 'The importance of structure in beginning reading', in *Reading Skills, Theory and Practice,* UKRA/Ward Lock Educational, 1970.
7. MANNING, K. and SHARP, A., *Structuring Play in the Early Years,* Ward Lock Educational, 1977.
8. JACKSON, S., MAHON, S., and WHEELER, E., 'Sand and Water', E. J. Arnold, 1978.
9. *Language for Learning,* ILEA Media Resources Centre, 1976.

# 4. The organization of the infant classroom

Although every school situation is different, it is essential to make some detailed suggestions for classroom organization and we hope these guidelines will help by outlining the main issues needing consideration.

Obviously, experienced teachers will already be using many if not all of the ideas incorporated in this chapter; nevertheless, a little time spent on it could prove rewarding. For the less experienced the practical advice may offer a great deal of support.

This chapter should be read in conjunction with Chapter 10, 'Organization of the junior/middle classroom', which examines further principles in organization and is complementary to this section.

## 4.1 General organization of space

It is best to divide the classroom into areas, some of which will provide opportunities for work that makes no mess, some for quiet activities, and some where sand, paint, and clay may be used freely.

The following list of areas may be useful:

1. *'Messy areas'*—i.e., sand, water, clay, painting, and crafts.
2. *'Quiet areas'*—i.e., mathematics, reading and writing, book corner.
3. *Other areas*—i.e., small-scale constructions, large-scale constructions, home corner, shop, interest table, music corner, woodwork bench.

This list contains a great many items, and if space in the classroom does not allow all these activities to take place at the same time, alternatives must be considered. For example, a clay and water table may be provided outside on a fine day; two easels may be set up in the classroom near the sink if you have one, or perhaps in a corridor, provided it is near enough to ensure supervision. All these activities provide experiences that will lead to the effective development of learning at the infant stage and will provide the basis for promoting language growth.

Other ways of alternating activities are to consider the possibility of using the home corner as a shop for half the term, or as a music room for part of the day. If there is a carpeted area the additional provision of a few colourful cushions will make it an inviting place to enjoy books. This area could also be used for part of the day for large constructions built with floor bricks and construction toys, and the carpet will deaden much of the noise, making it possible for children to talk to each other about their constructions and to collaborate in some ventures, as well as deadening the sound of falling bricks.

## 4.2 Organization of areas

Having decided upon the most practical way of utilizing the available classroom space, the furniture and equipment necessary for each area must also be organized with care. Tables will be needed for writing, mathematics, interest, and display, and for small-scale construction work. They may also be necessary if the sand and water trays have no stands, and for use as shop counters, puppet stages, and other occasional special activities. These activities all involve social interaction through talk, as well as providing a focus for intellectual and imaginative development through discussion with teacher and peers.

## 4.3 Storage

Different types of storage will be needed for specific apparatus. Mathematics apparatus is best stored on open shelves within easy reach of the children, but it may be necessary to have a lockable cupboard for musical instruments to avoid accidental damage to them. Books should be displayed so that the attractive cover illustrations will arouse the children's interest and make it easy for them to find the books they need for reference (see page 42); a tightly packed collection with only the spine showing does not appear nearly as attractive. A very narrow ledge can provide suitable display space for thin books by using plastic-covered curtain wire to hold them in place. Wall pockets can be tailor-made to hold pictures and work cards in areas of the room convenient for the children's use. Where space is limited it is often possible to design some apparatus that can be folded for storage when not in use. A simple clothes-horse-type construction, for example, can become a home corner or a shop. The tops of low cupboards standing at right angles to the wall may be utilized as display spaces and the plain backs of these cupboards will provide additional areas for pictures, book covers, or wall pockets and charts. Wall racks that have a space for each article help to guard against loss and ensure training in tidiness, and a silhouette chart behind the rack will help children to match shape to object in the pre-reading stage.

Small items for collage work and junk modelling will need to be kept in labelled trays or drawers, and larger empty cartons can be housed in a tea chest or a sack hung on the back of a large cupboard door. Children will benefit from the sorting and grading activity of nesting boxes inside one another, and this will ensure economical use of space as well as providing excellent experience in judging sizes appropriate to specific purposes. All this experience will help the children to make sensible decisions at a later stage with regard to the best sizes and shapes of materials needed for diagrams and written communications of all kinds.

## 4.4 Detailed organization within the areas

The provision of labels is an essential introduction to one of the purposes of written language, as well as an aid to the efficient management of classroom resources. In the early stages labels for work areas should be in the form of sentences so that the children's attention is focused on the meaning of the written words. This will emphasize the use of context cues in reading rather than concentrating on decoding skills too soon; for example,

| 'Two children can play with the water' | rather than | 'water tray' |

At a later stage both single-word labels and sentences should be used. Hooks or racks for woodwork tools, scissors, etc., should have one hook or space for each item so that apparatus can be checked at a glance. A backing card with the 2D shape or silhouette of the article will provide a visual discrimination activity in matching a 3D shape to its 2D counterpart, and this is a prerequisite to success in the ability to interpret pictures and diagrams in books as well as in some mathematical skills. Baseboards for organizing the placement of articles on shelves and tables provide another easy checking device at the end of a session, for example, a money board and a pencil board, as shown in Fig. 4.1. The labelling of the baseboards also provides a matching exercise of 3D shape to 2D shape, and the matching of an article to its name or symbol. As stated in Chapter 1, this provides a filing pin on which the child can organize his associations and experiences.

Two examples of labelled baseboards.

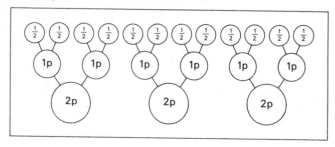

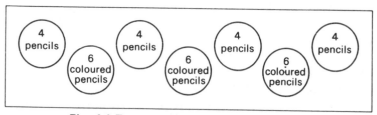

**Fig. 4.1** Two examples of labelled baseboards

Wherever possible the children should be involved in the activity of making the storage equipment required, as this provides opportunity for talking about the proposed organization and ensures that they are motivated towards using and maintaining equipment in an orderly and caring way. For instance, when introducing word sources it is helpful if the first set of wall pockets are made by the children, as this provides increased motivation to use them.

Several word sources are essential in any infant classroom. Their use promotes the children's independence in writing activities, saves the time of the children and teacher, aids success and fluency in written work and encourages an interest in words, leading to progress in alphabetical order and reference skills (further reference in Chapters 3 and 7).

### 4.5 Word sources

Word sources in the classroom are any places where words are written (either with pictures or without) that children can refer to when they want to know how a word is spelt.

The first word that a child learns to read and write is usually the one that is most meaningful to him—his name. In the early stages he will need to place tracing paper over his written name and trace it; later he will copy it and, later still, write it from memory. It is, therefore, important that he is provided with a name card which is clearly written in large print, possibly with a little picture which will help him to keep the card the right way up while he is tracing (see Fig. 4.2). If the picture is placed on the left-hand side he can be encouraged always to start his tracing on the left and work towards the right; 'start at the side where the picture is'. He should be encouraged to make downward strokes for a straight letter or part of a letter and anti-clockwise/clockwise strokes for curves.

**Fig. 4.2** A name card

Along with the name card it will be useful to provide cards that have a simple picture and a word or sentence. Some disadvantaged children will benefit from being provided with a card that has been made by sticking paper on to the background card to make a simple picture—the slight 'bump' of the edge of the paper will help to guide their pencils, giving them a better finished result which will encourage them to keep trying. When good control has been achieved with this method, a 'flat' picture-and-word card may be used (see Fig. 4.3).

(a)   (b)

House    Doll

**Fig. 4.3 (a)** A square card on to which is stuck paper 'windows' and a 'door'; a triangular card for the 'roof' is stuck on top of the square and the whole is mounted on another card
   **(b)** A line-drawing, coloured with paint or a felt pen, with solid black outlines for ease of tracing

A child can make six tracings, which can then be stapled together to make a 'book' which he can take home. In order to add his name to the book he can place his name card underneath a space on the first page and trace his name onto it. (Some children prefer to add their name to each sheet, so as to avoid mixing up their work with someone else's—this is of course very good practice for their writing skill.)

The picture-and word card is useful as a word source. When the child draws his own picture he can copy the word on to his page—if he draws a house he can find the card with a picture of a house on it, and copy the word without having had to ask the teacher what it said. Picture clues as an aid to finding words are very important at this stage. Once he can copy a word successfully, the child can become much more independent, even though he cannot yet write any words from memory.

Alongside the picture-and-word cards, which usually deal with isolated words, usually nouns, the child needs to see whole sentences and longer pieces of writing. In this context the nursery rhyme card is useful. A card with a picture and a short rhyme helps the child to connect the spoken word with the written word, and to see patterns in the words. Once the child is reading, he can use the nursery rhyme card to find words for his writing. If the child wants to write 'sat on a wall' he can find the card that has a picture of Humpty Dumpty on it and work out the words he needs by reading through it. A few examples are shown in Fig. 4.4.

At the same time the child will be looking at words in all kinds of contexts. Labels on objects in the room are very useful, for the child can learn new words and reinforce them every time he looks at the label. Both single words and sentences should be used.

In the early stages many children will profit from making their own book about anything that interests them. The child may draw a picture; when he describes it to the teacher, she writes the sentence or word for him. As he handles material like pencil and paper, crayons, paintbrush, scissors, jigsaw puzzles, construction toys, and manipulative apparatus of all kinds, the child will begin to develop greater control of the finer muscles of the hand, and will achieve better eye-hand co-ordination.

## 4.6 The child's responsibility

The most successful classroom organization is one that involves the children, making them responsible for the day-to-day tasks, demanding that they make sensible decisions so that the

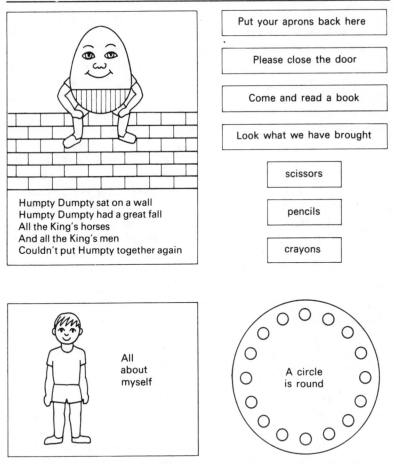

Put your aprons back here

Please close the door

Come and read a book

Look what we have brought

scissors

pencils

crayons

Humpty Dumpty sat on a wall
Humpty Dumpty had a great fall
All the King's horses
And all the King's men
Couldn't put Humpty together again

All
about
myself

A circle
is round

**Fig. 4.4** Examples of word, sentence, and nursery rhyme cards

development of personal autonomy is encouraged, and the teacher is left free to teach. The teacher will need to plan the children's involvement and the following decisions will be necessary:

1. The tasks to be delegated to children.
2. The period of time each child will have the task.
3. Who will take over if the child is absent (perhaps it is better to have two children responsible for each task)?
4. The occasions when children can make a personal choice.
5. Which activities may be pursued outside?
6. Who will fetch and carry for outdoor work?
7. Where 'noisy' activities and 'quiet' ones will be located.

## 4.7 Working out-of-doors

As well as providing space for movement, messy activities, and freedom to pursue noisy tasks, working out-of-doors extends the number of experiences that the class teacher can provide for her children. For example, a gardening or pond project may be possible if the school has its own grassed area. In addition, the freedom to move between indoor and outdoor activities is a normal experience for preschool children and their school experience in the nursery and infant situation should provide continuity. Although moving equipment takes time, it is a task that demands co-operation and responsibility on the part of the children and is therefore a valuable learning situation if suitably organized by the teacher. The following points may be useful for those wishing to introduce this activity for the first time. (Further help can be found in *Structuring Play Workshop* by K. Manning and A Sharp.[1])

It is a good idea to have painted wallboard fixed to the outside walls at a convenient height for pinning up the children's painting paper. This gives painting or chalking provision for many more children and saves carrying clumsy easels outside.

If the classroom has no direct access to the playground, this will make it difficult or perhaps impossible to move furniture outside. A suitable work surface for large-scale constructions may be provided by the use of mats which can be rolled up and carried easily. The mats will provide a defined area for different types of floor activities and children frequently enjoy sitting or lying on them to read their favourite books.

This saves moving furniture outside, and as lightweight mats are easily managed by young children this can be particularly useful when the weather may be changeable, necessitating a quick withdrawal indoors. The arrangement of outdoor activities should be such that the teacher can easily keep an eye on both indoor and outdoor events.

Clearing away is sometimes a lengthy task with young children, but a planned orderly end to a period of lively activity is necessary. A ready store of short stories, rhymes, and poetry provides a good basis for a quiet group session. The few spare moments available at such times may also provide the opportunity for comment and discussion linked to the children's immediate experiences and helps to refine concepts recently formed through activity.

## 4.8 Planning the daily routine

### Formal timetable

If you have a formal timetable, either because the head teacher provides it or because you prefer it, then the daily routine is already decided. However, as has already been stated, pupil talk is the raw material from which progress in education is produced, and it will therefore be necessary to change the routine a little in order to provide opportunity for profitable conversation, preferably with the participation of an adult. If at all possible the adult should be the teacher, but on some occasions it may be appropriate for the nursery nurse, or a parent who has had some guidance from you, to lead a group. It may be possible to rearrange things slightly so that a semi-formal programme can be followed, and work on a circulatory basis can help to bridge the gap from the rigid timetable to the integrated day.

### Semi-formal timetable

If the class is divided into three mixed-ability groups and the day into roughly three sessions, then by rotation it can be ensured that the children have a balanced programme. Although some time may be taken from each session by such things as assemblies, hall

|  | Day 1 | | Day 2 | | Day 3 | |
|---|---|---|---|---|---|---|
| a.m. before play | Literacy | 1 | Mathematical activities | 1 | Creative activities | 1 |
| | Mathematical activities | 2 | Creative activities | 2 | Literacy | 2 |
| | Creative activities | 3 | Literacy | 3 | Mathematical activities | 3 |
| a.m. after play | Mathematical activities | 1 | Creative activities | 1 | Literacy | 1 |
| | Creative activities | 2 | Literacy | 2 | Mathematical activities | 2 |
| | Literacy | 3 | Mathematical activities | 3 | Creative activities | 3 |
| p.m. before play | Creative activities | 1 | Literacy | 1 | Mathematical activities | 1 |
| | Literacy | 2 | Mathematical activities | 2 | Creative activities | 2 |
| | Mathematical activities | 3 | Creative activities | 3 | Literacy | 3 |

**Fig. 4.5** A possible semi-formal timetable

times, television, etc., over a period the amount of time each group spends on each area of the curriculum evens out. A possible scheme is shown in Fig. 4.5. First-year infant children during part of their literacy period will be developing early reading skills concerned with picture books and auditory and visual discrimination work, as well as work with picture sequences.

Young children need to be reminded of things every day because they easily forget what happened yesterday. It is good to begin or end the morning or afternoon with a class session—talking about anything exciting that has happened, and spending a little time reading information around the room.

Many games can be invented for this, some proving more popular than others. During the first week it will be necessary to concentrate on training the children in the organization that has been planned. If things do not work out as expected try some variation during week 2. Be adaptable but do not be in too much of a hurry, because young children need time to adjust to school and to adjust to new people and the organization of their time.

If children have come from a teacher who has operated an entirely integrated day there may be no need for the intermediate plan above. In this case, however, careful records of progress are essential to ensure that there is a clear picture of progression in basic skills emerging.

### Integrated day

This system makes great demands upon the teachers because they must be able to plan a programme and yet be flexible enough to capitalize on spontaneous interests. Yet if they can overcome this difficulty the quality of learning is usually much improved because the children's motivation is greater and the provision of a wider curriculum leads to a greater variety of interests. The main problems that need to be considered are the organization of the *teacher's time* and the detailed record-keeping necessary for the organization of flexible groupings of children to ensure effective teaching (further reference in Chapter 11). The teacher must have a system for checking that each child completes a suitable amount of work, and this will be geared to each individual's capabilities.

## 4.9 Organization for reading, talking, and writing

The teacher must have in mind a clearly defined progression in all aspects of language growth, and also a number of alternative ways to help children through this progression (see Fig. 3.1 (a) 'Strategy for beginning reading with a new class').

It may help to organize the work by thinking about the grouping of children. If the class is divided into six groups, each group could pursue a different activity:

1. Talking, using a tape-recorder or with a trained adult.
2. Listening, using a tape-recorder with junction box and headphones.
3. Individual reading to the teacher.
4. Writing.
5. Structured games to develop skills in reading, writing, and talking.
6. Independent reading for pleasure.

These headings are elaborated in some detail below.

*Opportunity for talk*, using a tape-recorder or with a trained adult, should be provided for children at the early stages of expressive writing (further reference in Chapter 7). This could be a straightforward discussion about a visit, a television programme, a planned concert, or a puppet show. The list is almost limitless, and although in the early stages talk will be mainly concerned with the children's individual or shared experiences, further development will be stimulated by the use of topics such as 'An adventure we would like to have'. This will prepare the way for more imaginative expressive writing at a later stage. Co-operative group talk with young children is important also for the refinement of basic concepts, and it provides the basis for many social skills as well as developing the ability to discuss and make judgements, so important at later stages of education. Painting, sculpture, junk modelling, mathematics, drama, simple song writing, and further reading provide other alternatives for follow-up work.

It is important that the teacher provides a variety of ways in which events can be followed up, so that the usual cry of children, 'Do we *have* to write about it?', can be avoided.

*Listening* with the use of a tape-recorder together with junction box and headphones occupies a group of children and thereby reduces the noise level in the classroom and ensures that the teacher can attend to other tasks. It helps to resolve one of the problems in the classroom, which is the lack of time to spare for the individual child. Auditory discrimination games such as 'Sound Lotto',[2] 'Listening with Understanding',[3] or taped stories from familiar books will provide ideas for those who have not yet used a group listening device (further reference in Chapter 5).

*Individual reading* to the teacher has always been a traditional priority in infant classes. Recent developments in research have stressed the importance of the teacher's diagnosis of reading difficulties during this individual session. The dangers of dwelling too much on the decoding process have also led to the recognition that context cues need to be stressed more than phonic teaching. The teacher must however know the structure of phonic progressions in order to balance the programme of reading for individuals according to the specific areas of difficulty (further reference in Chapter 3).

*Writing* needs to be developed and encouraged with the greatest of care. Children are frequently reluctant to write independently because they have been discouraged at an early age by teachers demanding written work too soon. Expressive written work is the result of progress in many skills, including oral expression, the ability to sequence events, physical skills for the mechanics of writing, visual memory for letter shapes, auditory memory for isolating sounds, knowledge of spelling and punctuation, vocabulary development, and thinking skills. There is a stage of 'readiness' needed for each step in recording expressive language, and the teacher must be sure that the child has all the prerequisite skills before proceeding to the next stage. Success at every stage is essential if the child is to progress satisfactorily. Oral language development must precede written language, and a variety of ways of recording expressive language should be used.

Ideas for stages in the development of expressive writing are given in Chapter 7, and handwriting is also discussed in more detail in that chapter.

*Structured games* to develop skills in reading, writing, and talking can be developed by the teacher to suit individual children or groups of children. Ideas on which to build can be found in *Language for Learning*[4] and the Communication Unit of 'Concept Seven to Nine'.

*Independent reading for pleasure* should be provided regularly for every child. The non-readers should have access to many picture story-books and it is important that all children should be provided with books that are at an easier level of readability than the book that they read to their teacher. This group could also be trained to use a simple film-strip projector so that film strips of award-winning books can add to their enjoyment.[5]

The dangers of colour-coding books according to the readability levels are discussed in Chapter 13. As with most infant activities, it is important that the child is given a wide choice, but this must be engineered by the teachers so that the choice is right for the child's stage of development. Readability is best measured by the use of cloze procedure (see further references in Chapter 8, also the writing modes shown in para. 6 page 198 and in Chapter 7).

## 4.10 Organization for independence

This is the keynote of a well-organized classroom. The children should be trained to use simple battery-operated tape-recorders so that the talking and listening groups can proceed without the teacher. The writing group will need a number of word sources if the teacher is not to be constantly interrupted to provide spellings. A 'word bank' or 'wall pocket dictionary' is useful, as well as the individual word book and collection of picture dictionaries. The teacher will also need to have in mind a simple progression for developing independence in expressive writing.

If an integrated day is used, the teacher must ensure that children can work independently at some stages of the day in all areas of the curriculum. One of the main problems arises when children cannot read the work cards provided. Here the teacher must bear in mind the progression needed in the reading material. Care must be taken to see that instruction sheets, reading material, and mathematical work cards are at the correct level for the individual child.

## 4.11 Structuring work cards

Although in the initial stages of learning to read it is beneficial to use a Language Experience Approach with little limitation in the vocabulary, when children are working independently in other areas of the curriculum control of vocabulary content will be a key factor in their ability to work from work cards or books, without the teacher's constant attention.

Some teachers may find the following outline of stages useful.

### Stage 1 Teaching vocabulary

The teacher must compile a short list of words that will be used in the early stages. For example in early mathematics work cards the teacher may decide to use 'count', 'draw', 'how many'? Flash cards should be made using good infant script and avoiding the use of capital letters in the early stages, as shown in Fig. 4.6. These cards can then be used for word games; and, when the teacher is confident that a group of children can read them, work cards using this vocabulary can be introduced (see Fig. 4.7).

| count | draw | how many? |

**Fig. 4.6** Infant script flash cards

**Fig. 4.7** Work cards

At this stage careful thought must be given to the ways and means the children are able to use to record information. Some possibilities are:

1. Using actual objects and matching numbers on cards.
2. Tracing the card and tracing numbers on separate cards (this requires quite a high degree of manual dexterity).
3. Drawing cards and copying numbers.
4. Using rubber printing stamps such as those that accompany the 'Happy Venture' scheme and matching numbers.

### Stage 2 Pictorial cards

It is useful for the teacher to produce small templates corresponding to the apparatus the children will use. For example, in work

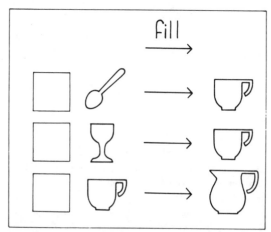

**Fig. 4.8** For work concerning volume and capacity

concerning volume and capacity, templates for a spoon, a cup, an eggcup, and a jug will make it easier to plan, and quicker to produce, work cards. The mapping arrow can be used with a word to give a direct function or instruction (see Fig. 4.8).

The children's recording may now take the form of tracing or copying the cards as before, and numbers on separate cards may still be provided for the child to copy if necessary. In addition, if the child has the necessary skill he may also use the templates made by the teacher. Care should be taken to see that the children do not become dependent upon any one method of recording. They should always be encouraged to have confidence in their ability to make progress in writing and drawing as their physical development continues. The ability to draw can be retarded or frustrated by over-dependence on drawing aids such as templates.

### Stage 3 Introducing written statements

As the children make progress in reading it is helpful to provide a written statement as well as the pictorial instruction, as shown in Fig. 4.9. The statement for the child to copy should be printed in a contrasting colour for clarity.

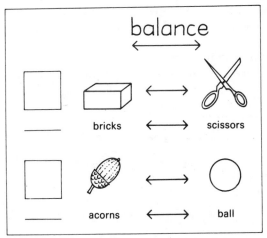

**Fig. 4.9** Introducing written statements

Recording will be similar to that at stage 2. If boxes in which objects are kept are clearly labelled 'bricks', 'acorns', 'pencils', etc. this will reinforce the reading necessary for work cards.

**Stage 4 Written instructions with statements for completion**
Most teachers of young children will be familiar with the problem
many children have when confronted with work cards or
comprehension cards—not knowing what to write. This frequently
results in the child copying the question as well as, or instead of,
giving the answer. This can be overcome by printing instructions
in black ink and providing a statement for the child to complete,
printed in a contrasting colour (see Fig. 4.10).

Can you weigh milk?

Weigh an empty cup.

The empty cup weighs..........

Weigh the cup full of milk.

The full cup weighs.............

So the milk weighs..............

**Fig. 4.10** The child copies and completes the statement printed in colour

The child records by copying the statement printed in the
contrasting colour and completing it.

**Stage 5 Information and questions**
At this stage information is given and then a question asked (see
Fig. 4.11). As before, a statement for completion is provided,

1 apple costs 2p.

How much do 2 apples cost?

2 apples cost.............

1 orange costs 3p.

How much do 3 oranges cost?

3 oranges cost ...........

Write some questions for your friend.

**Fig. 4.11** The child responds by copying and completing statements

printed in a contrasting colour. Red is usually a good colour to use as it tends to stand out well.

When the children are capable, it is good to finish with an open-ended assignment. By this stage the children should be reasonably fluent readers and writers, but teachers should always check that the vocabulary content used at each stage is within the capabilities of each member of the group.

### Stage 6  Question cards
These are similar to the cards used at stage 5, but the statement for the child to copy is omitted. This type of card should be used only with children who are confident and fluent readers and writers.

The above examples are based on work cards for mathematics, but the principles can be applied to the production of work cards for any subject. The aim of such a scheme of easy stages is to enable the child to work as independently as possible.

It should be remembered that basic skills are more efficiently learned in the context of the wider curriculum. The use of work cards tends to lead towards the practice of skills in isolation, and there is doubt about the ability of children to transfer these skills to everyday problems. Teachers must, therefore, ensure that their use contributes towards the achievement of teaching objectives.

Whenever possible oral discussions in practical situations is likely to be more fruitful than the use of work cards, particularly if the teacher gives attention to the choice of appropriate questions (further reference in Chapter 2).

### 4.12 The teacher's task
Each teacher will need to make her own decisions about organization within the classroom. These decisions will relate to inanimate things such as space, storage, equipment, sources of reference, movement of materials, and the use of time. The way in which these things are organized will affect the people within the classroom, and it is important that the children's stage of development is kept firmly in mind while decisions are being taken.

Children will benefit greatly from a careful progression in social and organizational skills, and the ultimate aim is that they will become independent learners at the later primary stage, so that the transition to the secondary stage is facilitated.

Other factors that the teacher must consider are the kind of organization the last teacher and the next teacher use, the way in which she herself prefers to work, and the abilities of the children in her class.

All the organization decided upon should facilitate the use of talk as a foundation for progress in all areas of the curriculum for each individual child, and the provision of written material at the appropriate level.

## References

1. MANNING, K. and SHARP, A., *Structuring Play Workshop*, Schools Council Publications, 1978.
2. 'Sound Lotto', Remedial Supply Co., Wolverhampton.
3. WRIGHT, J., *Concept Seven to Nine*, 'Listening with Understanding', E. J. Arnold, 1972.
4. *Language for Learning*, Media Resources Centre, ILEA.
5. 'Filmstrips and Tapes', Weston Woods Ltd.

# 5. Developing talk

Most teachers believe that language is of major importance in education. Unfortunately, for many, particularly those who teach children upwards of seven years of age, this has come to mean the skills of reading and writing only. Indeed, as one experienced teacher said recently, 'These children come from their infant school chattering nineteen to the dozen, and even helping one another with their work. I soon put a stop to that.' Of course, there is a time for silence, for individual work, for listening attentively; but all teachers must bring themselves up to date with the knowledge of how learning takes place and what motivates it, and the vitally important part that speech has to play in the process.

## 5.1 The importance of talk

There are many reasons, obvious to the perceptive teacher, why talk in classrooms is so necessary. A child's lack of ability to express himself, his ideas, and his feelings to his peer group leads often to deep frustration, which manifests itself sometimes in temper tantrums or sulks, or in his withdrawal from the mainstream of life. A child who cannot communicate cannot make friends easily, or share his joys or sorrows or ideas with others, or join in with free drama or creative play; indeed, he is in danger of becoming an isolate.

Children need speech not only to form relationships with others but also to organize themselves, to play a part in the life of school, to become integrated into the peer group. Without it they are denied much that is important in life.

Language also helps the child to explore his environment, to understand his experiences, and to come to terms with them. Help is frequently needed, and here the requirement is a good relationship with his teacher; confidence is of great importance.

We must ensure first that he has something to talk about, second that he is motivated to speak, and third that he has someone to talk to—and other children are not always a satisfactory audience. Interesting things around the classroom help, or perhaps pictures of the area around the school of children playing games, of themselves, of their families, friends and animals, of models they may have made. A camera producing instant pictures has great value when meeting difficulty with a reluctant talker. Other good starting points are the senses—touching, tasting, observing, and listening.

There is a place, even in the classroom, for what has been referred to in the United States as 'non-task-orientated talk' or, even better, 'relatively unstructured interpersonal intercommunication', which is frequently stigmatized as 'idle chat'. Maybe the former terms are more correct in spite of their rather high-flown language, for this is the speech that enables the child to play a vital part among his peers.

The pre-school child whose parents have talked to him and have also encouraged him to talk has a flying start in building a rich and extensive vocabulary. In school a child needs to sense the sympathetic understanding of his teacher before he will put his trust in her. He also needs to feel trusted and respected and, above all, encouraged. If we believe that children learn through experience, we must guard against giving them too many second-hand experiences in the junior and middle schools. They still need a stimulating and interesting environment for development in this area; and, unfortunately, there are often classrooms where discussion, conversation, and play activities do not take place because teachers regard them as solely infant experiences. The junior schoolchild still needs to express himself, to verbalize his thoughts, and to reason out situations, often in words not internalized. If language is to be an efficient tool of communication, then there is no substitute for usage. It is, after all, one of the activities that is uniquely human, and it is part of the total experience of all normal activities.

## 5.2 The language of learning

Conversation among friends is not, however, the only language that teachers must help to develop. Far more is involved in the language of learning, the language one needs for the formation of concepts, and for the higher cognitive skills of problem-solving and complex thinking.

During the last three decades there has been an upsurge of knowledge of the way in which people learn and of the enormous contribution that language has to make, yet very little of this knowledge has been put into practice in schools.

Teachers have a positive role to play in the development of the child's cognitive powers. No easy matter! It calls for knowledge of the theory and for down-to-earth detailed classroom organization of activities and time (particularly the teacher's own time). It needs also skilled use of language (again, particularly the teacher's own) in all aspects of teaching, but perhaps most in discussion and the use of questions.

Speech matters. (We are talking here not about dialect, or voice production, or elocution, but of the ability to use the language fluently.) Currently there are many demands, both locally and nationally, for assessment and accountability. These create pressure and cause anxieties. Teachers sometimes feel that if they are not taking a class lesson they are not using their time profitably, and that if children have not produced a mass of written evidence at the end of a day, they also have not worked fully.

It is useful to ask why talking so much seems to have become an occupational hazard. For some teachers it may well be because they enjoy holding the centre of the stage and find the greatest satisfaction in uttering themselves!

Or do they give way to a feeling of guilt if they allow the children time to learn, and, for an hour at a time, cease to 'inform'?

Or do they feel pressured by lack of time and take what appears to be the quickest way, explaining everything and not remembering that the material will probably be as quickly forgotten by most listeners?

Or is it, indeed, more satisfactory to teachers to give an answer rather than to discuss; does this give a warm glow of omniscience when the use of skilled questions would enable the child to tease out the solution to a problem for himself?

Speech has a heuristic function—that is, we learn by talking. It is important to remember at all times that not by any means all silent children are learning from the teacher's words of wisdom, and to realize the amount of forgetting that takes place if no active participation in the lesson is allowed.

### 5.3 The use of talk

As far as assessment is concerned, how is it possible to know how much of what is taught is assimilated by the pupil unless he is encouraged to talk about his learning in the type of speech that comes most easily to him? He must, for this, use the language nearest to him. Short regurgitated phrases of rote-learnt sequences or monosyllabic answers to closed-ended questions will not inform the teacher of the child's understanding. Children quickly learn to receive messages from some teachers as to whether or not their answer is the one required. These communications do not have to be verbal—the raised eyebrows, the jerk of the head, or the body posture are adequate non-linguistic gestures for most children. Furthermore, use of a word is not conclusive evidence that the word has been understood, and what is being played is often a kind of guessing game.

There are many books of howlers on the market, and teachers could all offer contributions ('obstacle illusions'—where an eight-year-old had tried to make sense of an unknown word; likewise, 'an infernal combustion engine'), 'My Dad plays the cornet in the Starvation Army', said a six-year-old whose parents are deeply concerned with work for the poor. 'My favourite hymn is "Pretty mice in plicity", said small girl, translating words far above her understanding which she had only learnt by hearing older children singing. Unfortunately, many of these books are indebted to an authoritarian style of teaching.

During a discussion with a group of six-year-olds the question 'What is science?' was asked. The teacher explained very carefully how science involved finding out by experiments, and pointed out that the children themselves had been doing just this earlier in the week (a) when they had planted seeds and bulbs, and (b) when they had been blowing bubbles, examining their flight, bursting point, colours, and the rest. One keenly interested, but sadly deprived, small boy announced delightedly, 'I know what a speriment is, you drop it in water and see if it comes out in bubbles.' Had his teacher been satisfied (as so many are) that her explanation was sufficient, and not encouraged the further discussion which she then initiated, she would never have known the gross misinterpretation of her explanation.

And if this is a danger in school, how much larger does it loom in later life? We pondered on a note left by a milkman recently: 'UOI 17p'. Words are used nowadays to influence, persuade, and indoctrinate in ways that were undreamed of prior to this century. Radio and television bring other people's voices into our homes as never before; it is imperative that today's children grow up able to assess the worth of heard statements and not be deluded by voice or by emotionally loaded words. Indeed, never before have people in all walks of life so needed the ability to understand and quantify the words of others. And again, never before has it been so necessary to be able to express oneself in terms that can be clearly understood by those listening.

This raises the whole question of classroom organization and of relationships between teacher and taught. In a most subtle way it demands a more honest relationship, where the child feels safe to explore ideas without risk of ridicule or reprimand. From active participation in lessons, from opportunities devised by the teacher to ensure that the child discusses his experiences, can come the sparking-off of ideas from other children, can develop communication, can come the gradual assimilation of new forms of language—indeed, of new ways of thinking. Details of organization in the classroom that will help to promote work of this kind will be found in Chapters 4 and 10, but a few examples will illustrate the points at issue.

## 5.4 Practical applications

With the younger children a great deal of speech arises naturally out of the type of activities suggested in Chapters 2 and 3. As children get older it is necessary to ensure that discussion in small groups does not disappear from the timetable, but conversely that a wide range of opportunities for talking is provided.

When a child brings an article of interest to himself to school to show his teacher it can be an exciting starting point for good discussion. It may be that the teacher is preoccupied first thing in the morning by administrative detail, or hurried by the necessity of getting to the hall on time for the start of the school assembly. Nevertheless, by cavalier postponement of attention, important teaching contact can be lost for ever. Time must be made for talk on these occasions and it should be friendly and informal, with the teacher listening and accepting the ideas and information offered, and participating in a genuine conversation between two people. Her own contribution should be offered without pontification, and further enquiry may be aroused by skilful questioning. Children must be encouraged to share their out-of-school interests in this way. Problem-solving is a spur to discussion, and talk in itself is a help towards effective learning for it enables the speaker to sort out his ideas for himself.

Similar opportunities for exchange of ideas occur when a class or a group of children are out of school, perhaps on a 'discovery walk' when something interesting or unfamiliar is seen. Walks through mixed woodlands full of flowers or over seaweed-covered rocks are wonderful, of course, but so too are explorations of city streets, slum clearance sites, busy shopping centres and village communities. Indeed, there are always many exciting starting points to be found in the environment, however drab it may at first appear. A few suggestions here will show how easy they are to find:

1. Street names.

2. Traffic.
3. Playground games.
4. Weeds.
5. How a village developed (using an urban traverse initially).
6. An old graveyard. (The high infant mortality rate of the last century is an almost certain spur!).
7. Architectural features, good or bad.
8. A rubbish dump; a village pond which has become an eyesore.
9. Play-areas and facilities (or lack of them).
10. Plant habitats.
11. Building sites (with care!).
12. The effects of trampling on plants and grass.
13. Plant growth in pavements, cracks, and walls.
14. Holes.
15. What can be found in park litter.
16. Hedges.
17. A patch of waste ground.

The teacher must not underestimate herself or the part she has to play in all of this, even though we would recommend that groups of children are sometimes left to work alone. It is in the direction of the exercise towards a suitable outcome that most children need guidance and support. (There are the exceptions, of course; a few children can motivate their own learning with very little outside help.) Unprepared group work, particularly if children are new to the idea, can be a waste of time and make their behaviour potentially difficult to handle. Prepared work cards can be of the utmost importance initially. Planned results are also necessary, one of the most obvious being to ask the group to report its findings to the rest of the class. (For the various methods in which this might be done see Chapter 9.)

This necessitates decision-making about methods, note-making during the exercise to facilitate accurate recording, and, last, justification of conclusions made during their work.

There is a two-fold aim implicit here. First, there is the sorting out of the learning by the group in discussion using their own terms—dialect forms, hesitations, repetitions, the fumbling towards the solution of the problem set. It is easier for most children to assimilate new ideas if they are allowed to use non-standard speech. Second, there is the reporting back, with its demand for explicitness and clear exposition, in correct and more formal language suited to a different occasion and different audience. This is in itself a daunting challenge to many children, and confidence can come only by practice, and by teacher encouragement.

Small group discussion in thematic work will be referred to in detail in Chapter 9, but when a small number of children have gained a fair amount of knowledge about their subject from their books, from their teacher, and from their research, it is good to ask one or two questions demanding that the group bring to their deliberations a depth of thought that will be much more than the recall of learned facts. For example:

1. The 9-, 10-, and 11-year-old children in one primary school took as their theme for the term 'The Life of Tutankhamen'. The question they were asked to consider in depth was, 'How would the boy Pharaoh have felt when, forced by his generals and his powerful priests, he had to change his religion from the worship of one god back to the old pantheistic religion?'
2. A mixed-ability class of 7- to 9-year-olds who had been studying the development of printing (see Chapter 9) were challenged to think deeply when asked, 'If radio communication and television had been invented before the art of printing, would this have affected out present way of life? Could it have changed the course of history?'
3. Following a field study expedition during which several 10-year-olds went down an old coal mine in the Forest of Dean, the children were asked to consider the conditions in which child miners were employed during the eighteenth and nineteenth centuries.

Even mistakes can prove to be valuable. The following two instances show how errors in mathematics were exploited to stimulate both discussion and further work.

A class of 6-year-old children had recorded graphically their favourite 'school dinner'. Because their graph had failed to have a uniform base line, an unpopular menu was apparently the winner, and the children knew that this could not be correct. But why? An animated conversation, with many opportunities for logical reasoning, quickly arose.

Two 11-year-olds who were mapping a building (using a Silva compass) made a two-degree error in their compass reading. This tiny mistake was so magnified when the plan was drawn to scale that they were immediately alerted and forced by their amazement into considering why this had happened and how it could be avoided in the future. Indeed, this led them to draw up a long list of recommendations and conclusions which they wrote out in detail for the rest of their classmates, to save them from falling into a similar trap.

Group work in experimental science presents another excellent opportunity for oral language development. The children should be asked to hypothesize, to select and reject from experience, to follow a logical train of thought and to discuss together their conclusions.

There is no lack of help on this subject (*Nuffield Science 5–13* is full of suggestions). As children work together, for instance exploring possibilities with batteries and circuits or discovering the properties of magnets, they should be encouraged to use the language most familiar to them, but it is on these occasions that the teacher can introduce the correct technical terms which most children love and quickly adopt as part of their own fully understood vocabulary. It is therefore essential, when planning group work for the class, that the teacher plans her day so that at times the rest of the class are gainfully occupied in some work that does not need her full attention. Her contribution to group discussion is of the utmost importance—as a receptive listener, as a catalyst, and as an asker of pertinent questions leading to clarification of thought and further ideas.

These learning situations need to be planned so that both doing and thinking are required, and where talk will mean that the experiences are being explored together. For one thing, the verbalization of thought helps concept formation. For another, children who have not learnt from their parents how to think logically towards the solution of problems can be greatly helped by following the train of thought as others verbalize their way through.

We are certainly not suggesting that the child never ventures forward; it is the teacher's task to use her skills to improve the child's use of language, to introduce new patterns of speech, to develop vocabulary, and to teach essential technical terms. We are saying that children need to use them, to take a full part in the talking that accompanies the work, if these new ways of using language are to become part and parcel of their own speech, and if they are to be enabled to select appropriate language for different situations and different material. Active participation is the best method of ensuring learning. (It may well be that mental, not physical, activity is what is needed at the time, so long as it can be ensured that it is indeed taking place.) This may challenge the whole of a teacher's style.

Discussion among a group who have either read, or have had read to them, one particular story helps them to 'read beyond the lines', to understand the careful sequencing necessary for plot development, and to recognize traits of character. Group prediction is a major aid in helping children think ahead. This is fully explained in Chapter 8.

So, too, a deeper appreciation of an author's intentions comes when a group of children read together, and then talk about, for instance, a poem or an extract from literature. Together the children will sort out their problems using the rest of the group as a bouncing wall; together they will relate the ideas the author expresses to their own experiences, so understanding not only the poem better, but also themselves.

When first asked to undertake this kind of exploratory talk the children's efforts may seem somewhat purposeless. Teachers should not be discouraged by the discursive and wide-ranging nature of the arguments, or by the introduction of apparent trivialities and irrelevancies into the conversation. The more often children are given the opportunity to read and discuss together in this way, the greater will be their appreciation of the author's viewpoint, and they will grow in awareness and sensitivity if they are constantly encouraged to remember their previous readings and refer back to them.

Drama, too, is an excellent stimulus for linguistic expression, as can be seen in Chapter 12.

Teachers must therefore work out for themselves, and their schools, their aims and objectives in oral work, and a means of recording them.

## 5.5 The teaching style

Teachers should analyse and evaluate not only the performance of children—attention to their own performance is essential. Those carefully thought out aims and objectives help greatly in this evaluation. If, as we believe, the use of spoken language is an important aid to literacy, then opportunities for speech in the classroom are an essential part of development. For this, thought given to the formation of groups is vital, because children need to learn to talk not only with their friends, not only with their intellectual peers, but with all manner of people. There are some children who are able to mix easily; there are a few who are natural leaders; but there are many who need the teacher's help.

To this end the pattern of group formation needs planning.

Sometimes they should be friendship groups, sometimes they should be composed of children of like ability—these two are frequently very similar to one another, and care for the isolate is a necessary corollary. Nowadays, too, it is imperative, wherever possible, that sometimes the group crosses the barriers, not only of class, but of race and creed. And there is a time, when the type of work to be done makes it practicable, to form groups of children whose ability varies widely, or groups that embrace members whose handicaps, either physical or mental, or whose attitude and temperament make them difficult to work with.

Children can be helped by this towards an understanding both of others and of themselves. Differing group formation also helps children to consider the appropriate language for the needs of their particular audience.

Obviously not everything that is done in one day in school is organized in groups, though probably much will be. Each teacher must resolve for herself what lessons are best taken with the class as a whole: the teaching of some skills, possibly (as a saving of teaching time), the introduction to new work on topics, the sharing of knowledge gained, short, stimulating question-and-answer sessions, the rounding-off of a task completed, and the shared experience of well-read stories are obvious examples on the language side.

There will also be occasions too numerous to categorize completely when children need individual attention—maybe for direct teaching of something not fully comprehended, or for some new learning not appropriate for the whole class; maybe for the development of growth points noted in writing; or perhaps for discussion of hypotheses in a science experiment. Every teacher must consider how the children in her care are best motivated, and plan her approach accordingly. There is no sharp division, either, between formal and informal: the best method is that which best suits the teacher, the learner, the subject, and the moment.

What of our language? One of the arts of speech that the child's attention must be focused upon is that of listening with understanding, and remembering what has been said. Does the teacher's own register help or hinder the development of this art? A tape-recorder (an essential tool in every classroom) left running throughout the day and the resulting tape analysed in depth can be of the utmost help in finding out how learning takes place, and can be used to great effect in the improvement of many teaching skills. (A video tape-recording is even more salutary.)

It is the quality of the child's thinking that is of paramount importance, and the development of this is greatly dependent upon the quality of the talk that takes place in the classroom—which, in turn, is greatly influenced by the teacher's own contribution.

## 5.6 Discussion in the classroom (or lost opportunities)

Much that is designated 'discussion' by teachers is far from this, as many tape-recordings show. Frequently so-called 'class discussion lessons' are nothing more than question-and-answer sessions dominated by the teacher and shared in a small way by a few able children. This is particularly true of the type of lesson in which the teacher is asking for replies to closed-ended questions whose answers have been previously taught. The teacher here has a clear view of the answer she requires, and is prone to dismiss, to ignore, and so to underestimate, any answer that does not conform. There is a grave danger of missing any contribution from the pragmatic experience of child and of becoming too like that unpleasant caricature—Charles Dickens's Mr Gradgrind:

'Thomas Gradgrind, sir. A man of realities. A man of facts and calculations.'

Indeed, as he eagerly sparkled at them . . . he seemed a kind of cannon loaded to the muzzle with facts, and prepared to blow them clear out of the regions of childhood at one discharge.

'Girl number twenty,' said Mr Gradgrind. 'What is your father?'

'He belongs to the horse-riding, if you please, sir.'

'Mr Gradgrind frowned, and waved off the objectionable calling with his hand. 'We don't want to know anything about that here. You mustn't tell us about that, here. Your father breaks horses, don't he?'

'If you please, sir, when they can get any to break, they do break horses in the ring, sir.'

'You mustn't tell us about the ring, here. Very well then. Describe your father as a horsebreaker. He doctors sick horses, I dare say?'

'Oh yes, sir.'

'Very well then. He is a veterinary surgeon, a farrier, and horsebreaker. Give me your definition of a horse.'

(Sissy Jupe thrown into great alarm by this demand.)

'Girl number twenty unable to define a horse!' said Mr Gradgrind for the general behoof of all the little pitchers. 'Girl number twenty possessed of no facts in reference to one of the commonest animals! Some boy's definition of a horse. Bitzer, yours.'

'Quadruped. Graminivorous. Forty teeth, namely twenty-four grinders, four eye-tooth, and twelve incisive. Sheds coat in Spring;

in marshy counties sheds hoofs, too. Hoofs hard, but requiring to be shod with iron. Age known by marks in mouth.'

Thus (and much more) Bitzer.

'Now girl number twenty,' said Mr Gradgrind, 'You know what a horse is.'[1]

Here is Sissy Jupe, full of practical knowledge of horses gained from everyday contact with them, yet all she might have to offer is dismissed out of hand, to be replaced by Bitzer's string of learned facts, totally unrelated to experience. Mr Gradgrind's unspoken message was cruel, the spoken one scarcely less so. Sissy Jupe would certainly feel that anything she had to say was worthless. Unfortunate for her, hardly less so for Master Bitzer, who was given to understand that rote-learning constituted wisdom.

Mr Gradgrind missed also an ideal opportunity for referring his pupils to books: children love to check their personal observations by the printed word, and often, in so doing, read on, and find out more.

Unfortunately, we all recognize Mr Gradgrind—there are many teachers like him; it is when we recognize something of ourselves in him that we feel most aware of our deficiencies.

We are not condemning all class lessons, of course. There is a place for them; but the retiring, the diffident, the academically less able, often find it intensely difficult to speak out in these circumstances (as any shy adults will appreciate). In a small group, children may be able to utter, to ask questions, to offer ideas, to explain their tentative hypotheses without fear of ridicule. By exchange with others they will gain confidence, courage, and the ability to range backwards and forwards in argument. Therefore we would recommend that an appreciable amount of time each week be spent in small group work, and that each teacher plans her own time in detail so that she is able to join each group at some period. To join, yes! Not to dominate the discussion that is taking place, but to play an apparently minor role.

What to listen for? Speech defects? It is possible—though many so-called defects clear up as children mature and the last thing a teacher would wish to do is to call attention to them. (Of course, if they are really handicapping the child then help from the support services should be sought.)

A major concern should be to note the use of vocabulary and to widen it; even more vital, to note and record the use of structures and patterns of language, Then, by carefully planned intervention, exploration into new forms can be encouraged. Children learn to use language by using it, and this first and foremost in speech. The teacher also needs to join each group to encourage the children by sympathetic and interested listening, or to further the thought processes by leading the children with skilled questions to the opening-up of further courses of enquiry.

It has been suggested that when children are encouraged to pursue their own questions these are not rigorous enough to form a basis for further work. It can happen. Part of the teacher's task is to see that her contribution to the discussion helps children to formulate significant questions which will lead to investigation in depth—the skills of enquiry form an important part of learning. These are referred to in greater detail in Chapters 7 and 8. Many questions arising in this matter will not have the convenient type of answer so often contrived by textbook questions, but they will certainly motivate interest, arising as they do from the children themselves.

### 5.7 Questions as an aid to discussion

What kind of questions must the teacher learn to ask to ensure that they are thought-provoking? We would suggest that they should be questions without predetermined answer. They may require the child to draw upon his own observation or experience. They may ask him to reflect upon his feelings in response to experience. They may be questions to which there is no single correct answer but which are asking the child for his ideas on the subject, in this way helping him to express his ideas and lead on to further questions. They may indeed be questions where the answer is unknown, but which will challenge the child to think deeply. He should sometimes be put in the position of taking some decision for himself.

The difference is clearly marked in comparison with closed-ended questions where the only appropriate answer the child can give is 'Yes' or 'No' or a rote-learned sequence. The solution to a problem is often reached more quickly if we are able to discuss it, sometimes even with a person who can offer no apparent help, for frequently it is the ordering of one's own ideas through speech and the clarification of one's thoughts that point the way ahead. There must be many occasions when a child comes to a teacher with a problem, starts to ask for help, and then, with little or no assistance, reaches a solution as he explains his difficulties. We would suggest that, if only adults were prepared to listen, this would happen frequently. Alternatively, children should be challenged to resolve the problems by group discussion.

Here a group of 10-year-old children had been reading Dylan Thomas's *'Memories of Christmas'*.[2] They had enjoyed it but had missed a deal of meaning, so they were asked to talk about it together, without the presence of their teacher.

D  (*reads*) 'All Christmases roll down the hill towards the Welsh-speaking sea' Eh? The Welsh-speaking sea? It must be the noise of the waves rolling on the shore.

B  The sea is different in Wales; it makes different noises.

S  But, but, but. . . .

R  I know, it says Welshshshsh, as the waves roll back.

J  No, it's set in Wales. You see . . . there's an English-speaking sea and a Welsh-speaking sea which means they're both the same but speak a different language.

S  What, the sea?

J  No the people. . . .

P  Oh. It means it's *set* in Wales, I see. . . .

D  (*reads*) ' . . . Christmases roll down the hill towards the Welsh-speaking sea, like a snowball growing whiter and bigger and rounder.' Christmases rolling down the hill—but we're talking about one Christmas really.

J  (*in a very puzzled voice*) Ye-es. 'Christmases rolling down the hill'.

D  'Rolling down the hill'. Oh—that must be all the fun and the parties and. . . .

J  Of *all* the Christmases gone by.

D  No—we're talking about one Christmas in this thing, you know.

J  I'm not sure, I think he's putting them all together.

D  Christmases piling down the hill, all built up . . . .

B  Together you mean.

D  Yes, all the things built up, the parties and the games have built up into one big massive Christmas.

D  'Like a snowball growing whiter and bigger and rounder'—that just means all the joys.

S  And the excitement.

D  And the excitement getting more and more building up.

During these discussion periods it is a good idea to have a tape-recorder running at the centre of each group. This initially might lead to some self-consciousness on the part of the children, but they quickly become accustomed to the presence of the equipment. Listening and analysing the tapes afterwards gives the necessary insight to the teacher for recording and future planning. (They can be looked at from many different aspects—social acceptance, participation, dominance—not solely from a language standpoint.)

Children also need more than simple discussion with their peer group if they are going to make good progress. They must be given the opportunity to talk with adults. Discussion must take place about events, outings, topic or project work, day-to-day happenings, their current reading in fiction. Discussion about what they have learnt from textbooks, too, is essential; it is so easy to be misled into thinking that book knowledge for the able child is learning. A small excerpt from a taped discussion points the message.

A group of mixed-ability children were experimenting with an inverted jam jar placed over a lighted candle standing in a saucer of water. They were intrigued with the resulting effect, and discussed it at length.

S   It's hard to explain.
D   I expect the air in the jar sucks the water up.
S   Heat sucks up the water.
P   No, heat pressurizes the air, that's what it said about space.
D   Perhaps the candle warmed the water (*he feels it*). No, it hasn't.
S   (*tries it again with the candle unlit*) Oh. It must be because of the flame, it doesn't do it when it's not alight.
P   I told you, heat pressurizes the air, do you understand?
D   No, not really.
P   It's like they say about space, heat pressurizes the air and the oxygen goes somewhere.
D   I still don't get it. How do you know?
P   It said so in one of my Dad's books so I know it's right.

At this point the teacher joined in the conversation. P had obviously been looking into an out-of-date science book, and, although an able reader, had not understood the text.

Talk is essential. 'A priority objective for all schools is a commitment to the speech needs of their pupils and a serious study of the role of oral language in learning.'[3]

### References

1. DICKENS, CHARLES, *Hard Times*, Oxford University Press, 1955.
2. THOMAS, DYLAN, 'Memories of Christmas', *Quite Early One Morning*, J. M. Dent, 1967.
3. *A Language for Life* (the Bullock Report), HMSO, 1975, Ch. 10, para. 30.

### Suggested reading

BARNES, D., BRITTON, J., and ROSEN, H., *Language, the Learner, and the school*, Penguin, 1969. A secondary school study—but relevant none the less.

, J., *Language and Learning*, Penguin, 1970. Professor Britton
e traces the development of language through childhood
d stresses its importance to the individual.

, P., *Lost for Words*, Penguin, 1962.

GAHAGAN, D. M. and G. A., *Talk Reform*, Routledge & Kegan Paul, 1970.

LEE, V. *et al.*, *Language Development*, Croom Helm, London, Open University Press, 1980.

LURIA, A. R. and F. la YUDOVITCH, *Speech: The Development of Mental Processes in the Child*, Penguin, 1971.

MARTIN, N. *et al.*, *Understanding Children Talking*, Penguin, 1976.

ROSEN, C. and H., *The Language of Primary School Children*, Penguin, 1973

SLOBIN, D. I., *Psycholinguistics*, Scott Foresman, 1971. A handbook for those teachers who wish to look more deeply into the psychological study of language and speech.

SMITH NEIL and WILSON DEIRDRE, *Modern Linguistics*, Pelican, 1979. A readable introduction to much modern knowledge about language and linguistics. Telling examples make for ease of understanding.

TOUGH, JOAN, *Focus on Meaning*, Allen & Unwin, 1973.

TOUGH, JOAN, *Listening to Children Talking*, Ward Lock Educational, 1976.

TOUGH, JOAN, *Talking and Learning*, Ward Lock Educational, 1977.

WILKINSON, A., *Language and Education*, Oxford University Press, 1975.

*Nuffield Science 5–13*, McDonald Educational Publishers.

*A Language for Life* (the Bullock Report), HMSO, 1975, Ch. 10.

# 6. Talk into writing

Unusual, perhaps, to start a chapter entitled 'Talk into writing' with a section on listening. But speaking, writing, reading, and listening are very closely intertwined, and lend support and encouragement one to another. There is no better incentive to good talk than an appreciative audience, who, by their interest and ability to listen, help the speaker on towards confidence, competence, and coherent utterance. It is out of this fruitful soil that writing develops.

## 6.1 Listening skills

Communication, of course, is a two-way matter, depending both upon the sender and upon the receiver. The art of listening must be founded upon attention. The healthy child, with no physical hearing problems, who is interested in most things around him will probably develop his span of attention and his skill as a listener without additional help as he matures. Nevertheless, it must not be taken for granted that this will be true of all children, and the teacher may well have to work hard to foster the art. Progress is difficult to track and to record, for listening is a personal thing, depending much on mood and outside distractions in the immediate surroundings. And, of course, 'There's none so deaf as those that will not hear'.

Teachers must, therefore, be alert to recognize any lack of listening skills and to work towards development whenever necessary.

Recent research has shown that, on the whole, as adults we are poor listeners. There is, of course, a limit to how long we can listen at one stretch, and there is little doubt in our minds that this limit is frequently exceeded in almost every educational establishment. Teachers do far too much talking and encourage children to talk far too little. In 1950 it was stated that: 'Primary school children were found to be listening for two hours thirty-eight minutes each day, that is 57.5% of school time.'[1] We would hope that since that time the situation has improved, but doubt that any similar research undertaken today would reveal a marked improvement. Naturally the background experience infant children bring to the task of identifying everyday sounds will vary enormously. Not all everyday sounds are common to all children, for example the telephone ringing or the kettle whistling. This is true of all oral communication. If the listener has not got the necessary background of knowledge and experience, then information received can be totally incomprehensible. We have all experienced the garbled versions of messages children bring home from school.

The old party game often gives rise to much merriment as whispered messages become more and more distorted, but it is a serious matter in school when children are not understanding because of the complexity of the language involved. It is important for teachers to be aware of how listening to and identifying everyday sounds can be linked to language development generally by the careful use of questions.

A brief list of ploys that can help will trigger off in the teacher's mind many more of a similar type.

1. Giving instructions, at first only one or two, the list gradually lengthening in complexity (this can then be developed by altering the style of the instruction, using a more compound form of sentence).
2. Playing games which demand listening skills like 'O'Grady says', 'Who am I?', or 'Messages' (a whispered message being passed round a group of children).
3. A minute of complete silence, with children being asked to remember every sound heard.
4. Identifying sounds made by the teacher out of sight (actual sound is better than recorded sound for this because of distortion made electronically).
5. Drawing geometric shapes (two children, one on either side of some visual barrier, one having a sheet of paper on which the shapes are already drawn, the receiver having a blank sheet on which to draw as instructed by his partner).
6. Arranging model animals on a previously drawn 'map' of their likely habitat.

Much of this instruction-type material lends itself to preparation of tapes, recorded by the teacher for use by the children, singly or in groups, using head-sets at listening centres.

## 6.2 Auditory skills

Most children, by the time they get to the first year junior level, will have the ability to recognize everyday sounds and to be able to match them to pictures. Some children will already have developed a level of phonic ability. It is worth considering that such ability is in part linked to a developing maturity. The necessary prerequisite to the phonic approach to reading and spelling is that the child must be able to discriminate between sounds at the beginning, middle, and end of words. For children who have yet to acquire this ability, the following auditory discrimination activities may be useful.

1. Children can be asked to sort and match pictures that have the same sound at beginning, middle, or end.
2. Bingo games using the same principle as above can be used.
3. Pictures can be spread on a table, the child selecting those pictures that have the same sound as the word that is provided by the teacher.
4. With the addition of paper clips this activity can be developed into a magnetic fishing game.
5. A group of children can be given picture cards. They are then asked to hold up cards that have the sound that the teacher gives.
6. Variations on 'I spy' are useful.
7. Rhymes can be read to the children who then supply the words omitted.
8. Rhyming riddles are also useful, and the teacher may ask, 'What rhymes with cat and rat and is worn on the head?'

When this discrimination is well established, the child is ready to benefit from a phonic programme and to develop the skills of matching phoneme to grapheme. In spelling this ability is needed in the reverse direction, matching grapheme to phoneme.

The logical progression can be seen from the gross form of auditory discrimination, matching sounds to pictures, to a more refined form needed to discriminate sounds of parts of words and match them to the printed or written symbol. Sentence complexity is another factor to be noted, especially where younger children are involved. Listening and the development of language are so closely interrelated that equal emphasis needs to be given to them. What is said must be within the powers of reasoning and abstraction by the individual child—this we believe raises questions about the validity of the 'class lesson' as a major component of a child's educational experience in school. Finally, listening is most effective when we are required to do something as a result.

'The child needs to speak, but he needs to listen as well. He learns to speak through listening and listening is where language experience begins.'[2]

## 6.3 Stories

Good narrative, well read or told, is possibly the greatest stimulus to concentrated listening. We cannot over-emphasize the preparation a teacher needs to make in order to tell a story effectively, and it is best if this is done by the teacher herself, though recorded stories and poems allow children to re-hear their favourites, or work in small groups on new material. One time-saving ploy is to record as one reads to the class, the laughter and other reactions which are heard on the replay frequently being an added bonus (further reference in Chapter 2).

Stories in sound can be prepared on tape. These can be fun for the class to draw up. It can be equally entertaining for the children to record interesting story possibilities for one another. 'Sound banks' should be prepared of a variety of sounds which children might find inspiring but which would be difficult for them to record at the time they find them necessary. Such sounds as the waves breaking on the shore, seagulls mewing, a fairground's noises, trains departing or rushing by, a busy railway station, traffic, the police or ambulance siren may all be useful, and many more may suggest themselves to teachers and children who embark on this type of material. Here is an example that led to a surprising result. The sounds were taped in this order:

 a. A dog whimpering.
 b. Footsteps on gravel.
 c. An owl hooting.
 d. A window being opened.
 e. Wind.
 f. The window being closed—all outside noises ceasing.
 g. Stealthy footsteps.
 h. Jangle of keys.
 i. Drawer being opened.
 j. Rushing footsteps down stairs.
 k. Click of light switch.
 l. Scream.

This was played over by a group of older junior children, and one of them wrote:

> A dog whimpers.
> The gravel path crackles.
> As someone creeps nearer, nearer.
> In the next room the door bangs.
> A window closes gently as the wind howls around it.
> The window creaks again, I can hear the pounding of my heart.
> The night is dark.

The old gnarled tree sends shadows to the far wall.
Suddenly.
The night is shattered into pieces of fear.

As you can see, this stimulated a child to pen an exciting piece of writing, though in this instance this was not the primary purpose.

For all this time is needed.

There is no time?

Then planning needs improvement. Some teachers fail to reach their full potential because they do not define their aims clearly enough to themselves, and because they do not plan their own time efficiently.

### 6.4 Individual assignment cards

Would assignment cards solve the problem? At least the individual child can work at his own preferred speed (which may, or may not, be an advantage).

Also, he can decide if and when he needs assistance. This can work very well at the beginning of a lesson, when all of the class are working from prepared cards and only one or two children opt for help. What usually happens as time progresses is that more and more children run into difficulties and a queue forms. The enthusiasm that most children bring to new learning may well be dissipated if help is not fairly quickly available.

Sometimes assignment cards are used to employ part of the class while the teacher gives his attention to another group. In these circumstances the difficulty of teacher contact becomes even greater.

Yet curiosity, questioning, and interchange of ideas with an adult are a driving force to learning and must be encouraged and sustained.

Classroom pressures often dictate that these potentially valuable discussion periods between teacher and child, when they do occur, are of a very short duration, frequently two or three minutes at most. There are also other dangers inherent within this system. We found one such difficulty in a class when a gifted teacher was using individual assignments for almost all her teaching. Becoming worried about the length of time she was spending with individual children, she decided to record every time she taught a child or stimulated a worthwhile discussion out of which learning arose. At the end of each four weeks she found that the academically able and those children at the opposite end of the spectrum had dominated her time at the expense of those in the middle band.

The other worry we all have about individual cards (which have their uses when used in conjunction with a variety of other ploys) is that they *are* so individual, and do not offer opportunity for discussion with others, for explanation, or for argument, or even for the sharing of knowledge with one's peers. They are not necessarily a sign of thoughtful enlightened ideas, and can be as stultifying as the worst of class exercise books. They remain only one of many teaching styles we must be able to adopt, and change frequently, in the course of our involvement with the class.

## 6.5 Interview techniques

We have suggested the value of tape-recorders. In one school recently they have proved invaluable in a project that arose out of a class discussion on playground games, when the teacher was amazed to find that her class of eleven-year-olds could not supply five different outdoor games apart from the organized school ones of football, netball, etc. This quickly grew into an interest in times recently past—the times of the children's parents and grandparents, in fact.

It was obvious that an excellent contribution to the school's library/resource centre could be supplied by channelling this interest. So, first, the children found out as much as possible from their relations, made notes, compared facts, and drew up a somewhat incomplete document about life in a time only recently past. The class then realized that a great deal more research was necessary, so the co-operation of every elderly person in their vicinity was sought (and most of these older citizens were delighted to co-operate).

The children were going to take tape-recorders to the houses of these people and interview them, but interview techniques need practice, so detailed instruction cards were prepared explaining all necessary technical details for the making of a good-quality recording.

At various times during the following days children were heard around the school building interviewing anybody and everybody who would co-operate (and many of their candidates had been briefed beforehand to answer the questions asked!).

Boy to cook

    B  Can we ask you some questions?
    C  Certainly.
    B  How long have you worked here?

C Ten years.
B Do you like it here?
C Yes.
B Do you like cooking?
C Yes.
B How many meals do you make?
C About three hundred and eighty a day.
B Ooh, that's a lot. (*long silence*) Is it hard work?
C Yes.
B (*another long pause*) What time do you come to work?
C Eight o'clock.
B Oh thanks. (*end of interview*)

This interview reflects beautifully the effect that questions have upon answers. A number of these interviews were played back in class and discussed in groups. The shortcomings were identified, and the children were asked to listen to one or two television or radio interviews and try to analyse the types of questions that led to more enlightenment, and which were likely to elicit freely given information.

## 6.6 Interview assignments

After further discussion various interviews took place in the class between friends; the results were played back, reviewed, and criticized. Only after much work did the teacher feel that the children were able to put their interviewee at ease, and were really prepared for the extramural visits.

The children went in pairs, at prearranged times, to the houses of every elder citizen who had expressed a willingness to take part. If only as an exercise in public relations it was a great success, but most valuable contributions were made to language development, to the sensitivity to audience, to flexibility in thought, to the development of discussion, and with it the ability to recall parts of the dialogue and to realize how it was developing, all this necessitating an extended span of concentration.

The organization of the visits was not difficult, but a number of necessary preparations had, of course, to be taken—parental permission obtained, supervision arranged on main roads, and the rest of the safeguards that are familiar to every teacher.

Each pair of interviewers was briefed not only in the techniques of actual tape-recording, but in the simple politeness of offering to play back the resulting tape, and eliminate or rectify any part of it. Social graces are important in adult life.

Back at school, the tapes had to be transcribed, collated, written up, typed in duplicate (this last not undertaken by a child), and bound. The resulting set of eighteen books made an excellent contribution to the school's resource material.

Many different subjects would lend themselves readily to this type of exercise: a study of the locality, the local shops, parental occupations, race or creed (if handled with sensitivity), a building site, a village or town survey—indeed, almost any project involving people lends itself to the use of interviews. If this work forms part of an integrated topic, the links with the major areas of the curriculum—not just with language, but with mathematics, science, religion, history, geography, art and craft—are readily apparent in most cases, and made meaningful to the child.

### An extract from one of the interviews
*M and Y interviewing Mrs X on life when she was eleven*

Mrs X, where did you live as a child?
Mostly at Cardiff in Wales.

Did you get any pocket money?
I think I used to get about sixpence a week.

What did you spend it on?
Oh just sweets, or we used to buy these little dolls—you can't get them now—about six inches tall, and all these girls about my age used to buy them and we would dress them and take them to school and put them in our desks. I've been caught before now and the teacher used to take them from us and put them in the stove and burn them. We used to see who could dress them the best.

What were they made of?
Oh, sort of china, little china heads.

How much did they cost?
About tuppence, threepence each. I spent a lot of time playing with these dolls and dressing them up.

Did you ever go abroad?
No, couldn't afford it.

Didn't you ever go to England from Wales?
Oh I dare say I did that as I'd uncles and aunties over here.

So it was a treat when you came here?
Yes, and as our Sunday school treat we went to Abergavenny. It is rather a lovely part of Wales and there's a mountain called Sugar Loaf. Nearly every year we went to the same place and that was our Sunday school outing.

In all this work the teacher was constantly aiming to make the children heighten one another's abilities, to awaken their critical faculties, and to show them how valuable their own contributions were to a sustained conversation.

The same type of exchange with trusted friends can be used with great effect to improve the quality of the written word.

## 6.7 First-time perfection?

When writing an important document—a letter of application, for example—do you first make a model, plan out a skeleton, or jot down ideas before making a fair copy? Have you ever looked at the rough drafts of the manuscripts of some of our great writers? If so, you will have seen how frequently they have improved on their first trials, adding or altering words, substituting whole phrases, changing sentence order completely, and so on, the result being the best words in the most satisfying order.

These masters of the English language usually cared enough about their style to work upon it. Yet how frequently teachers ask the child to write his ideas in an exercise book, in good handwriting, well spelt (and for preference using a good vocabulary), correctly punctuated, and, withal, fluent?

We would suggest that these teachers, in so doing, are gravely handicapping the writer.

Naturally, in the long run we want to ensure that the children spell well and write legibly, for poor calligraphy and incompetent spelling interfere with fluency and also, during the last century, the latter has become almost a social gaffe. Incorrect punctuation can make nonsense of the written word, and if a piece is unreadable it is worthless; it is obvious that these skills are important (further reference in Chapter 8).

Nevertheless, fluency is the first essential. Any normal child will limit his output, his turn of phrase, and his vocabulary if he is over-corrected and underpraised. (No intelligent six-year-old will attempt to spell 'saturate' when he is sure about how to spell 'wet' if he knows he may be taken to task for his error.)

Only the skill and sensitivity of the individual teacher who knows the capabilities of the children in her care can tell her when it is time to insist upon correctness. If the child has written well and enjoyed so doing, then maybe it is time to work upon the techniques.

## 6.8 Rough drafts

When a group of older junior children are asked to undertake free personal writing we would suggest that they be allowed to write a rough draft which will be for their eyes alone. On its completion they should be required, with the aid of a dictionary, or other help if this is too difficult a skill, to correct those words they used and understood but did not know how to spell. In a rapidly expanding vocabulary these are many, and children must be encouraged to be adventurous and try out new words and new forms of language. They ought to re-read, insert or alter words, add maybe, adjectives or adverbs, perhaps put phrases in apposition, or completely re-order their sentences.

During this 'proof-reading' attention should also be paid to such punctuation as they know. Children do not actually re-read and correct their work unless specifically asked to do so, and so they lose one of the advantages that the written word has over the spoken—that it can be erased, corrected, and improved upon.

## 6.9 Constructive criticism by a peer

When the individual child is satisfied that his work is the best he can make of it, peer group discussion can be of great value. If the piece is then read over to one or two friends and discussed this can prove an excellent exercise in critical appreciation. One or two firm rules have been found helpful here.

1. In order to avoid that devastating condemnation of which children are past masters, the listener must first select a part of the passage which he considered good in some way and offer praise, as all good teachers do.
2. Then he ought to select a part of the work he wishes to criticize adversely but on one condition alone: that he offers what he considers to be a better alternative. This may or may not be, to the original author, an acceptable amendment, but with children who are accustomed to this type of work the resulting discussions can bring a heightened awareness of that elusive quality, style.

This example is taken from a tape-recording made when children were preparing a part of the school's Christmas concert on the theme 'Christmas Thoughts' (further reference in Chapter 5).

They had read and discussed Dylan Thomas's *Christmas Memories* and were composing a piece of prose to be read as a link between two carols. Two boys reflect together on a rough draft:

*( P read rough draft aloud for second hearing)*

P   As I was eating my dinner . . .

M   How about 'my scrumptious dinner'?

P   Yes, that's O.K.

M   Or—'as I was eating my scrumptious dinner stuffing roast potatoes into my mouth'?

P   No. That seems a bit revolting.

M   Well—er—'filling myself. . . .'

P   This has got to be read for our Christmas thing remember, with grown-ups there. You've got to make them enjoy it, haven't you?

M   Mmmm.

P   It's hard to do that. *(Continues reading aloud)* '. . . and the harmony and the. . . .'

M   There's too many 'and's really—just like I do when I write.

P   Yes, you're right. Let's read it right through and get rid of some. Don't need this one for a start 'sound at night, comma, the dazzle, comma, the harmony and the'—yes I need that one—'angels'. Full stop. *(reads on)* 'How scared the unimportant shepherd that stood. . . .'

M   '*Un*important'? I thought, played—played quite a big part in the story.

P   Ah yes, but not compared to the kings and majestic people.

M   Ah. No. But they are to the farmers, and in the story.

P   Yeah, really.

M   They would not be unimportant because if they didn't have shepherds. . . .

P   I see what you mean.

M   'Little known'? Yes?

P   'Little known'! Yes, I'll put little known, it fits better than 'unimportant'.

## 6.10 Constructive criticism from a teacher

When the children are satisfied that their rough drafts are as good as they can possibly make them, they should be encouraged to discuss them with their teachers, for this is when they can best be helped to prepare a final polished piece of work, be it prose or poetry. It is now that it can be of great value to discuss style, to comment on good vocabulary or phraseology, and to assist where confused syntax had bedevilled clarity.

If each author reads his work aloud, with his teacher following the script, the need for punctuation becomes self-evident, and the required techniques can be taught in context. They are far more likely to be remembered in this way than in any practice exercises, especially if it can be pointed out what nonsense can be made of a manuscript if it is not correctly punctuated.

Hoary chestnuts such as 'Wanted, a piano, for a lady with carved oak legs' or absurdities like the following four lines can point the message:

> King John entered on his head
> A crown upon his feet
> His riding boots on either hand
> His gauntlets leather-made.

Children need to appreciate that all written language has to be far more precise and explicit than the spoken word because the writer has no personal contact to help him to convey his meaning. Emphasis in conversation, for example, can be made by gesture and expression; these are unavailable to the writer, who therefore has to develop many other skills to overcome this loss.

It is a paradox that sustained and well-developed speech is of the greatest help in becoming a fluent writer, yet if the style remains too close to the spoken word it becomes a handicap.

Would re-ordering his words help?

Skilfully led discussion will often elicit from the child himself new ways to express his meaning more clearly. Better turns of phrase are frequently forthcoming, and the subtlety and the range of our English vocabulary can be remarked.

For instance, in spoken dialogue the mood of a speaker in a reported utterance is easily conveyed by the tone of voice used; in written forms the little word 'said' needs to be replaced by a more descriptive verb—'muttered', 'shouted', 'mumbled', 'whispered', or 'screamed' carry the writer's meaning far more vividly.

One of the gains of writing is that the author does have the time to search for the exact words he needs (in speech he would be interrupted if he paused for long to search). Children must be prevailed upon to seek for the best words for their purpose.

## 6.11 Precision in writing

The necessity for precision in writing can be stressed in many ways, and children have to be convinced of the need to be explicit. It is often difficult for them to understand this need, particularly when they are writing for someone who will obviously be aware of all they are trying to explain. (One example of an adult in a circumstance of this kind is illuminating. The school cook, excellent in all practical ways, failed her cookery examination year after year. On one occasion she had successfully bottled 100 pounds of blackberries, yet ploughed on her written account of how to bottle fruit. As she said, 'Why tell the examiner you have to look for cracks and chips? He knows that much don't he?')

Let the children invent a game, perhaps a variation on a playground activity or a board game. Next, let them write out the rules and instructions, and give these to other children in the peer group for them to peruse and to act upon. It is usually a salutary lesson. If the participants fail to understand the written instructions, the children can then resort to verbal explanations. They should be asked to monitor their own need for gesture, diagram, or demonstration. A second attempt at coherent exposition is valid, and usually produces good results.

For some children it is imperative to prove the need for clear, full accounts, for example of scientific experiment. All too soon the need to satisfy an examiner will press upon them. One instance will serve to exemplify what we mean. James, interested in all things electrical, had to describe the workings of an electric light bulb. He wrote tersely and too concisely to make his meaning clear, but he was unwilling to accept this fact. To bring home to James the need for more explanation and clearer description his teacher asked him to select just two friends in his class who were likely to be able to understand his meaning. He was not to say what he was describing—merely to read his brief passage to them, and ask them what he was writing about. The result was hilarious, and the message accepted. It must be added that in this group of three friends James was not made to feel inadequate or self-conscious, and the task of describing the bulb adequately was subsequently given to all three of them.

An exercise of this kind does not have to spring from science, for obviously there are many occasions when accurate accounts are needed.

For many children who find the actual writing difficult a valid alternative is to record on to tape. This may then be worked on in much the same way. If a written record is required it might well be transcribed by an adult, perhaps to be copied, if the need arises, by the author himself.

Using tape-recorders instead of pencil and paper can prove just the spur that some children need. Forcing unready children to write can at times be a form of torture, and a task with no hopes of success. No child is ever helped by being put in a failure situation frequently. Moreover, preparation for recording means practising good speech and intonation—it is not a 'soft option'—and the making of simple programmes for the entertainment of the other children is an excellent motivation towards production.

## 6.12 Towards a policy

It might sound as if we are advocating a most haphazard method of teaching techniques. Nothing of the kind. When working in this apparently informal way it is imperative that each teacher (or, better still, each school) works out a check list of techniques and skills for the pupils—geared, of course, not to chronological ages but to developmental stages. In order to do this the makers of the policy must have a sound knowledge of language, and a clear idea of their objectives in the development of writing in their school (further reference in Chapter 15). But the teacher must always look for the potential in the child's work, and should never allow the correction of grammatical errors or mistakes in spelling to take precedence over the more important ability to express ideas or thoughts with clarity.

It is evident from a child's writing just where he is along the line of progression, and the teaching can be tuned accurately. Naturally, it will save a teacher's time if she can deal with a number of children together, for example when teaching a particular form of punctuation. Good recording can make it possible to select a group of children who are ready at the same time for new knowledge in this field (further reference in Chapter 11).

## 6.13 Should one always comment ?

Although children are usually disappointed if their chosen recipient does not respond positively, the teacher should not feel that she must intervene at every juncture. As always, sensitivity is needed when criticizing children's work; there are occasions when any interference is unwarranted, perhaps unforgivable. These are the times when a child allows his deepest feelings to shine through his writing. He must have trust in his audience, and to betray this trust could be both hurtful and damaging.

A tragedy occurred to a family in one school. There were five children of primary school age and a new baby one month old, when father, who had been unemployed for some time, was taken ill during the night. Neighbours were called, the house was in a turmoil; the nurse, the doctor, and the ambulance followed, but the massive coronary unfortunately proved fatal.

The following day the five children were sent to school, aware of disturbances but not knowing the truth. Half-way through the morning their grandmother arrived at the school to plead with the head to tell the children of their father's death. Reluctantly, she undertook the unwelcome task.

In the ensuing months the eldest boy became 'the man of the house', the eldest girl matured, but the third child in the family, Tom, a boy of eight, a poor performer academically, had a very bad reaction. He had been his father's favourite, and had, in turn, adored his father and followed him whenever it was possible. His suffering was acute, and his trauma evident from his anti-social and sometimes violent behaviour. His peer group and his teacher all suffered to some extent, though they were tolerant because they understood the cause.

About three months later his gifted young teacher went to talk to the head of the school. After serious discussion and careful preparation, it was decided to risk allowing a group of children in her class to write about 'Fear': a risk, because they felt it was not really a suitable subject for the age group; a risk taken because they felt that discussion and writing on the subject might help one child.

Tom wrote (ill-spelled, but set out in this form):

Very cold,
Thunder,
Black,
Very frightened.
The stairs creaking under many feet.
I shiver in my bed.
All the doors keep opening.
Very scared.
In that night.
Dark, dark, always.

As soon as he had completed his work he leapt to his feet, screwed up his writing paper, and with tears in his eyes ran out of the room, throwing a crumpled ball of paper into the waste-paper basket as he passed. Two minutes later he returned to the room, rescued his poem, smoothed the creases from it and threw it on his teacher's desk saying, 'You can have that, Miss.'

The school would not claim that Tom immediately became a model pupil, but the rapport with his teacher, and his complete faith in her, had enabled him to express and share his fears and so, to some extent, to come to terms with his experience. Gradually his behaviour problems were solved.

Throughout the school Tom and his class had been read to, at least once daily, from a wide range of books. From this, and from much spoken work in the class, he had developed resources of language that enabled him to express his inner self. Comment on his work, on his change of tense, on his handwriting would have been unthinkable.

## 6.14 Fair copies

There are, then, many times when 'Thank you' is the only response.

With this proviso in mind we should like to look again at the rough draft.

By this time it should be a finished piece of writing which is satisfactory to the author—the best he can make of it. Must it now be copied out?

It may well be that a fully corrected and much-worked-upon draft is enough, and that to ask for a well-presented copy would be to undo some of the joy of writing. But if the need can be made evident and the outcome positive, then a fair copy, as beautifully presented as possible, can be a most worthwhile ploy, and a valid handwriting exercise into the bargain.

An alternative, if the need can be engineered, is to record the finished result on tape (further reference in Chapter 9).

## 6.15 Environmental studies

While we think that environmental studies rank high in import-ance for today's children, there is little value in studying the growth in a hedge with northern and southern aspects, of drawing pictures of houses in a street, of making mathematical calculations of weeds in a lawn or of sorting litter into sets, unless conclusions are drawn and lessons are learnt from these conclusions.

As with discovery work in science, so too with environmental studies, the discussion with the adult plays a major role. With guidance children can become quite adept at logical thought, and towards the mental age of 11 and 12 they can begin to make abstractions from experiments and from observations.

One example will suffice.

> The wall study completed at camp proved the point that if a lot of random samples are taken it is possible to have a reasonable summary of the plants that grow on the various pieces of land or wall.

Our wall study gave us these conclusions. Moss was the dominant type of plant, covering one-third of the wall surface. Flowering plants, twenty-five per cent, and grasses, twenty-three per cent, followed, but these tended to grow in the richer and damper areas between the stones. Over half the plants we found on the wall were non-flowering (mosses, lichens, and ferns) and this is probably because they have adapted themselves for growing in poor conditions. Many of the other plants could not survive without richer soil and more water.

This shows a thoughtful approach by an 11-year-old to what is a difficult concept, an approach he would not have been able to make unless he had been guided in the ways we have suggested.

## References

1. WILT, M., *Journal of Education Research*, 1950.
2. YARDLEY, A., *Exploration and Language*, Evans Brothers, 1970.

## Suggested Reading

DONALDSON, MARGARET, *Children's Minds*, Fontana, 1978. A most thoughtful and stimulating book about children and learning; an essential 'read'.

MARTIN, N. *et al.*, *Writing and Learning across the Curriculum 11–16*, Ward Lock Educational, 1976. The role of language in all aspects of learning is looked at in this book which is a follow-up to the Schools Council work on the development of writing abilities. Although primarily for secondary school teachers, there is much that is relevant to the primary child.

WILKINSON, A., STRATTA, L., and DUDDLEY, P., *The Quality of Listening*, Macmillan, 1974.

# 7. Writing

The title of this chapter calls to mind two distinct and separate skills: calligraphy on the one hand, and the ability to communicate through the medium of the written word on the other.

## 7.1 Handwriting

Lack of the ability to write quickly, legibly, and easily can have a detrimental effect on the whole quality as well as the quantity of a child's written output, for it hampers the flow of his thoughts and in so doing severely limits his fluency; hence it must be account.

Calligraphy is an art, yet also a disciplined skill in itself, and time must be spent by the teacher to teach it and by the child to practise it. Handwriting, like road safety, is a subject not for discovery learning, but for direct instruction. If this is not forthcoming the child will be unlikely to develop a running hand that is legible, swift, individual in character, and so much a part of himself that it will serve him all his life.

### Style

First of all, schools must give professional consideration to their selection of the style of handwriting they wish to adopt. Agreement should be reached through discussion not only in one staff room, but across the range of infant, junior, and secondary years, to ensure some conformity.

There are two main forms in use in infant school today: a print script and a broken cursive or italic hand. There are valid arguments for the adoption of either one. The people who opt for print script reason that children will find the letter characters in the books in the reading schemes similar, and that by having fewer forms to remember they will have an advantage. (And, certainly, type faces in common use are many and varied, giving strength to this argument.) As opposed to this, other teachers reason that the modified cursive, with its more fluid style and its future joins already in evidence, make the inevitable change to a full running hand an easy stage. There is an increase in speed, and no pattern of writing to unlearn.

There is good, sound reasoning on either side—what really matters is that the schools policy ensures continuity of style and method throughout the formative years.

## Position

Some things are of common concern whatever the form of the handwriting style selected.

1. Suitable tools should be provided, and care taken to ensure that they are correctly held. Edward Johnstone, one of our great calligraphers, recommended that the pen or pencil should be held by looping the thumb and forefinger on to and slightly gripping the shaft, supporting it from below with the second finger. The third and fourth fingers are then tucked out of the way, into the palm of the hand. This correct hold must be encouraged from the outset. As with all bad habits, if an incorrect grip is permitted it may prove difficult to change later on.

2. The tool must be held so that it meets the paper at a sensible angle, not more than 45° to the plane of the paper. (The exact angle obviously varies with the type of writing point, as well as with individual taste.)

3. The relaxation of the muscles is important, particularly those of the fingers, hand, and forearm. Tension leads quickly to fatigue and to writer's cramp. Here especially the tool is important—a softish pencil, a firm point to nib, are necessary.

4. Appropriate height of table and its complementary chair should be checked automatically by the teacher along with correct sitting posture.

5. Unlined paper large enough to ensure freedom of choice of letter size should be provided at the outset because of the variety of physical development found within any class. Lines may well detract from the task in hand because of the difficulty of following them and of positioning each letter on the line correctly.

Nevertheless, ascenders and descenders need attention, for they are the clues by which many adults recognize words. Therefore, when the mechanics of letter formation have become automatic, lined paper can help to focus attention on these ascenders and descenders, and on letter spacing and proportion—all of which are needed for good presentation.

Perhaps the best method at this stage is to use heavily marked under-paper to show through as guidelines. This is a solution to the problem of appearance adopted by many adults.

6. Left-handed children are certainly at a slight disadvantage initially. Ideally their writing should be taught by a left-handed teacher, but where even a demonstration is not possible the teacher must adapt herself to recognize their specific needs.

The paper must be placed differently on the desk, at a far greater angle to the writer. The pencil should be held in such a position that the writer can see what he has written (usually the grip needs to be further up the 'barrel'), instead of obscuring his words immediately by moving his left hand directly across it. And, when he comes to use ink, if ever, he must be provided with reverse oblique nibs. The 'look' of a word helps correct spelling; to obscure it or smudge it offers no assistance whatever.

The actual sitting position of the left-hander is also different from the right-handed writer. He should turn his whole body at a greater angle to the edge of the desk so that his left hand reaches easily across it.

## Stages of children's writing

At the very beginning the child will draw pictures or make models and talk about them.

1. When the teacher feels the child is ready, the caption is written by the teacher, using the child's own words.

The teacher will need to demonstrate the correct formation of letters to individual children or to small groups, and it is helpful if she states explicitly how each letter is formed. Children must be encouraged to start their letters at the 'correct place'. It does seem to be easier and more natural at the outset to make an upward movement, but this habit should not be allowed to grow for ultimately it will be a handicap.

Brushwork, pattern-making, tactile kinaesthetic methods (writing in sand, tracing with the fingers around letters formed in glass-paper, furry fabric, or velvet), all help to establish correct techniques. They may be slow to develop, and may call for much intervention by the teacher, and encouragement to persevere in what so often appears to the child to be an unnatural way of forming letters and an awkward way of holding a pencil. It is obvious that much tuition must be individual; it is equally obvious that a good deal of practice is necessary, but it must be short and frequent and never leading to boredom or to tired fingers.

An overhead projector is an excellent visual aid for the teaching of correct letter formation.

When the child can copy letter shapes fairly adequately, he may begin to copy the words that the teacher has written for him. It would seem more helpful at this stage for the teacher to write the child's words on a strip of paper for him to copy. This does not demand the visual memory needed for copying from a chalk-board. Also, the strip can be moved down to the paper, which ensures that children do not copy their own mistakes. If the words are copied from paper that is then destroyed, the child can feel that the book is 'all his own work' and he will achieve greater confidence in his own capabilities. A desire for independence grows and it will not be long before the child makes progress and writes words from memory 'by himself'. For the beginner it is helpful if the piece of paper is placed under his book projecting along the top edge of the page, possibly with a red spot or other significant mark which will encourage him to start at the left-hand side of the page rather than the right. The teacher will need to suit the size of her writing to that of the child: large writing at first, becoming smaller as time passes and the child acquires more control (see Fig. 7.1).

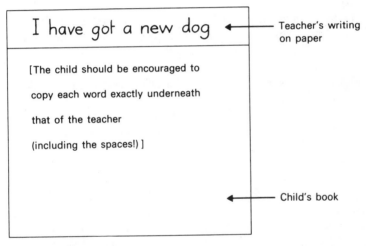

I have got a new dog ← Teacher's writing on paper

[The child should be encouraged to copy each word exactly underneath that of the teacher (including the spaces!)]

← Child's book

**Fig. 7.1** Copying from a paper strip prepared by the teacher

For longer pieces of writing, the child's second line would need to be written on another strip of paper, which can then be placed over the first one: each word and space can then be copied accurately, as before.

It goes without saying that a stock of ready-prepared strips must be to hand, and that the teacher should always pay attention to the standard of her own writing, letter shapes, formation and spacing, in order to encourage good writing habits in the child.

2. The child writes over the teacher's writing while watched by

the teacher (or another knowledgeable adult) to ensure that he is forming the letters correctly and is writing in a left-to-right direction. (Some children have been observed to pick out all the 'o's to copy first because they liked them. Habits such as these may well lead to confusion at a later stage in reading.)

Poor speech patterns should be accepted at the outset, as the child dictates his thoughts to the teacher, but should be phased out very gradually and sympathetically.

3. The child copies underneath the teacher's writing. At this stage he must have the ability to hold a pencil, to copy letters using the correct formation, to follow a left-to-right direction on each line, and to write the lines from the top to the bottom of the page.

The teacher will be able to use those mistakes the child makes to analyse any difficulties he is meeting and so help him to overcome them.

The way in which letters are formed in writing is a positive guide to the child in discriminating between similar letters like 'p' and 'q' or 'b' and 'd'.

Care must be taken to see that children start at the right place, and also that closed letters are in fact closed—so that, for instance, an 'o' is never mistaken for a 'c'.

4. The child writes his own words using reference sources and dictionary skills referred to later in this chapter and in the chapter on extended reading skills.

This step marks an important progression from the copying of his teacher's writing to a more independent stage.

It will be helpful if he has a personal collection of written words to which he can refer each time he is writing. However, at first, many children are not ready for their own 'word books' with a page for each letter of the alphabet; their lack of knowledge of alphabetical order prevents them from finding the correct page for the teacher to write the word and hinders them in their own searches.

It is more useful at this stage to provide each child with a single sheet of card approximately 24 cm by 18 cm which has been ruled into 12 squares on each side, providing spaces for 'Aa' to 'Ll' on one side and 'Mm' to 'Zz' on the reverse, with 'Xx', 'Yy', 'Zz' sharing the final space. (These squares are wide enough to allow for two columns of words.) By this means a child can scan all the words in his word bank easily. It has been suggested that the whole alphabet might be on one side of the card, but this means either too large a piece of card for convenience or words written in too small a script to be of use. The child learns incidentally which half of the alphabet contains which letters, and sees the sequence they follow.

It would probably not be necessary to fill more than one card with words in this way unless the child was really still struggling with his writing, because by the time some of these squares were full the child would normally be ready to go on to the next stage, the 'word book' (see Fig. 7.2). This will help to develop dictionary skills; alongside the word book (which is not a dictionary, because it doesn't give definitions of words, but only lists of words) the child

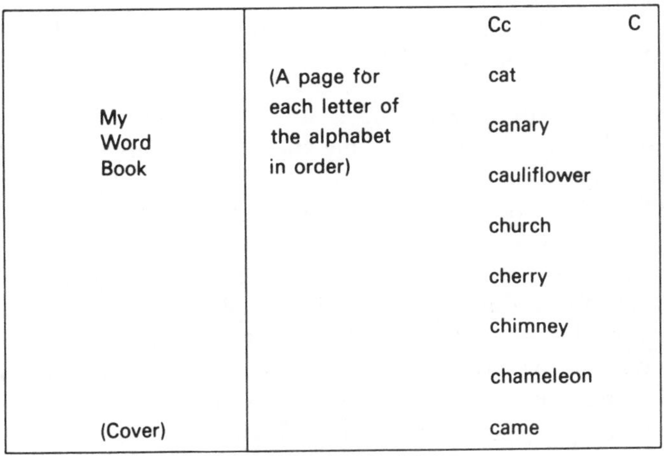

| | | Cc | C |
|---|---|---|---|
| My Word Book | (A page for each letter of the alphabet in order) | cat canary cauliflower church cherry chimney chameleon | |
| (Cover) | | came | |

**Fig. 7.2** The 'word book'

should also be using simple picture dictionaries to find the words that he needs. Because knowledge of alphabetical order takes a long time to develop, it is helpful if the child is provided with information sheets with pictures and words that he can see at a glance. Occasionally these should be prepared as large charts on the wall, but this needs a lot of space and small information cards are usually preferable. These can be stored in shoe boxes. It helps a child if a card can be carried back to the desk so that he can copy difficult words precisely.

These cards could be 'tailored' to fit on a theme. On animals, for example, there could be cards providing pictures and names of a variety of animals, a different card for each type—animals that live in burrows, forest animals, fresh-water fish, insects, domestic animals, sea birds, etc. Thus each child could be carrying out his own programme of work.

Children *may* need work cards to tell them which questions to ask—they often need information cards, not only to find the answers to the work cards, but also to find out the answers to their own questions and as a stimulus for 'personal writing'.

Having used separate cards, which are easy to find, and satisfying, the child will be encouraged to go to all kinds of books for his information, including dictionaries and encyclopedias. These will involve the skill of selection from a larger amount of material in order to find the information he needs.

5. The child writes independently, building some words phonically, writing some from memory, and copying some from reference sources.

During this time, when he is using words constantly in his writing, the child will develop the skill of spelling his own words. A useful aid at this point is a card with the alphabet written on it (in order) with the capital letter and lower-case form of each letter. If a child wants to write a word, but needs to get away from the dependent stage of copying each whole word, he can ask the teacher to show him how the word is 'built up'. The teacher will point to each letter in turn, at the same time saying the *sound* (not the name) of the letter. The child can then build the word with small letter cards as in the 'Breakthrough to Literacy Word Builder' and have it checked before copying the correct version:

### cook

In this way the child will be helped to learn the spellings of a large variety of words.

At all stages children need to be provided with attractive books, to be read to frequently, to see good examples of the teacher's writing, and to be constantly encouraged, so that they think of reading and writing with enjoyment and with expectation of success.

### In the junior years

Handwriting practice should certainly not cease at the end of the infant years—indeed it becomes particularly necessary at the stage of changeover to a full cursive hand, and again when pens are introduced.

Ligaturing, or the linking of letters together, needs special attention to ensure that the movement is both quick and clear.

An analysis of the school's chosen style will reveal sets of letters whose joining movement is similar. These might well be taught together, making sure that they are always linked to comfortable partners (for instance, 'e d', 'ing', 'e a'—never a rarity like 'd b' or 'c g').

The next step should put together letter groupings that use a variety of ligatures, again selecting those letters frequently found together—e.g. 'tion', 'sion', 'ough', 'igh', 'ttle', 'ble', 'ous', 'dge'.

Handwriting practice then has a two-fold use, for it not only helps the child to develop a fast-flowing attractive hand, but also teaches kinaesthetically, some common English spelling patterns. There are many non-phonetic letter groupings in the English language, which are stumbling blocks for many children when they wish to write a word correctly. To practise them regularly during handwriting periods helps the child to 'feel' correct when he uses them.

It is important to organize short but regular practice sessions; it is equally important that material to be copied has meaning for the child.

It is plain that the most 'telling' material is that which is of concern to the individual himself. One example might be the building up of an anthology of poetry, perhaps containing the child's own personal writings, those of some of his friends and/or some published works which have appealed to him. Another example is the fair copy of those pieces of his work that have involved personal investigation, the results of which need to be communicated and which therefore have highlighted the need for clear, precise exposition. There are many opportunities in a normal junior school classroom for this type of dissemination of knowledge.

The great writers frequently re-drafted their work. Children, too, need opportunities provided for such critical appraisal, preferably in consultation with a teacher, or member of their peer group; when satisfied with the first draft of a fair copy is the natural outcome.

## Presentation

Care in presentation of work, both by the teacher and by the child, has a most definite influence on the desire to produce good work, and this time spent on good production is time well spent.

Children need to be made aware of the total view of a page, and to be taught how to make the layout attractive. Titling, proportion of height of letter to length of line, width of margins in proportion to each other and to the amount of text, paragraph indentations, style of headings, and possible decorative treatment all deserve attention.

Often young children choose to decorate their own work, border patterns being a frequent choice. This inclination can usefully be encouraged and developed. Teachers may wish to refer to some of the illuminated manuscripts of the early handwritten books for examples of the potential beauty of the written page.

The development of calligraphy as an art form in this manner is not quite the same as the development of an economic and swift style of handwriting which requires systematic speed practice, yet it in no way detracts from it. Indeed, the awareness of form, rhythm, flow, and unity strengthen the ability to write at speed.

The main objective ought to be an individual, fast-flowing, attractive, legible style for each person, so that he can communicate his ideas to his audience without being handicapped either by fatigue or by lack of speed.

Instruction and correction should at all times be reserved for definite handwriting times, and should not interrupt the concentration needed for personal writing.

## 7.2 Writing to communicate

The other aspect evoked by the term 'writing' is communication.

### Why write?

There should always be two over-riding considerations when thinking of writing:

> First: *Audience* — for whom am I writing?
> Second: *Function* — why am I writing?

The sad comment is that for thousands of schoolchildren the answer to the first question is 'for my teacher' and to the second, 'because my teacher told me to'.

There is but little incentive here to write at all, let alone to write well.

This could quite easily be remedied: it is not difficult, with a little careful thought and preparation, to provide other audiences and to make sound reason for almost all the written work required of children in school.

### Modes of writing

It seems to us that Professor James Britton's categories of modes of writing used in the Schools Council publication on the development of writing abilities[1] and in the Bullock Report (*A Language for Life*[2]) have yet to be improved upon. This method of classification of writing has its detractors, but to date nothing better has been offered in its place. It certainly helps children, from about nine years upwards, to recognize suitability of style to subject matter: it helps to prepare them for the type of writing that may well be demanded of them when they come, for instance, to write up a scientific experiment, to organize the presentation of data in a geographical essay, or, in a different vein answering a different demand, to produce a considered and polished piece of prose or poetry.

Herewith, then, is a brief summary.

## Expressive mode

Imagine 'writing' to be a continuum. If we take this to be an imaginary line, in the centre lies the 'expressive' mode. (As with any set of terms, one has to define one's meaning and exclude those aspects that one does not intend. This word, 'expressive', has overtones that are not required in this context.) By this is meant the natural easy expression of the writer in the language nearest to himself. It is the mode in which the young child first writes down his ideas for his teacher; it is the mode the pupil uses when struggling to come to terms with a new idea; it is the mode the adult uses when writing to a friend in conversational manner.

Three examples will make this clear:

*Example 1*

*Writing by a six-year-old about herself*

I live in a shop. The sounds I hear are cars and buses and vans and coaches and the bell on the shop door. It's fun in a shop. I hear my dog go 'woof, woof'. My dog is lovely. When I touch him his fur is so soft, he is a lovely big cuddly Labrador.

*Example 2*

*Writing by a nine-year-old trying to explain 'moving pictures' during a topic on optical illusions*

### Moving Pictures

I have made a little book with lots and lots of pages. On every page I drew a footballer. On the first page he was just going to kick a football. In the next picture I drew he was nearer still. Next he had almost got to it. In the next he had kicked it. I went on like this until the ball had gone out of sight. If you get the book and flick over the pages it will look like the footballer's kicking the ball. I don't quite get how this works but I think it is because your eye can not see the pictures separately when they flick fast so it looks as if they are moving but they're not really. . . .

*Example 3*

*Report of an experience when staying at a Colonie de Vacance in Normandy written by an 11-year-old*

We all march into the dinner hall. But then I stop still, there are other children in our places.

We have to sit on different tables than usual with two unknown girls facing us.

I start giggling, probably because I couldn't think of anything else to do.

Milly, Jane, Anna, and I say 'Hullo', to these girls, but they don't reply.

'Very polite', I think to myself in a sarcastic way.

Then, just as we are going to ask if they have tongues in their heads or not our teacher stands up and explains that the children are French and don't speak a word of English so it was up to us to start a conversation with the amount of French we knew.

After a lot of confusion and giggling Jane manages to say, 'Bonjour'. They start having hysterics. I do not think it is funny at all. I think Jane ought to be jolly annoyed, I certainly would have been if it had been me. They start off into a long blabber of French.

I feel out for something to say to them but the words don't come out of my mouth.

We try again to get through to them, this time we succeed.

Victory at last!

We try a bit harder and they respond.

But then we start talking about things in English; they sit there, blank-looking, just how we'd felt. I know how they feel—lost in a sea of different language. So I make another effort, and soon we are all firm friends and talk by voice and actions.

We are pleased at our breakthrough.

## Transactional mode

Children move out along the continuum towards the transactional as they become aware of the need to marshall facts, and organize them into logical order as in project or scientific work. Here, too, fits the writing of historical or geographical data, as before demanding accuracy and precision.

If good non-fiction is read aloud to children, as well as the more usual stories and poems, it helps them to become familiar with the type of language used in this more formal style. It not only widens their vocabulary of technical terms but introduces them to other forms and constructions of sentences.

*Example 1*

The class had been studying 'Ourselves'. One group had a skeleton to examine. Jane, a member of this group, was asked to contribute information about her observations for the completed report.

> In a skeleton there are exactly 206 bones altogether. Bones can be separated into families, for instance the femur is a long bone and so is the fibula and the humerus and the radius. Some bones are flat bones: your ribs and your shoulder blades. Some people think that your spine is a long bone but really it is lots of small bones joined together; they are called vertebral bones. There are also some short bones, and they are obviously the carpal and the tarsal bones of the hands and feet.
>
> If all bones and muscles were taken out of your body you would drop to the floor like seaweed on the shore.
>
> The pelvis is a bone that is like a baby's cradle or a food bowl. There are no other bones like that in the skeleton.

*Example 2*

This writing is by an 11-year-old, who had been with his school on a week's field study expedition to the Forest of Dean. Here he is using his own very recent experiences and combining them with book research to write an account of the early history of the Forest. This was to be put together with the work of the whole group to form a complete study, to share with other classes.

> [Short extract from]
> *The Early History of the Forest of Dean*
>
> There are signs of Early Stone Age man in certain caves in the hills and cliffs near the River Wye. In these are the remains of mammoth, cave bear, and the woolly rhinoceros. The flint flakes that have also been found prove that even at that time, long, long, ago, there must have been trade between Wiltshire and Dean, because the nearest place that flint is found is in Wiltshire.
>
> Bronze axe heads have been brought out of these caves.
>
> There are menhirs standing here too. It is thought they were put here either for religious reasons, or else to mark the way from the River Severn up to Hereford.
>
> In the Iron Age the forest became very important because iron ore was found. The Celts dug great 'scowles' to get the ore out. ('Scowles' means the pits the Celts dug: we saw some at Puzzlewood.)
>
> The Romans came, probably for the iron ore. They paved the tracks (some of their roads can still be seen) and they covered the whole Forest of Dean.

## Poetic mode

Dispense with pictures of children struggling to produce rhyming verse, or 'purple passages' full of high-sounding words, artificial and insincere, written solely to please the teacher.

The term 'poetic' on this continuum means that writing which has much in common with the language of literature. Here the writer stands back as an observer of the world, commenting, using his creative ability, choosing the best words, putting them in the best order, shaping and polishing, in an endeavour to form a satisfying whole, satisfying to himself and to his potential audience.

The reading of good literature to children is one of the mainsprings of inspiration.

### Example 1

This delightful piece was incorporated in an 'individual topic' on horses. The children, 10-year-olds, had obviously heard, at some time during their time at school, Paul Dehn's poem, 'How to Paint the Portrait of a Bird'.

#### A Portrait of a Horse

First you paint a field with fresh green grass in it. Paint some trees and a sun.

If you want a horse paint some food in the middle of the field and then paint an open gate. Then all you have to do is wait and wait until you hear the sound of hoofs.

The hoofs belong to a wild horse. He sees the food and he comes in. When he is in, quickly close the gate and start to paint. Get the smallest brush you have and then paint every hair on the horse. When you have painted him put your name in the corner of the picture. Now it is done.

### Example 2

Written by an 11-year-old while sitting in a plantation of evergreens. The class were staying at a field study centre in the Quantock Forest.

#### Coniferous Forest

Nothing stirred!
No bird was in sight.
Then the trees swayed
And a wave like a mighty ocean
Tumbled through the winding branches.
The brown light,
Floating like a mist in heavy skirts,
Dappled on the tree trunks.
A cobweb hung sagging on a branch
And way down below hung a silver thread

That glinted in the light.
The ground was covered in a carpet of needles.
And seemed to move
Trembling and shaking.
The peck, peck of a woodpecker
Broke the silence
And then was gone.
The cold filtered in through a never-shut door
And rushed into the silence.
As I neared the edge of the forest
The warmth struck me full in the face.
It came to greet me.
A bird sang in a beautiful brilliant beech tree.
The sun shone
And my eyes squinted in the glare.
Heather had sprung up around the path
Had lined it.
The dappled pattern on the ground
Was like an never-ending rump of a rocking horse.

It will be obvious that from the expressive mode out along the continuum towards the transactional end the writer plays a part in the action, weighing up pros and cons, hypothesizing, giving information, issuing commands or requests; involved, in fact, in the world about him.

This is not true of the writing along the continuum from expressive out towards the poetic. Here the writer gets further and further removed from the centre of the action, and becomes a spectator, a commentator on life. Imagination and fantasy may well play a part here in helping the writer to create something completely new.

## Using the modes

As children grow through the junior years their appreciation of these types of writing should mature. They should come to recognize which form is most suitable for the subject in hand.

An excerpt from a tape of nine-year-old children discussing their work illustrates the point. Paul had visited a paper mill and had written an account of paper making.

Teacher  Yes, that's a good try, though I don't think every one else in the class will understand the process fully. Can you put some more into it?

Tamsin  Put your thoughts into it, Paul.

Paul  No, my thoughts won't help anyone understand. It's just how machines worked and what really happened that I've got to explain.

His teacher was delighted with his reply, which demonstrated that he fully realized the requirement, and was moving well along the continuum from the egocentric writing of the expressive mode to the less personal informative style that the subject demanded.

It must be emphasized that, although we have identified three categories, we are writing of a whole continuous range, and that nowhere along the continuum will be found hard dividing lines. Indeed, most children in primary schools, even in the older classes, will certainly not have mastered the art of writing to the extent that their work could be firmly classified as purely 'transactional' or as purely 'poetic'. What the teacher must aim for is that children should begin to recognize congruity of style both for subject matter and audience.

Here is an example of writing by an eight-year-old just beginning to move from the expressive mode out along the continuum towards the transactional, It came as a result of a study of Early Man. To help the children envisage what life might have been like they had tried to make artefacts (tools, weapons, clothing, pottery, etc.) using only those methods and materials that research had told them had been in use during the Stone Age.

The report is an experience very close to the writer, but nevertheless care has been taken to see that the sequence is evident throughout, that the detail is correct, and the writing factual and unembellished by irrelevances.

I have been making things like Stone Age men did.

I have woven and twisted. I started by twisting. I got some wild clematis and plaited it. I had a problem. It was what shall I use to tie the end of the wild clematis so it won't undo. I used three bits of grass and plaited them to tie with.

I decided to make a pot for carrying water because every time I tried to carry it with my hands the water ran through. First I went and dug a hole in the ground to find some clay and then I dried it a bit in the sun. After that I rolled it into a big ball. And I put my clenched fist in it and swivelled it round and shaped the clay. I put it near the entrance of our cave to dry. Some days later I rubbed it shiny. To shine it is best to use a smooth, shiny stone.

Next follows a piece of prose (or poetry, call it what you will) written by an 11-year-old. It is firmly rooted in expressive mode— personal, chatty— yet there are signs of the careful selection of words, and a sense of both form and rhythm.

*Housework at a Youth Hostel*

Dust and mud,
Dust and mud,

From Wellington boots.
Look at the stairs
All to be swept.
Down the stairs I go
Along the corridor,
Into the broom cupboard.
Collect the dust pan and brush.
Back to those stairs again.
Sweeping side to side
Into the dust pan!
Side to side
Into the dust pan!
Side to side
Into the dust pan
Goes the routine.
I yawn and get slower and slower
But at last I reach the bottom
And look at my nice
clean sparkling stairs.
A crowd of people come
scampering down,
Dust and mud,
Dust and mud,
I go very hot with
anger inside.

## Practical application of the modes

The very last thing to do when trying to encourage good writing is to set children to practise in each of the three modes. This could be disastrous.

There must come a gradual realization of style and its suitability to demand and circumstance, but this ability to differentiate depends upon the child's skilled use of language in the expressive mode, when he is using it well for his own personal needs.

## 7.3 The teacher's role

The teacher should never at any time underestimate herself and her influence: here she has a decisive role to play in the development of the child as a writer. It is her skill that counts in leading the child onward, from the initial idea of putting down his thoughts in words as he would utter them, through the under-standing that writing is so very much more than this, to the realization that it has to be shaped and refined. The child must also be gradually brought to recognize that the writing of a factual report needs a very different approach from the writing of a story or a poem, and that the very subject matter or the people he has in mind as his audience also affect the mode, the language, and the whole style of his writing.

## 7.4 Writing in the infant years

There are two essential rules for success at the outset of written work: (1) the young child must first want to write, and (2) he must have something to write about (further reference in Chapter 3). Some infant pupils are reluctant to attempt independent writing because demands have been made upon them too early; they have found themselves suffering from failure because unrealistic goals have been set for them. The teacher must be sure that the child is ready to attempt to write (further reference in Chapter 2) before he is asked to do so.

The purpose of writing is communication, and this presupposes that the finished product will be read. By whom, other than the teacher? What use, also, will be made of the child's written work? And is there something worth talking and writing about?

At first one should expect that almost all a child's writing will be written-down speech; a young school child's utterances are frequently quite complicated in syntax, for by school age most have learnt to handle language in its spoken form competently.

Any insistence upon short sentences is a retrograde step, preventing a child from using his linguistic ability ably even if he does learn about full stops. Far better to allow the thoughts to flow, joined by 'and then' and 'and then'. It is much easier at a later stage to develop style in a fluent, willing writer than in a child who has been inhibited by constant correction.

Relationships, as in all teaching, are most important; children will develop best as fluent writers when they have trust in the person in charge, when the atmosphere is encouraging, and the environment stimulating.

### Personal experiences (shared)

At first personal experience is the main starting point for most writing; it may be shared experience arising out of a happening in the classroom itself, or from a planned visit to a place of interest in the neighbourhood.

> Cooking.
> Planting seeds.
> Playtime.

The engine-driver's visit.
Harvest Festival.
Blowing bubbles.
A topic on American Indians.

These are all examples of the normal day's activities which could be used to stimulate children's writing; similar opportunities can be found in every school. A little more planning is needed to organize visits to, for example,

A farm.
A tropical bird collection.
A wildlife park.
A derelict clearance area.
A canal bank.
A wharf.
A market.

or a 'seeing walk' in the immediate vicinity of the school itself.

It is better with young children to restrict the journeys to places easily get-at-able, so that the trip itself is neither tiring nor expensive. It should be borne in mind that spontaneous activity frequently provides a better starting point than planned stimuli.

## Personal experience (individual)

Many young children, still very much in the egocentric stage, wish to make their own individual contribution to the day's records, and deserve every encouragement so to do. They may well wish to write about their own models, their particular mathematical or scientific discoveries, or their recent play activities.

Not all writing is school-centred, of course; experiences from home will be reported:

Buying new clothes.
The birth of a sibling.
When I got lost.
My pets.
Visits to or from relatives.
Going to the fair.

Unfortunately, not all children's experiences are of this nature, and we find them writing of the family row, the pet thrown out, drunken scenes, visits to the pub, cruelty, and so on. And how beneficial it is that they can indeed write of them, for the aid it gives is two-fold. First, the very fact of reviewing the happenings helps the child to come to terms with them; second, the knowledge of the child's background revealed to the teacher helps her to understand the child's problems more fully.

**119**

### The writing of stories

There are some children who either cannot or do not wish to bring their fears and anxieties directly into view, but who need to dwell for a time at least in fantasy.

All children love to hear stories, very often demanding the same story again and again until its sequence is thoroughly familiar; a few children delight in creating their own (for others it proves an almost impossible task, and should not be demanded of them). There are other children, however, for whom it is therapeutic to translate their inquietudes and terrors into witches, goblins, ghosts, and 'all things that go bump in the night', and the opportunities should be provided.

Story-writing initially ought also to be in the child's own natural register; it is fairly easy to teach children to manipulate adult phrases, but to no purpose; they ought to be allowed to use their own forms and constructions at first. The best corrective comes indirectly from well-written and well-read stories in a rich reading-aloud programme.

The opportunity must be given for the hearers to retell the stories, and it is then that one notices their style being modified, their vocabulary enlarged, their sentence construction improved, and their sequencing ability developed as they learn to sustain the story line.

Authorship begins, of course, by listening to stories, and progresses by dictating them, preferably to an adult who will type them out. They can then be made into a book which can be illustrated by the author, and used by other children in the class, taken home to show parents, and generally treasured. Something, therefore, that would have been lost if only spoken has been captured and a powerful motive towards the written word demonstrated, namely, that one can preserve in words an experience, an idea, or a celebration that is memorable.

Fig. 7.3 charts suggested stages for story writing in the infant years.

### 7.5 Writing in the junior and middle years

There is no magic in the transfer from infant to junior years, and no sudden difference in writing should be expected.

The expressive mode will still be the major one used by most seven-year-olds, for they will still be verbalizing their own personal experiences and preoccupations. So the speech of home with its dialect forms should not be suppressed.

| | Stage 1 | Stage 2 | Stage 3 | Stage 4 | Stage 5 | Stage 6 |
|---|---|---|---|---|---|---|
| Starting point | Story told by teacher to class or group | Story told by teacher or shared experience retold by teacher, e.g. visit to the zoo retold in sequence | Experience or story well known to the group | Teacher begins an imaginative story. Each child in turn adds to it | Teacher gives same starting point of story to both sub-groups | Discussion or experience to stimulate story writing; perhaps several starting points from which children can choose |
| Organization | Group of up to six children | As stage 1 | Group of children who have formed basic concepts for reading and have limited sight vocabulary based on own talk | As stage 3 | Large group sub-divided into two smaller groups | Group for discussion followed by individual work |
| Skills needed by children | Ability to chat | Ability to chat about recalled experience | Basic concepts for reading plus limited sight vocabulary based on own language | As stage 3 plus the ability to match printed sentences | As stage 4 plus ability to identify initial letters and sounds of words | As stage 5 plus the ability to build up regular phonic words |
| Materials | Tape recorder; art materials for children | As stage 1 plus large felt pen for teacher | As stage 2 plus list of children's basic sight vocabulary for teacher's reference | As stage 3 plus teacher's sentence-maker (magnetic board or flannelgraph or Breakthrough type) | Two tape recorders (one for each sub-group) plus Wall Pocket Dictionary and materials for stage 4 | As stage 5 plus word builder for each child |
| Procedure | Story discussed and sequence identified; each child produces picture for one part of sequence | Teacher begins story and each child adds next part. Pictures produced as stage 1 | As stage 2 | As stage 3 | Each sub-group develops story independently of other sub-group | Each child develops own story |
| Recording | Children's oral contributions recorded on tape | Recording on tape plus sentence written by teacher underneath each picture | Teacher records as stage 2 but uses children's sight vocabulary as much as possible | Original group story-telling recorded on tape; then recorded pictorially; then recorded by children with aid of sentence maker or Wall Pocket Dictionary | As stage 4 | Some children tape record story, some record pictorially, and some record graphically according to ability and/or choice of children |
| Production | Picture story book or wall story plus tape recording | As stage 1 | As stage 2 plus separate cards for matching sentences | Picture story book plus tape recording plus sentence and word matching strips | Two books and tapes produced | Separate story book for each child. Could be typed on 'Jumbo' typewriter, then illustrated by child and used in book corner |
| Skills developed or practised by children during production | 1. Oral expression 2. Recall of story 3. Physical manipulation of large drawing materials 4. Pictorial expression | As stage 1 plus 5. Group reading of teacher's writing (helps to form concept that printed squiggles convey a meaning) | As stage 2 plus 6. Sentence-matching with teacher's help | As stage 3 plus 7. Word matching with teacher's help 7a. If able, children copy own text | As stage 4 plus 8. Comparison of story development 9. Use of Wall Pocket Dictionary 10. Use of finer tool for writing | As stage 5 plus 11. Phonic analysis of words |
| Skills developed or practised by children using finished product | 1. Listening skills when using tape recording 2. Picture interpretation 3. Progression through a book, or, if wall story, left-to-right orientation | As stage 1 plus 4. Attaching a meaning to the printed word (does not have to be as accurate as reading at this stage) | As stage 2 plus 5. Ability to match sentence strip to printed sequence | As stage 3 plus 6. Ability to match words to teacher's printing | As stage 4 plus 7. Ability to compare a story sequence | As stage 4 plus 8. Reading a simple story told in the language of their peers |

**Fig. 7.3 Suggested stages for development in story writing**

121

And we would suggest that this writing in the language nearest to the writer should be encouraged throughout school life whenever the pupil is struggling to master new concepts. There are two main reasons for advocating a continuing use of the expressive mode. First, the writing in itself helps the learning, just as talk does. Second, it is essential for teachers to know when a concept has been understood, and no amount of regurgitated phrases from a notebook or copied words from a text will ever reveal true mastery.

The 'shared thinking' of the seven-year-old's writing should, as he matures as a writer, gradually move out along the continuum. When the writing is informing as opposed to sharing, or when it is towards the language of literature, then the dialect speech, the incorrect forms, can and should be screened out.

What must one look for in all writing? Over the last decade two schools of thought have arisen. One group thinks the aim in the teaching of writing should be to generate a vivid outpouring of ideas, showing originality, force, simplicity, and a wide vocabulary. The opposers suggest that perfection in grammar, punctuation, spelling, and handwriting is what should be sought. Surely this is a false dichotomy. Children need to be free to write fluently, but the teacher must then work upon the child's intentions, look for growth points, select teaching matter, and so overcome the danger of polarization.

## 7.6 Marking

What then to correct? One important suggestion was made in Chapter 6 about discussion of first drafts. We would suggest that marking 'in absentio' is a useless ploy for the teacher of young children. A policy of perfection is for the teacher to mark every child's work with the author at her side. This, of course, is not always possible or practicable, but we would suggest that it is better to mark half the class's work in this way on one occasion, and the other half on the next. The unmarked work should be read through, and a positive comment written at the end, because many children would feel frustrated if they thought that their teacher had not read and appreciated their efforts.

As one glances through scripts it is a good idea to select teaching points that are common to a group of children. Nevertheless, care must be taken not to be seen only in the light of tester and assessor, but also in the light of trusted recipient and appreciative audience.

If the teacher knows that a second draft would be a wearisome exercise, as it may be for the young junior or the slow older child, other methods of achieving a good finished effort must be adopted. One such is to rule a wide margin down the left-hand side of the paper to be left blank by the child, who will write in pencil on the right-hand side. When the teacher marks the work she puts in the margin such spelling corrections as the child is capable of learning, discussing with the writer such things as spelling rules, or word families as she does so. The child then, on his own, erases his mistakes, learns the spelling of the word to be inserted, covers the teacher's writing of this word, and writes the correction in place. Finally, he cuts off the margin, and so finishes with a corrected piece of work and a word list, which can either be clipped to his others, or copied into his own word book.

## 7.7 Spelling

Until quite recently in our country's history spelling remained highly personal; nowadays standardization of spelling is demanded, a difficult requirement when the irregularities of our language are taken into account. The small, frequently used 'function' words cause untold difficulty (or, one, of, off, some, he, her, the, them, they, those, there, their) and they make up about one-third of most running text. They provide problems for several reasons—they are frequently phonically irregular; they are usually glossed over very quickly in speech so the child does not hear them aright; and they have no emotive associations to assist the memory. (Hence any reading scheme based on these as 'key words' is, by definition, difficult.)

Despite this, a good phonic framework built into the school's language policy is essential, and familiarity with this coding system is half the battle (further reference in Chapter 3). For the rest, children have to be taught, according to their ability and their present needs and interests. Again, the school needs a coherent and on-going programme so that this teaching is not haphazard, but is undertaken frequently, in very short bursts, with children grouped according to ability. A class spelling list, issued on Monday morning and tested on Fridays, is a useless waste of time for the great majority of children, though particular letter combinations practised in handwriting sessions do help.

### Letter sequences

These are important because one of the major skills in spelling well is the knowledge of large units of common letter sequences, whether learnt through motor skills or through visio-perceptual ones. Children should be made aware of the internal structure of words, and trained in visual perception as well as in motor skills. The span of letter-sequence imagery can be increased by simple practices, such as looking at a word on a flash card and, after removal of the image, writing it. The marking method suggested in the last section, where the child himself is responsible for looking at the word, covering it, and writing from memory, is another useful ploy. When young children are writing they should be encouraged to say the word—not letter by letter, but as their pencil moves along.

Phoneme–grapheme strategies are important also, so all children, even the ablest readers, should have worked right through the phonic programme in use in the school, paying particular attention to blends and digraphs, because spelling is not a 'spin-off' from reading, but a completely different kind of activity.

### Spelling rules

There are some spelling rules that do not have so many exceptions that they become handicaps. These are well worth introducing to third- and fourth-year juniors, preferably by engineering that the children discover them for themselves. They should then be recorded in a special notebook. (Some simple dicta for writing can also be treated in this manner—quotation marks, apostrophes, plurals, tense, and various other punctuation rules, particularly noting those that have been discussed with the teacher as she has marked work.) There must be in the teacher's mind rules for rules:

1. They must be widely applicable.
2. They must have few exceptions.
3. They must not be verbose or in unfamiliar technical terms.
4. They must be easily understood when referred to at a later date.
5. They must have examples with them to illustrate their point.

An excited interest in words themselves, in their roots and their derivations, can often be aroused in junior children. Those words derived from our Saxon ancestors as distinct from those originating from the Norman conquest form a simple example. (Compare, for instance, our words for various forms of meat: on the table, frequently the word brought by the Normans; in the field, the Saxon word kept alive by the conquered people, many of whom had to turn to the menial task of caring for the animals.) It follows from this that families of words should be considered too, and prefixes and suffixes understood. There are now many games on the market, ranging from the very simple to such adult entertainment as 'Scrabble', which are well worth having in school. Most of them, particularly in the early stages, gain in value if an adult oversees them, a worthwhile session for the assistant in the classroom or the helpful parent perhaps.

The teacher can, by analysis, classify errors in spelling, noting omissions, reversals, mishearings, local idiosyncrasies, lack of phonic knowledge, etc. Books that offer help in this field are listed at the end of this chapter.

Having said all this about spelling, it must nevertheless be stressed that the most excellent spelling is useless unless the child wishes to write. So the emphasis must, as always, lie here. Once the incentive to communicate is established, then the necessity to spell becomes apparent, for if the words cannot be read, communication fails. But, as we said earlier, over-correction can so easily stifle the desire to write. It is helpful to the child to understand when and where spelling matters (not in rough drafts, we would suggest). Explain about tolerances, and allow a generous measure when the children are writing freely.

It is perhaps unnecessary to add that children should be encouraged to refer at first to their own word books and later to dictionaries, which must be provided at suitable levels in every classroom, with at least one full adult dictionary to consult when others fail.

## 7.8 The teaching of techniques

There are many points of orthography which must be taught if a child's written communication skills are to improve. They may well have to be taught and practised in isolation, but only when the need has been recognized, and when they can be put to practical use as soon as they are mastered.

There are some skills, such as the inverted commas, exclamation marks, direct and indirect speech, that can be learned without the actual presence of a teacher, by means of carefully prepared structured programmes. These may possibly make use of sophisticated modern equipment in the form of electrically operated teaching machines or video tape using a television display screen; but more within the reach of most teachers are cassette tapes and slides, or display boxes through which a simple linear programme can be wound, or maybe just a single sheet of paper or card with a masking device on top. Material so presented has the benefit of allowing the child to follow at his individual speed, and to check and recheck until he has mastered the skill. It also provides opportunity to return for practice at a later date if need be.

On the other hand, the teacher may prefer to gather together a group of children who are at a similar stage so that she can explain the new learning herself. (For some of the more difficult skills and for a few children nothing can take the place of personal contact.) If the recording system recommended in Chapter 11 (Fig. 11.2) is used, it is a fairly simple matter to select groups who are ready to learn certain new techniques, and so save teaching time.

In either case, when taught, it is necessary for the children to have practice in their new-found skill. Work sheets are useful for this type of exercise, which can then be used as and when necessary. (Here note the distinction between work cards, which are usually prepared singly for individual or group work, and work sheets, which can be duplicated for any number of children.) It is an asset if the school can have master copies readily available. Work sheets with carefully prepared exercises may also be used diagnostically, so that the teacher can ensure understanding.

To be realistic, not all busy teachers feel able to prepare enough such resources. It is then a good idea to have a selection of the best that are currently on the market and use them selectively. Although we would not recommend using exercises from commercially prepared books for the whole class on a regular weekly basis without regard to individual need, there is a place for such material when used selectively as reinforcement of learning.

## 7.9 Cloze procedure

(This is a reading/writing procedure using a piece of text from which certain words have been omitted. The task is a skilled form of completion exercise demanding a reasoned, logical response to all the context cues available.)

### Readability

One most useful teaching aid, in our opinion of far more value than comprehension or vocabulary exercises, is cloze procedure. Initially this was used to test readability of text in the following manner. A certain number of words in a text were deleted on a systematic basis—say every tenth word. If the reader could supply a word that fitted, both syntactically and semantically, then the text was within his capabilities.

We still use cloze procedure for 'readability' on occasion, but the idea has been developed, extended, and used in a far wider field.

### Context cues

It is obvious that cloze procedure can be of the utmost use in helping the child to respond to context cues—there is no right answer; the child's chosen word indeed may be as fitting as that used by the author. (In one school where children were very familiar with this work, the teacher chose to use a rather badly written guide book; the children's own contributions were frequently better than those in the printed text, to their great delight. What a confidence boost they were given!) Of course, wrong answers can be given—and in group discussion after the completion of the exercise these can be commented upon. It is, of course, in this follow-up period that most of the gain accrues. Vocabulary can be enlarged and a sense of style heightened. Words chosen by some children can be shown to fit the context (they are therefore acceptable), yet they may not be the most fitting choice. Others in the group may offer different suggestions, justifying their choice and allowing the teacher to point out nuance of meaning, atmosphere, intention, character, and viewpoint, according to the understanding of her group.

### Parts of speech

Deletion exercises also offer opportunities for teaching correct grammatical terms and usage. For instance, all adjectives, all adverbs, or all verbs may be omitted. The smaller function words may also be highlighted in this way, or the pronouns deleted.

Syntactical agreement may be reinforced by leaving off word endings. Spelling rules learnt can be tried out, too, just as certain areas of knowledge can be tested if so desired.

On some occasions the teacher may wish to stress rhyme, or to discuss syllabification—cloze procedure can be easily adapted to these ends.

We have found it preferable to allow children to work in pairs so that discussion takes place about their insertions. This is followed by group discussion having, at a maximum, 10 children together.

If one really wishes to extend the ablest readers, a deletion of even one in three is possible if an interesting, simply written narrative is selected. This seems to prove that flow of non-technical language coupled with a good story line overcomes much readability difficulty, so making a nonsense of strict colour-coding on reading age for both fiction and interest books (further reference in Chapter 13).

All in all, cloze procedure offers innumerable possibilities for the enterprising teacher, and we recommend that a bank of ready-typed 'masters' should be built up for general use.

Exercises have been used in English schools for at least 70 years, yet there seems little proof of correlation between the results of these and the grammar actually used in other contexts.

## 7.10 Learning about words

Cloze procedure, of course, is not the only interesting way of improving a child's knowledge of the way in which language works. An interest in words for themselves should be fostered; puns and riddles, which have such an appeal to junior children, should have an important place. We have found that children love to collect ambiguities, too. A headline in a local paper took pride of place for some time: it ran, 'Fourteen stone giants play in Wiltshire Rugby Club'. (Members from Stonehenge RFC, possibly!)

Adjectives and adjectival phrases are easy, but have added interest if they were used in calligrams adapted for the purpose (see Fig. 7.4). A variation on the theme is to cut a shape jigsaw fashion, and, when each child has filled his part of the puzzle with descriptive words or phrases, reform and mount the original. Or again, the words could be affixed to a model.

**Fig. 7.4** A calligram

Children should be taught about syllables. They might then try to produce a poem in the Japanese Haiku style—with three unrhymed lines only, the first of five syllables, the second of seven, and the third line of five again.

The snow fell softly,
Melting to drops of water
On my anorak.

*(Brian, aged nine)*

The cinquain is a slightly harder form, consisting of five lines of two, four, six, eight, and two syllables respectively.

Raindrops
Stab the playground
Bouncing off the tarmac.
Thank goodness I am safe inside
And dry.

*(Ian, aged eleven)*

Other parts of speech might be used to form patterns—a five-line verse might be asked for, with the following desiderata:
First line, one word
Second line, two connecting adjectives
Third line, three verbs
Fourth line, four words descriptive of feelings
Final line, one word.

Books
Exciting, enjoyable,
Read, laugh, tremble.
Amused, afraid, scared, worried,
Library.

*(Jane, aged nine)*

Or one might ask for words forming a diamond, with these limitations: One noun, two adjectives, three participles, five nouns, three participles, two adjectives, one noun different from the original one, all words having some connection with the first.

Cat
Soft, Gentle.
Purring, Washing, Lapping,
Leopard, Lion, Cheetah, Puma, Tiger,
Stalking, Prowling, Pouncing,
Fierce, Proud,
Hunter.

*(Jill, aged ten)*

## 7.11 Writing stories

Story-writing, in itself of great importance to some children, can also help with reading. In 'Book time', when the teacher is meeting groups or individuals for discussion, it is worth paying attention to basic story patterns and progressions, knowledge of which can be used to assist in the location of information and in the sequencing of their own story lines. These, too, must be discussed with the adult who needs to draw close attention to the plot development and to portrayal of character.

Children's appreciation of style may be encouraged on occasion by taking an exciting paragraph from a story, and altering the emotive words to prosaic ones for a first reading. This is then followed by a reading of the original version, when debate will highlight the quality of words.

### The peer group as audience

The question of audience for stories is an easy one to answer. Children may well write for their peer group, and the knowledge that others will see their work will make the effort of the fair copy worth while. Nevertheless, frequent demand for re-copying may militate against output; other agencies may be employed (parents, general assistants, the teacher herself) to type out, preferably on a 'Jumbo' typewriter, the finished product.

At the top of the junior school, children should be capable of writing long, sustained novels, complete with chapters. Flow diagrams are a useful aid for the development of the plot.

Fig. 9.6 on page 175 shows how a group of children had planned to report their book research on Romans by using a very simple flow diagram to organize their ideas. Similar techniques can be adapted for the sequencing of the plot of a story. The form might be something like the chapter headings in Fig. 7.5, each possibly further subdivided into paragraphs detailing the subject matter. These can be corrected, preferably chapter by chapter, and then made into books for use in the classroom library.

Some children prefer to complete the whole task unaided, from the first few words through the rough draft and copying-out stages, the making of the contents list, end papers and illustrations to the final binding (further reference in Chapter 8). Others prefer assistance with the reproduction—and, indeed, if their actual handwriting is painstakingly slow or not easily readable, it is essential to provide help.

These long stories should not be attempted 'in one go' or even during one week, but should be kept as an on-going piece of writing, to be returned to, in the adult manner, on frequent occasions. It is preferable that this should be when the desire to

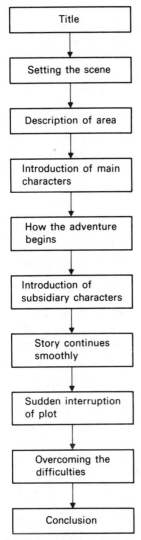

**Fig. 7.5** Outlining the plot of a story

write wells up within the author, and classroom organization should be flexible enough to permit and further this approach to workmanship.

### Writing for other children

During the upper junior years strong motivation for story-writing can come from writing for children for the infant school. Before embarking on their work the authors should, if possible, visit an infant classroom. There are many questions to be asked before putting pen to paper and these need to be puzzled out and reflected upon prior to the interviews with their potential audience.

A study of the books best liked in the classroom can also help. If the teacher wishes, this ploy can lead on to the study of language in some depth.

The finished stories, far better typed in large print in this instance, can then be mounted on card and illustrated. If then laminated they can be useful additions to the infant class reading corners.

One of the nicest aspects of this work is that so frequently the less able older child produces the stories most suitable for the five-year-olds and so gains in stature. Another benefit is that these books wear out quickly, and so there is genuine demand for more!

## 7.12 Co-operation between different ages

There is much to be gained from involving older children in the activities of the infant school. The older children gain in confidence, and learning how to communicate with younger children helps to develop their sense of audience. The younger children benefit from individual attention, and a purpose for talking, writing, and reading is provided for both age groups. In one primary school the fourth-year junior teacher and the reception teacher decided to work co-operatively. The children were paired for reading so that they read to each other and the juniors wrote stories for the infants. During the production a great deal of discussion took place. The juniors began to appreciate that they would have to use vocabulary that the younger children would understand, and the importance of sentence construction and overall length was also realized. Suitability of plot and character received attention, too. Some very good descriptive work was produced by the juniors after observing the infants making and eating pancakes on Shrove Tuesday.

Two other classes participated in a joint project on fairy tales. The infant class explored the stories through language and art and the juniors developed comprehension questions for the infants to answer. In order to do this it was necessary to find the main ideas in the stories, so a great deal of work on summarizing was accomplished. The story that they found most difficult to express succinctly was 'The Emperor's New Clothes'. The main point of this story is quite difficult to express, even for adults.

The teacher asked the children to devise some questions that the infants could answer by reading the story and some questions to which the answer could only be 'found in your head'. In this way the children were able to provide questions at the levels of inference and evaluation as well as literal questions. It was noticeable that, in order to frame questions, the children really had to understand the story first.

This method of work developed comprehension skills for both juniors and infants. Once again there was much discussion in the junior class about suitable vocabulary, and the need for appropriate sentence construction.

The whole project provided tremendous opportunities for both age groups to develop reading, writing, talking, and thinking skills at their own levels of development.

## 7.13 Continuity

Juniors writing for infants, secondary schoolchildren producing stories for juniors, and different age groups working together for a common end can all help smooth the path through school as well as towards literacy.

One junior school we know is fortunate enough to have close liaison with their comprehensive school which has an offset litho machine. Occasionally the best stories from the fourth-year junior classes are taken by their authors to the 'printers'. The proofs are sent back to be read, corrected, subheaded and illustrated in the junior school, returned to the presses, and printed. Some of the resulting copies are sold to defray expenses.

## 7.14 Personal writing

One very important stimulus for writing stays with a human being all his life. We mentioned its force during the infant years, but it remains a powerful motive for use in the post-infant school years. This is the writing of personal private impressions and experiences. As in the infant school, these may be classroom-stimulated, personal, or shared, such as the report of the school football match, or concert; or the visit to the school of the nurse, the doctor, or a travelling theatrical company. In one school the visit of fingerprint experts following a burglary gave wonderful firsthand experience for writing.

What about a visit to an infant classroom at Christmas? It can be magic, not only for the gold and glitter and the look of wonder on young faces, but for the memories and the nostalgia it all evokes. Response to music and pictures also plays a part.

Occasionally an object brought to school will trigger off vivid writing. Sometimes a poem or a short arresting phrase will be useful as starting points.

'The brakes screamed, tyres skidded. . . .'
'It lay there, sparkling in the sun.'
'With hardly a sound the knob turned.'

Children may want to write stories using these as opening sentences, or they may prefer to write down their thoughts and feelings.

For some children even titles help them to get started. Here are a few examples, not necessarily to be used, but merely as indicators:

Clearing out a cupboard.
Switching off the light at night.
High wind.
Bonfires.
Hallowe'en.
Heavy rain.
Heavy snow [at the right moment].
Nightmares.

Titles may elicit reports of the type of happening that so many children share outside school:

Going to the hospital.
Going to the dentist.
I'm in trouble.
When I fell into the pond.
The day I got home late.
The day I got lost.
I'm frightened of the gang.
I once borrowed Dad's saw.
Look what I've got.

Finally, and probably the most valuable stimulus, may be the personal recording which is about the private concerns of the individual. These may well be made explicit only when the atmosphere is supportive and the relationships sound. Into this category comes Tom's poem (see page 99), or the following outburst arising from a very different type of experience:

I woke one Sunday morning
Very early in the day.
I got out of bed and looked—
Out through the glass window.
To my surprise

I was face to face with cows!
Cows on the grass,
Cows trampling down the flowers,
Cows drinking the fish pond water,
Cows everywhere,
Everywhere you could possibly think of!
The cows had got through
The stonewall fence at the bottom of our garden,
Of our pretty garden,
The cows had spoiled our garden
I just sat at the window,
Staring.

Several important aspects are recognizable here: children are challenged to find ways of expressing thoughts and feelings that might otherwise remain implicit, and in a very safe context. There is no test, no question to answer, and so no fear of being wrong, and all children have within themselves experiences to draw upon, not least the underprivileged.

## Audience

It is, as we said, encouraging to the writers to be able to offer much of their work to a wider audience than just their teacher. Sometimes the reason for correctness and good handwriting can also be emphasized by mounting fair copies and displaying them in the classroom, corridor, or school hall for all to read. A class magazine, too, provides motivation: the method of using a spirit duplicator is easily taught; the production of a master copy is an exercise in neatness; and a team staffed by children alone can very soon become proficient in the publication of their own work. A bonus is added if the team are also asked to help select and reject material for inclusion in any one issue, for editorship encourages powers of literary criticism and discrimination.

Reports on school matches and outside visits are usually avidly read if put on the school notice-board. So, too, is information concerning vital interests, for instance where and when to meet the transport for the football match, what to take on a class outing, dates and times for swimming lessons, the choice on the menu for the week, and so on.

School rules might well also be displayed on the notice-board. (If left up too long no one sees them, but one or two succinct statements, well set out and changed at frequent intervals, help to reinforce the rules.)

Tests for qualifications such as those for BAGA awards,

swimming certificates, or cycling proficiency badges are obvious notices which deserve space where they can be easily seen, read, and referred to whenever necessary.

Letters are important, and here again there is no need to invent a recipient—many opportunities for 'real' letters arise during a normal school year. These may well include letters necessitated during preparations for an outing, the booking of a coach, the request for permission to visit a certain place, the obtaining of tickets, etc. They may be invitations to visiting speakers or thank-you notes after such an occasion. They may be requests for information on a subject that the writer cannot obtain from books. Frequently, though, they are letters to teachers or friends who are ill, perhaps in hospital and in need of cheer.

Book reviews are another form of writing that has an obvious readership. Other children are frequently persuaded to buy or borrow a book when it is highly recommended by a member of the class whose judgement they value.

Children need much help in understanding the demands made upon the writer by his audience, his subject matter, and his brief.

### Reporting

Reports, on the whole, should contain only verifiable facts, and all opinion should be rigorously excluded. One exercise to help children understand how to write in this manner is to make a study of accounts of events collected from various newspapers, note the places where opinion or bias have been included, and delete them. The information then remains, clear and uncoloured by the writer's prejudices. After this the preparation of notices containing important information prove a valuable practice. Further use can be made of newspapers to reinforce this teaching by using articles full of the reporters' own thoughts and feelings. One can, by teasing these out from the facts of the story, gather some idea of the personality of the writer, of his ideas and his preferences. This can be carried a stage further by comparing and contrasting whole newspapers and noting which incidents and what news they consider most important and how accounts can be slanted, not only by inclusion of comment but also by omission of some element. Indeed, newspapers comment quite clearly by their very selection of the news that they print.

School events, matches, sports days, happenings, and local occasions all lend themselves for the practice that children need in reporting, in representing faithfully what actually took place. A fair extension would be to ask for a separate paragraph, in which the reporter commented, and expressed his opinions, after having reflected on the event. Another practice exercise might entail writing first a factual account of an event (possibilities range from a quarrel between rival gangs to an imaginary sighting of a visitor from outer space). This can be followed by a second account, as from a very biased observer.

Advertisements almost always carry hidden persuaders. Not only is the written word in newspapers and magazines suspect, but the spoken word on television opens up a whole new field of study. As with the printed word, most children believe initially everything they hear to be true—they do indeed need to be taught to recognize the unreality of this belief, and to recognize, at least in part, the way in which they are being influenced.

In the previous chapter we looked briefly at other factual writing which needed precision. Rules and instructions are both good examples of the genre, needing opinion-free, accurate statements. Early attempts at setting down simple explanations should be limited to very simple tasks, entailing not more than five steps. (The same guideline should be followed when asking children to read and follow the teacher's instructions.) Gradually the stages can be extended and the children asked to prepare directions for various functions—marbling, book-binding, screen-printing, using a tape-recorder, cooking, using a protractor, using a clinometer, making an embroidery stitch—the ideas are legion. If diagrams help the clarity of the work, then they too should be encouraged.

The writing up of information gleaned from books, teachers, or the media is helped greatly by some practice in these skills, and will be looked at in greater depth in a later chapter.

### Letters

Letters, however, must have separate consideration; they are difficult, nay impossible, to categorize along the continuum because their style is affected by both audience and subject matter. They range from the business document, firmly in the transactional mode, through the friendly missive bearing news of everyday happenings, to the polished art form like the published letters of Charles Lamb.

From a very early age children become sensitive to the appropriateness of language for differing social situations. In part this is taught: consider the occasion in the home of a three-year-old when an adult visitor was greeted by his father in these terms: 'Hiya, Jo, you old blighter—where've you been lately?' The son, thinking to be like father, repeated the greeting. What happened? His parents reprimanded him immediately—'Don't you dare speak to your uncle like that, say hello in a proper way.' Throughout school life, too, considerable adjustment is demanded —the way to address a teacher, the correct behaviour at meal tables, how to speak to visitors to the school, and the form for answering the telephone politely and efficiently are examples.

The greater part of the child's awareness, however, is not taught in a positive manner but accrues gradually as he listens to the speech patterns he meets. Listen to any young child when he is involved in make-believe play; he changes register at will to suit the situation and rehearses his achievement frequently. And as he matures he will also develop several registers; his playground 'language', his in-school 'language', and his family 'language' may well be very different. This developing sensibility to the correct form for the situation can be encouraged in drama if it is taught in the way we suggest. It is a valuable felicity in adult life, not only in verbal communication, but also in writing, and it becomes invaluable in the composition of a letter.

Consider the following 'thank you' from a talented 10-year-old to his aunt, a rather awesome figure whom he did not know intimately.

Dear Aunty ——,

I was so greatly pleased by the 'mass' of coins you so very kindly gave me. I was very pleased especially about the Greek ones that are valuable to me! It was absolutely fantastic when dad gave me the coins and I greatly appreciated your trouble to go to the office to get them for me. I will look at them carefully and perhaps sketch them so I can find out about them at the library.

Thank you also for the carefully planned itinerary for letting us know where you are.

I am very pleased about the 10 pfennig which is German. I have the 1 pfennig and the 5 pfennig and I couldn't get the 10 pfennig anywhere so you can imagine how pleased I was when I saw it.

We will all be thinking of you when you are staying or flying or driving abroad. I hope it will be very nice and I hope you don't get 'jet lag'.

Once again thank you a million times for all those coins.

I hope you get this letter and I hope you are very well.

Lots of love,

Notice how he is put off-balance by his intended audience and vacillates between the formal transactional style and the purely personal. Phrases like 'that are valuable to me', 'greatly appreciated your trouble' and 'carefully planned itinerary' written as he struggles to impress with his style, strike a very different note from 'absolutely fantastic', and 'thank you a million times', where he allows his natural exuberance to show through.

By thirteen years of age this gifted youngster has got it almost right. Here is a copy of his letter to a gentleman, with whom he was barely acquainted, thanking him for some technical advice. Maturation, normal development in a caring home, and a sensitivity to the way language varies according to the dictates of audience and situation enable him to select the appropriate register, although the style is still easily recognizable as that of the same writer.

Dear Mr ——.

Thank you very much for taking the time and effort you did to test my Zero 1 Master Control Unit. I can assure you I appreciated your kind thoughts greatly. I am sorry I have not replied earlier but we have been away for Easter for quite some time and it has been difficult to find a moment to write.

Your tips and hints on more efficient use of my system were most helpful, especially the advice you gave me on track cleaning, etc., and I am confident that in the future my layout, with your advice, will be a vastly improved one.

The class 29 you suggested for my layout I have bought, and it is now fully operational. It was on special offer at Modeller's Den as you pointed out, and I saved a sizeable amount of money on it.

May I once again say how grateful I am to you for testing my locos and Zero 1 Master Control Unit, and for all the advice you gave me on better running for my layout, and how pleased I was to receive your superb letter.

Thank you very much,

Yours sincerely,

By no stretch of imagination do all children reach this level so naturally. Teachers must plan for this development and, by skilled intervention in structured play situations, in drama, and in discussions about written forms, encourage children to consider this subtle aspect of language.

## 7.15 Across the curriculum

In the main this chapter has looked upon writing as an attainment in itself.

However, attention to language must not be reserved for the 'English lesson'; must not be divorced from the rest of the curriculum. Indeed, an important incentive to write arises out of lively work in many other areas, which will be further developed in the chapter on thematic work.

Ruth, aged nine, puts it succinctly:

> Writing is important because if you say something that's important it's never remembered, but if you write it down on paper it can be passed on, being written out again and again so even when you're dead your writing can still live.
>
> Writing can be a communication of people, of things that are in the past, like history, and the Bible.
>
> Writing can make people laugh, excited or frightened.
>
> Writing gives information and it helps us to understand things.

## References

1. BRITTON, JAMES et al., The Development of Writing Abilities, 11–18 (Schools Council Research Studies), Macmillan, 1975.
2. A Language for Life (the Bullock Report), HMSO, 1975, Ch. 11.

## Suggested reading

BRITTON, JAMES et al., The Development of Writing Abilities 11–18 (Schools Council Research Studies), Macmillan, 1975.

BURGESS et al., Understanding Children Writing, Penguin, 1973.

CLARK, M. M., Teaching Left-Handed Children, University of London Press, 1974.

INGLIS, A. and CONNELL, E., The Teaching of Handwriting, Nelson, 1964.

JARMAN, C., The Development of Handwriting Skills, Blackwell, 1979.

PEEL, M., Seeing to the Heart, Chatto & Windus, 1967.

PETERS, M. L., Spelling Caught or Taught?, Routledge & Kegan Paul, 1967.

PETERS, M. L., Success in Spelling, Cambridge Institute of Education, 1970.

TORBE, MIKE, Teaching Spelling, Ward Lock Educational, 1977.

A Language for Life (the Bullock Report), HMSO, 1975, Ch. 11.

Children and Language, West Sussex County Council, 1976.

# 8. Study skills

The Bullock Report[1] highlights the fact that in many schools the teaching of reading ceases once a child has completed the last book of a reading scheme.

The latest Primary School Report (*Primary Education in England, A Survey by HM Inspectors of Schools*[2]) reiterates this worrying fact. It comments quite favourably on the attention given by teachers to the initial basic techniques of decoding, but states that little evidence was found of the teaching of the more advanced skills.

A basic competency in reading is essential, and teachers handicap both themselves and their pupils if they fail to teach the flexible strategies that are needed to obtain knowledge from books of the non-narrative type. The higher-order study skills must be taught and practised frequently in the junior school in contexts relevant and interesting to the child, for he will make techniques his own only if he sees them as necessary for his own purposes.

## 8.1 Teachers' own skills

Perhaps one of the reasons teachers neglect this extension of reading is that until recent years little was known about study skills, hence they themselves were not taught to vary their rate and type of reading for various circumstances and materials. This means a re-learning and re-thinking of approaches and strategies that are appropriate to developing activities that will ensure that today's children acquire extended reading skills.

## 8.2 What are these extended reading skills ?

First then, what do we mean by higher-order skills? These are the skills required by the child or adult when he wishes to find information on any subject for himself, and they increase in number when he is confronted with a wide range of books. He needs to be able to find his way around a library, to be able to obtain a quick opinion of the overall range of a selected book, to locate and extract the relevant material, to read and re-read if necessary until the problematic area is understood, and to read the book at his own particular level for enjoyment, if it appeals to him.

He must also be able to *understand* what he is reading, such understanding being in tune with his requirement and the demands imposed by his purpose.

Briefly, here is a list of those skills that can be started during the early and middle years.

**Extended reading skills**

    Uses contents tables.
    Uses index.
    Uses dictionary.
    Uses encyclopedia.
    Uses library system.
    Is able to sequence.
    Reads for pleasure.
    Surveys.
    Skims.
    Scans.
    Reads rapidly.
    Defines purpose for reading.
    Forms questions for reading.
    Assesses reliability in books.
    Assesses suitability in books.
    Recognizes bias.
    Can differentiate between fact and fiction.
    Can differentiate between truth and opinion.
    Indexes and cross-references.
    Makes notes.
    Collates information.
    Uses information read.
    Produces bibliography.
    Reads intensively.
    Constructs flow diagrams.

These will be referred to in detail in this chapter or the following one.

But first, comprehension, without which reading is useless.

## 8.3 Comprehension

Comprehension of the printed word should not really be classed as an advanced reading skill, nor should it be seen as the ability to work through comprehension exercises; it begins, or should begin, when a child first listens to a story, maybe when seated on his parent's knee.

For the young child in school even his first reading books should be read with understanding; mere decoding is not true reading. And how, but through comprehension, can he come to that useful ploy—contextual guessing (for to be sure, this is how most adults cope with new vocabulary)? Some children can comprehend at an amazingly accurate level without being able to read the actual words aloud; others, while able to pronounce every word in a given passage, do not understand in the least what they have read. This latter technique is of little use and makes the results of most so-styled reading age tests a nonsense.

## Some taxonomies

Some researchers of late years have postulated that comprehension can be separated into distinct sub-skills; for example, F. B. Davis:[3]
1. (a) identifying word meanings;
   (b) drawing inferences;
   (c) identifying the technique and mood of a passage;
   (d) finding answers to questions;
   or, again, Barrett:[4]
2. (a) literal comprehension;
   (b) reorganization;
   (c) inferential comprehension;
   (d) evaluation;
   (e) appreciation;
   or, yet again, A Melnik and J. Merritt:[5]
3. (a) understand word and sentence meaning;
   (b) find main ideas and related details;
   (c) organize and classify facts;
   (d) perceive sequence of ideas;
   (e) draw inferences and conclusions;
   (f) understand problems;
   (g) form judgements;
   (h) predict outcomes;
   (i) read critically, distinguishing fact from opinion;
   (j) read for appreciation;
   (k) understand relationships;
   (l) follow directions.

Most recently, E. A. Lunzer and W. K. Gardner,[6] despite search, found it impossibile to produce a trustworthy differential test of comprehensive sub-skills, but felt that it was nevertheless clearly apparent that comprehension operated on at least two levels. They arrived, too, at a very obvious conclusion—that comprehension tests and exercises have but a limited value, and that understanding is likely to be deeper when reading with objectives in mind that naturally motivate the reader. '[Comprehension] is a measure of the pupil's ability and willingness to reflect on whatever it is he is reading.'[7]

## The two main categories of comprehension

It can be seen that these sub-skills—whichever set one chooses—fall readily into two main sections:

1. Comprehension of almost a superficial type (if this is not a contradiction in terms), requiring only that the reader can make sense of the order and of the vocabulary (in other words, that he recognizes that syntactically the text is readable).

2. Comprehension that enables the reader not only to read the lines, but to read between them and beyond them.

To improve one's own teaching skills it is important to understand the difference that these two categories make in their demands on the reader.

### *Literal and reorganization comprehension*

Literal and reorganization questions refer the reader straight back to the text, the first to find a purely literal answer, the second to tease out and possibly reorganize information given in the passage, for instance about an event or a character.

Questions that need only these skills can be answered by any reader who can cope with the text itself; it is not necessary to understand the underlying ideas, or to bring any thought to bear on the questions. They are useful skills, of course, not to be spurned; but full comprehension is far more than this.

### *Full comprehension*

Comprehension of the sort we mean is a complex process demanding a high level of mental involvement and a willingness to think about the text. The reader has to pick out ideas, and recognize the pattern of the author's argument and the sequence he uses to elaborate it. He must be able to reason, to infer further details or cause and effect. Furthermore, he must gather together the information he already has on the subject (from many other sources) and use it to help him reflect upon what he is reading, so that he can make some judgement about it—whether it is fact or fiction, truth or opinion; whether it is biased; whether the character is acting wisely or no; and so on.

Finally, he needs to react thoughtfully to the whole writing, to respond to the author emotionally and sensitively.

## Developing the skills

One should not assume that children's skills of comprehension will develop automatically. Teachers must plan for growth and extend the thinking that takes place when children read.

But how?

The vocabulary they meet must be rich and varied, and understood. The children must gradually be introduced to units of increasing size—phrase, sentence, paragraph, chapter, and so on. They must be able to see the underlying plan. Their teacher must learn to ask problem-posing, open-ended, thought-provoking questions.

And the children must have a purpose for reading.

### Work cards

A desire for information contained in a book is of paramount importance, so a personal reason backed by vital curiosity is the most effective spur. Here the research into books demanded by interesting thematic work or study assignments (further reference in Chapter 9) on topics dear to the individual transcends the use of 'comprehensive exercises', whether in books or in so-called laboratories.

Children can become most adept at identifying a word or phrase in a passage that has been used in a question and writing a sensible sentence around it; this is no proof whatever of their having understood the text. There is much commercial material on the market, containing short printed excerpts followed by literal or reorganization questions, which do nothing to raise the level of the children's thinking.

What is more, the questions asked in this material are frequently ordered in the same way as the passage itself, making even thought or understanding unnecessary in the production of correct responses.

Any work cards prepared by the teacher should have at least some questions that demand thoughtful replies. (One or two questions that refer directly to the text may well be included: they give the reader confidence and, in any case, all the deeper skills of comprehension must be based on a sound reading of the text.)

Questions that begin with such words as 'Why do you think that . . . ?' require the reader to use mental effort to make explicit to himself that which is implicit in the text. The kind of logical reasoning found in science is a good example, though it must be borne in mind that the child must have some previous experience upon which to base his prediction. (A child who has never seen the sea may read about it, but he can never understand what it is like without real experience.)

It is important also to realize that much of the understanding of what is read comes from the continual internal reading process of anticipating, amending, concluding. So true comprehension must allow for realization at varying levels, according to context, past experience, and present vocabulary. Analysis of material read must therefore always be in terms of the initial questions and purposes. For instance, a child might reason to himself, 'I read this to find out what life was like in England when the Normans came. Have I achieved this, and, if so, did I choose the best book, and did I read it accurately and efficiently?' Simple 'literal comprehension-type' questions are thus completely valid if they were in the mind before the reading began; for instance, if 'Who was the King of England just prior to 1066?' was the only piece of information required.

Exercises that encourage the notion of reading first and asking questions afterwards are to be avoided.

### Modelling

A better method on some occasions might well be 'modelling'. Here the children are asked to make some sort of pictorial representation of what they have read: this can be in the form of a diagram, possibly with labels, a web, a flow diagram, a sketch, a cartoon, a strip-cartoon, or a painting. Modelling can prove to be of great value with those children for whom the written word proves difficult.

Children may be asked to put into their work only those facts that they glean from the text, or they may be asked for inferential detail also.

### Questions about narrative

Stories, too, are fertile material for depth of comprehension.

During the reading of *Terry on the Fence*,[8] for instance, a question like, 'Terry has been put into a very awkward situation. How do you think he will behave now?' is a hint to project into the feeling of a boy caught and driven by a gang of bullies. A debate on the opening chapters of *The Worst Kids in the World*[9] might, if well chaired, evoke thoughtful discussion about children who do not conform to the norm of the neighbourhood. Evaluation of conduct, as well as of information, is an important skill; throughout our lives we need to be able to weigh up pros and cons, to understand our fellow men, and to bring our own experience and values to the fore to help us to form judgements. (One must, of course, remember the likely background of the particular children for whom we are preparing the questions and not expect adult judgements.) It is imperative to find time to discuss children's own reading with them, not merely asking for precise versions of the story line or recall of favourite incidents, but querying the understanding of the characters, their actions, and their feelings.

Many teachers are skilled when it comes to asking good questions, particularly when discussing stories. This skill should be thoughtfully extended so that all work cards are aimed towards encouraging all children to think in depth about their reading.

## 8.4 Skills

The Primary School Survey reports that 'there was a tendency at all ages for children to receive insufficient encouragement to extend the range of their reading'.[10]

Indeed, in three-quarters of the classes observed there was no teaching of the more advanced skills at all, and what little was seen elsewhere usually lacked planning and practice. Most children were unable to use books as real sources of learning.

The report highlights the fact also that the 'match' of reading material to the child's ability, which is so important, is at its weakest with the ablest readers. In almost all the cases books were not well matched and were too simple.

Many study skills should be introduced at a simple level during the very early years of school (further reference in Chapter 3), but now we should like to consider them systematically and at a more advanced level. It is important to accept from the start that, while these skills may be taught incidentally, the child must recognize the techniques he is using and the teacher should record how far the child has mastered them.

He needs to be taught to select, to analyse, and to criticize. He needs to be able to locate and select appropriate materials, to evaluate purposes and strategies for reading these items, and to evaluate them with regard to himself and the material chosen.

For example, a child embarking on a piece of investigation connected with a school journey needs an overall framework planned with teacher help and a clear sense of intent in reading the necessary material. Once he has located the book, he needs to know how to check quickly that it is appropriate to him as a reader and suitable for the task he has in front of him. He then must be able to find the correct section of the book, read it, and assess the outcome in terms of his original intentions. The questions he must ask himself are:

1. Is this book suitable?

2. Must I read it all?
3. Does this section require very close reading?
4. How valuable has this book been to me?
5. Shall I go on and read it now for enjoyment?

The task for the teacher is to ensure that the child who is a 'good reader' makes continuous progress by a combination of explanation and activity. He must be made aware of the ways in which his reading can become more efficient without a loss of involvement. It is imperative to teach techniques when they are *needed* by the child, because techniques or skills practised in isolation are worthless. Interest and purpose are essential. In the lively classroom these can emanate from a current topic such as a theme based on children's literature, a school journey, or an exciting event in the locality (further reference in Chapter 9). In this way books will be there as of right, to be used and enjoyed by the reader and not merely as artificial containers of sets of exercises to be worked or collections of transitory information. Skills must develop from purposeful activities tied to reading needs.

### Dictionary skills

This term is self-explanatory, of course, but it must be remembered that less able readers need lots of help when confronted with several words whose initial letter is identical. Search for second- and third-letter order is something that needs to be practised. Words needed for use in their own written work are the best type of list to work on. Children should be encouraged to go to their dictionaries not only for correct spelling, but for meanings, pronunciation, and derivations of words. When they do use the dictionary they must be encouraged to search thoroughly and to make informed guesses as to the initial group of letters. This will give pause for thought to the child who looks up, or instance, the word 'accidentally' under 'axe', and immediately reports that it is not in his dictionary. He should be encouraged to speculate, and then try again.

Words collected for use with topics can be arranged alphabetically by groups of children before being displayed. A further refinement with older children is to separate nouns, adjectives, verbs, and adverbs, and then arrange these groups in alphabetical order. One or two published school dictionaries do have practices ready prepared; these are limited, of course, and not always very relevant, but occasionally of some use.

Means must be devised to help children select the correct definition when they look up a word with more than one meaning.

Several sentences, each containing one particular word, but using it in a different way, can be prepared; then children will have to select the right phrase from their dictionaries to put after each sentence. An old Victorian party game called 'Teapots' provides another variation on the theme, when sentences are spoken in which the multi-meaning word is substituted by the key—'teapot', leaving the hearer to identify, with as few clue-sentences as possible, the master word.

A further dictionary skill, which has been termed 'concept hopping', can prove useful, particularly when searching in an index prior to turning up information on any given topic. This involves seeking first the known word, then, if it cannot be found, another word with which the first has obvious connections. For instance, in a list of contents, if the child fails to find any reference to 'trebuchets' he might locate information he needs under 'siege', or 'weapons', or even under 'warfare'. The use of a simple thesaurus helps a broadening of written vocabulary, and is not to be overlooked as an aid to lively writing. (It can also, by discussion with the teacher, highlight the amazing subtleties of the English language.)

### Library skills

These are the skills needed to help a child find his way around the bookshelves, to locate the subject area, and to home in on the actual books in which he is likely to find the information he is seeking. But the extent to which they can be taught in the school depends very largely upon a number of other factors—where, for instance the school library is located; what sort of cataloguing system is used. Reference to Chapter 13 is important.

Nevertheless, successful searches for books can be started in early years; the dust jacket of any book can be mounted on card and the child asked to find the matching cover picture (provided the books are displayed with this showing and not merely placed so that the spines are visible).

With the use of prepared work cards the tracking game can go further; having located the required book the child can then be asked to find a stated page and answer simple questions about the text.

For beginning readers, or very slow ones, it is an excellent idea to provide cassette tape-recordings of the passages to be read, so that the reader can play it and replay it as necessary while also following the actual printed words. (It is preferable to have access to a listening centre for this ploy, then no one nearby is distracted by the recording.) In this manner children can follow the text, do some research from books without the help of the adult, learn the skills of comprehension, and contribute to the general work of the class without being too hindered by their lack of ability to decode.

Although at the outset this may seem far too time-consuming for the teacher who prepares the cassette recordings, a bank is surprisingly quickly established. Furthermore, the making of the recordings can be turned into an excellent reading-aloud exercise for the more able readers in the school.

## 8.5 Reading rates

Good readers need several rates of reading in order to cope with the many levels of material encountered. Teachers wishing to improve reading skills must consider the pupil's individual performance in each area—recreational reading, surveying, skimming, scanning, rapid reading, and intensive reading—and the children themselves need to be able to recognize when to use each different type. This appropriateness can be developed by practices in the classroom with a well-planned theme that provides learning opportunities requiring many reading rates at different times and with different materials. A clear pattern of progression needs to be drawn up, and ways in which the basic reading rates are explained and attempted need to be varied.

### Recreational reading

One of the major aims of the middle years should surely be to see that the children are 'hooked on books', to ensure that each and every one of them realizes what joy can come from the printed page (further reference in Chapter 12). Many good readers will have come to this knowledge for themselves and will go to books for sheer pleasure, though not all children who read fluently do this.

Unfortunately, the recreational reading rate can easily become the only one in the repertoire, and material that needs intensive study may be tackled at a leisurely pace and dismissed as being too complicated or boring. The habit of reading all required material at the same speed and from cover to cover in strict order must be guarded against when searching for information. Even adult students sometimes commence a course of study by settling down to read every set book from page 1 onwards as though it were narrative, instead of surveying, skimming, then scanning the essential sections in depth, and reading intensively only where necessary.

With the majority of readers the aim must be to establish a recreational rate and build upon it in terms of other speeds. Ideas for encouraging recreational reading abound, and range from book-centred topics or themes to the regular book sale or club.

The acid test is whether or not the reader can select the right rate for the material and the purpose. It is vitally important to teach that there are other rates that might be more appropriate for the task in hand.

In all of this the teacher is a very important influence. Matching the book to the reader at all levels is essential if progress is to be made. Indeed, the child who tells his teacher that his book is 'boring' is often one who can decode the words but cannot read the text at a level that allows him to respond to the author.

### Surveying
Surveying is a reading skill that involves a quick appraisal of the whole book, locating such items as author, contents, index, overall number of pages, chapter headings, and the spread, or otherwise, of illustrations.

### Skimming
The next step, when examining a book for its relevance, is skim-reading, whereby one can obtain an overall idea of what the book is about. Surveying and skimming together can then form the basis for partner or group discussion about the range of the book.

Able readers may well be asked to use these two skills as efficiency techniques to assess and form opinions of a number of books. They will be doing what the librarian does—quickly comparing a wide range of similar material. Their comments can be noted and kept on cards in pockets in the back of the books. These may be folded so that their opinions remain concealed; they may then be read together when the opportunity arises and used as a starting point for further work.

Skimming needs to be explained to and practised by children, who could be asked to form a mental image of a key word or phrase and then look rapidly down the page until their eyes light upon it. This helps to give a clue to the whereabouts of information required and can be of great help to the slow reader in any type of research, for he can find quickly the place where he needs to scan or read in depth.

### Scanning
Scanning is 'reading in such a way as to locate specific information without having to read the material in its entirety'.[11] As such, it is

essentially a practical reading skill that all developed readers need, but it must be kept in perspective; to encourage 'digest reading' *only* would be a retrograde step.

Scanning must therefore be explained as a short-cut that is needed to cope with a mass of printed material, and that is appropriate only in certain recognizable circumstances.

Such circumstances need to be engineered at first in order to encourage children to pick up the necessary background cues that will enable the skilled reader to select the information he needs quickly.

### Activities to encourage these reading habits

Skimming and scanning can be encouraged in a number of ways; the finding of information can become an enjoyable game.

The teacher may read out the passage to be located, asking the children to indicate when they have found it and leaving time for everyone to succeed. As a class activity this would have obvious drawbacks, for it would need at least one set of books; and, of course, the very good readers would always be first.

A better way is to make it a group activity, selecting readers of the same approximate level of ability and speed for each group, and to have also a further ploy for the first finders while the rest are still searching. (They might, for instance, be asked to paraphrase the information in the passage in order to give the original one plus an explanation of its meaning in their own words.)

Another group activity might well start at the survey level and aim to get children to say briefly what the book is about. Initial generalized comments can be deepened by questioning; for example, 'What does the blurb state is the purpose of the book?' 'Which chapter is most concerned with this purpose?' (A good many books fill half their pages with background or explanation.) 'Within this chapter, which paragraph is the key one?' Surveying thus becomes skimming, and then scanning for more specific detail; and it helps children also to begin to recognize the normal pattern of an information book—that is, background history or explanation first, then expansion and new information, then speculation, summary, or conclusion.

During work on topics—individual, class, or group—a five-minute break can be made to enable individual children to show their peers how they can locate and explain material quickly. This can be taken a stage further via group discussion around the information selected, and with skilful distribution of books can lead to discussion of the accuracy and quality of various authors and sets of books. (Greek gods, their names, and their powers seem to vary considerably; so do the Pharaohs, according to some authors.) Children should be encouraged to recognize fallibility.

They also need to realize that different authors or different publishers will give a different type of information, albeit about the same subject.

Again, during any work from information books, an interruption may be made for one child to give a short explanation of an aspect of the work in progress with reference to a particular book and section of a book; for instance, 'John, tell us quickly how Nelson's navy obtained the sailors to man their ships—remember to say the books you've consulted and the section of particular use to you.'

Groups of children may work on reading material, preparing questions for their peer group to answer, and trying to compose 'thinking questions'.

Again, they might search the text for statements of fact and statements of opinion. If they list these in random order a good group discussion with other children could well develop, and sequencing skills be improved.

Bias in writers is also worth alerting able readers to. (Try using various newspaper accounts of football matches—the home team support is often very apparent.)

### Rapid reading

Rapid reading may also be practised; many children respond to its challenge and like to know their own speed and how it can be improved. First, though, it must be emphasized that rapid reading is, like skimming and scanning, for a particular purpose, and not for any kind of prize other than achieving more efficient reading in the right situation.

Initially, a group can be started using the same books, reading as quickly as possible for a set time, possibly three minutes; a simple line count can give an idea of word coverage.

Members of the group can then test each other to check on understanding and retention of the major points. Children should also be encouraged to monitor their own reading patterns by simply following their progress down the side of the page with a light pencil on a matching sheet of paper, and back-tracking, stopping, and starting the pencil again as and when their eyes do. More sophisticated aids can be made by the children in the form of masking or uncovering devices, though it must be emphasized that a reasonable section of the text must be revealed at all times in order to ensure that full use of context is made. There are on the market various electronic devices designed to improve speedreading, but we would suggest that homemade improvizations are sufficient.

### Intensive reading

Intensive reading is the obvious progression in the skill of learning and researching from books. Here the reader needs to read with concentration and maybe re-read the passage he has located to be absolutely certain of its meaning.

This activity is very much against many of the habits of childhood, so when planning work in this area the necessity for reading in depth has to be obvious, and the outcome easily verifiable. The examination of evidence in an imaginery court case, a search for treasure with clues hidden in the text, and journey directions demanding detailed reading are three types of activity that ensure that good readers encounter particular passages that have to be read many times in a search for understanding. So, too, do instruction cards designed to teach techniques—for instance, how to use a tape-recorder, interview instructions, or the exacting sequence for putting together some complicated model. Many more work cards of this type will readily suggest themselves.

### 8.6 Sequencing

The term 'sequencing' is often applied to early reading but can also be used in a far wider sense as being part of the convention of the writing of fact and of fiction. Children, if asked, will be able to relate four or five basic 'story lines', their recounting being based on convention and expectation. If they are asked to do the same, after some experience of surveying books, they will come to realize that standard patterns exist in this field as well. These can be discussed to form the basis of patterns of prediction for the child. For example, most encyclopaedia-type books can be worked through alphabetically; specialist books usually begin with a general outline; and illustrated books can be sequenced by the pictures and their captions listed at the beginning.

Directions of many types lend themselves for help in the teaching of sequencing. For instance, recipes are an ideal source for practice in this skill. The instructions can be written in sentences, which are then mounted separately on cards, shuffled, sorted, and rearranged before the cookery begins.

Stories with an obvious plot can be used in the same manner. These may be introduced initially in cartoon form or comic strip, then in sentences, but ultimately in paragraphs which usually form the best units. In comprehension exercises the demand for writing skills often masks the ability of the good reader who is not also a fluent writer. In the sorting of cards into a sequence the competent reader can use his skills to the full.

When children have completed their rearrangement of the cards it helps their appreciation of sequence if they are asked to explain how they decided, for example, which, was the opening paragraph, how they recognized what followed, and what led them to choose the concluding section. All of this helps to raise the level of children's thinking.

Good readers to a large extent rely on guessing ahead, their guesses based on past experience with story lines and information patterns. Poor and reluctant readers are often in a trap. They cannot read sufficiently well to build up a basis for prediction because their problem with decoding or comprehension make them concentrate on the words immediately in front of them. They therefore do not by themselves build up any book or story outline. These children need much planned experience in anticipation. One of the best ways to give this practice is by group prediction.

### Group prediction

Select an interesting story or passage which the children will be able to read; break it into parts at suitable points; have each section typed out (preferably on a Jumbo typewriter) on a separate sheet; and staple the sheets together in the correct sequence. Then ask the group to read the first page only. Follow this up with a general discussion intended to draw out predictions for the next section of the story or piece of prose. Treat each excerpt in the same way, remaining as little involved in the discussion as possible and using only such questions as:

'What was that about?'
'Why do you think that?'
'What part of the passage indicated that?'

It is important to remember to give encouragement at all times, even with the most unlikely prediction! The children must be referred back to the text to support their guesses and thus will be shown the power of context cues to influence an interpretation of a passage and its predicted outcome. The emphasis must be placed on the developing aspect of language in use, rather than on 'guessing correctly'.

During such work the teacher and group will be continually suggesting, hypothesizing, supporting, and amending in accord with group and individual opinion. Practice is therefore given in reading, re-reading, reflecting, discussing, responding, and interpreting.

Anticipation is a useful way of introducing a story and of focusing attention upon an important incident, character, or theme. At first it is advisable for the teacher to chair the group, but with experience children can sometimes be left with a child as chairman. This is an activity worth doing often. It gives practice in recognizing sequence and in spotting detail, it widens vocabulary, and it encourages discussion. It can also help deepen insight into character and plot development, and into author's intent.

The success of this work depends upon certain organizational factors that need to be taken into account before prediction activities are used. First consider—must we always use typed or printed material? One recommended method of group involvement is by using an overhead projector with a group of approximately ten children. This poses obvious problems if the rest of the class are within hearing and seeing range; inevitably they become interested in what is going on and distracted from their own work. Yet a lesson taken with a whole class would mean less participation by the very children who need the most practice, although many reluctant readers do learn a great deal from listening to classmates explaining reasoning in response to context.

Perhaps the greatest problem with this kind of work lies in the selection of passages to be used. The teacher may prefer to write her own short stories, or to adapt pieces of prose from magazines, always ensuring that any material thus produced has a developmental pattern in itself. Writing these pieces is a worthwhile activity for the teacher, and a collection of such material could be made available to all staff.

On the other hand, if text from books is chosen, and facilities or time for preparing it on separate sheets are not available, one short-cut is suggested. The set of books may be opened at the first page to read, and a rubber band stretched over each book enclosing the following pages, so that the temptation to look ahead is forestalled.

We have recommended the use of group prediction and sequencing and, in Chapter 7, cloze procedure. There are, however, two reservations about their use that must be borne in mind. First, employed with a lack of understanding and without sensitive discussion, they can be as sterile and as unconducive to real learning as any other set of exercises. Second, and most important, all these ploys make the reader pay regard to all kinds of aspects of the test which, if good fiction is being used, may divert his attention away from the affective quality of the writing. This presents a paradox: on the one hand, to introduce an exciting piece of fiction by using, for instance, group prediction can inspire many children with a desire to read further and a knowledge that more can be gained from text if one reads deeply and thoughtfully. On the other hand, there is the possibility of reducing the poetic to the transactional by taking apart what should be essentially a whole. There are now on the market several books of reference which present their information in narrative form; perhaps excerpts from material of this type would help to resolve the dilemma.

### Context cues

In group prediction work the importance of context cues is obvious. All able readers have a subconscious grasp of context, but poor readers are usually unable to see the subtleties of word position and emphasis and have difficulty in retaining enough information to allow them to cast back and forth over the text. They need encouragement and practice in the use of context cues.

First, a simplified form of anticipation based on one sentence at a time will focus attention on the effects that single words have on the suggestions for the next sentence.

Second, sentences with a straightforward pattern can be used to indicate cues that act to show answers coming late in the statement: 'The King sat down on the——.'

The place of the omission can then be varied to show that some cues have to be searched for and remembered because they act on earlier material: 'The——had been a family treasure for many years.'

Third, a great deal of fun may be had by taking a sentence or a paragraph, altering the nouns or verbs in it, and then exploring the effect upon other parts of the context and upon the predicted follow-on.

Finally, much can be gleaned by a brief but regular look at the text the children are using so that they come to recognize the cues.

> Where in the sentence does the main character appear?
> Where is the important information?

**157**

Is there a similar pattern in paragraphs?
Can you recall the main points of a sentence or paragraph?

## 8.7 Survey, question (SQR)

To sum up the chapter, we have freely adapted a study technique (SQ3R) advocated by the Open University.

Children need to be taught how to study, and SQR is a useful framework, recognizing, of course, the need to select from it according to the ability of the children.

### Survey

These techniques can best be tackled at the book selection stage of thematic work and developed via class, or preferably group, discussion of appropriate and inappropriate material quickly surveyed and commented upon.

A framework for the children could gradually be built up to read something like the following:

1. Having used your library skills to select a book you feel might be of use to you, do not rush away with it, but first study it.
2. Is it illustrated? If so, look through quickly to see what you can learn about the contents of the book from the pictures. Does it seem useful for your quest?
3. Is there a publisher's blurb? If so, read it quickly.
4. Has the book a table of contents? If so, look down it.
5. Has the book an index? (Note that some indexes have differing type faces denoting illustrations, plates, diagrams, etc.) Check to see if the book contains at least some references you need.
6. Has the book got chapter headings? Read them through quickly.
7. Is this a volume of an encyclopedia? If so, remember that the index is probably in the last volume.
8. Who is the author? Do you know anything about him?
9. What is the date of publication? Is this important for your topic?
10. Is the text suitable for you? In other words, can you read it and understand it? If not, put it back on the shelves and try a different book.

### Question

Look at the title of the book and then think carefully.

1. How much do you already know about this subject? Probably quite a lot, if you think about it, so collect up in your mind all

your previous knowledge gained from your own experience and from other sources (teleision, teachers, other people, magazines, and other books).

2. Form the questions that you want answered so that, in a way, you can treat the book as a person and interrogate it.

3. Using index and contents table, quickly skim-read to check if this book will help you to the answers. Footnotes, illustrations, and chapter headings will also help to tell you if the book contains the specific items you need. If it does not, put it back on the shelves and start again. If it seems useful, take it away to your work area, and continue to study the book there.

4. *Chapters.* In most books the opening paragraph of a chapter gives a lead to its contents, and the concluding one is often a summary, so you probably do not need to read the chapter right through to start with.

5. *Paragraphs.* The opening sentence usually states the theme of the paragraph, and there are salient words and phrases that point to vital information, or to turning points in the writer's argument: 'first', 'second', 'next', 'therefore', 'because', 'although', 'nevertheless', 'on the other hand', etc. This knowledge helps you to identify and extract the main ideas more quickly.

*(Note to teachers.* Two or three books may be selected by competent readers, but do not let children be overwhelmed. Relevance is the test, and the formation of questions by the reader himself is the key.)

## Read

*(Note to teachers.* Initially skimming and scanning techniques must be explained and practised with a few children who are about to use books in a situation where these skills will be of help to them.)

1. Use skimming and scanning techniques to locate the information yo require.

2. Select the correct reading rates for your purposes.

3. Make simple notes (reference in Chapter 9).

4. Collate your material (reference in Chapter 9).

5. Learn how to quote correctly. (*Note to teachers.* Why not, provided the text is thoroughly understood?)

6. Use simple diagrams to plan your work (reference in Chapter 9).

7. Make a bibliography.

## References

1. *A Language for Life* (the Bullock Report), HMSO, 1975.
2. *Primary Education in England, A Survey by HM Inspectors of Schools*, HMSO, 1978
3. DAVIS, F. B., 'Research in Comprehension in Reading', *Reading Research Quarterly*, Summer, 511–12, 1968.
4. BARRETT, T. C., 'Taxonomy of the cognitive and affective dimensions of reading comprehension, unpublished article quoted in MELNIK, A. and MERRITT, J., *Reading Today and Tomorrow*, University of London Press, 1972.
5. MELNIK, A. and MERRITT, J., *The Reading Curriculum*, University of London Press, 1972, Chs 1 and 2.
6. LUNZER, E. A. and GARDNER, W. K., *The Effective Use of Reading* (Schools Council Development Project), Heinemann, 1979.
7. Ibid.
8. ASHLEY, B., *Terry on the Fence*, Oxford University Press, 1975.
9. ROBINSON, B., *The Worst Kids in the World*, Beaver Books, 1974.
10. *Primary Education in England.*
11. *A Language for Life.*

## Suggested reading

GILLILAND, J., *Readability*, University of London Press, 1972.

HARRISON, C., *Readability in the Classroom*, Cambridge University Press, 1980.

MELNIK, A. and MERRITT, J., *The Reading Curriculum*, University of London Press, 1972.

MELNIK, A. and MERRITT, J., *Reading Today and Tomorrow*, University of Lonodn Press, 1972.

STAUFFER, R. G., *Teaching as a Thinking Process*, Harper and Row, 1969.

WALKER, C., *Reading Development and Extension*, Ward Lock Educational, 1974, Chs 1, 2, 3, 4, 5, and 7.

WEAVER, C., *Psycholinguistics and Reading; From Process to Practice*, Winthrop Publishers Inc., 1980.

# 9. Thematic work

## 9.1 Some of the reasons for this teaching mode

Subject divisions are a very adult concept; in thematic work these artificial divisions can be eliminated, and many varying concepts and skills integrated and arranged in a way that makes more sense to a child.

We believe that it is more important to teach children how to learn, how to research, and how to record than to put over a given body of knowledge. Some knowledge is important, of course, but the main emphasis in the junior and middle years ought to be on the *mode of learning* in a carefully planned sequential programme.

An additional advantage is that, within this framework of learning, children can work at their own level and teachers can establish a simple programme of development for each child within the general curriculum of the school, so catering for the wide variance in ability found in many classrooms.

There is a good deal of uninformed criticism of educational method by people who use such terms as 'formal' and 'informal' (or 'progressive', which they appear to have confused with 'permissive').

To a good teacher these methods are not polar opposites; she uses the approach that will best help the individual child at a particular moment to a particular piece of learning that he needs.

This must be structured very firmly in the mind of the teacher. Her role must be one of planned intervention with definite aims in view. These will include, in the language component, increasing the complexity of a child's thinking, enabling him to ask good questions as well as answer them, encouraging him to use language in all its forms, to research for himself and record, to share his findings with others, to work in depth, and to remain curious, observant, and sensitive.

Nevertheless, research into one particular interest does not, of necessity, mean working in an integrated style. Study skills can be put into practice in any work requiring book knowledge, be it from a historical, geographical, topical, or scientific viewpoint.

In a book on language and its use in school it is not possible to explore fully the planning, preparation, and organization required for thematic work in general, or all its possibilities, so we shall merely examine the opportunities it offers for the advancement of literacy.

## 9.2 A planned topic on 'Books'

'A child learns language primarily by using the four modes of talking, listening, writing and reading in close relationship with one another.' So stated the Bullock Committee: it is the responsibility of the school to provide an environment that will nurture language. To us, work woven around a central theme can do this excellently.

To illustrate we have first taken one particular theme, namely 'Books', and shown how it was most successfully developed in one school, with a mixed-ability class covering the wide range of seven to ten-year-olds.

The teacher had in mind the following key statements from *A Language for Life*:

> There are certain important inferences to be drawn from a study of the relationship between language and learning:
>
> (i)  all genuine learning involves discovery, and it is ridiculous to suppose that teaching begins and ends with 'instruction' as it is to suppose that 'learning by discovery' means leaving children to their own resources;
>
> (ii)  language has a heuristic function; that is to say, a child can learn by talking and writing as certainly as he can by listening and reading;
>
> (iii)  to exploit the process of discovery through language in all its uses is the surest means to enabling a child to master his mother tongue.[1]

### Introduction

The topic was introduced by making a collection of favourite reading material ranging from comics to adult books of information. These were handled and discussed; excerpts were read, cartoons enjoyed, television serialization mentioned; and a vocabulary concerned with books became familiar, including words like 'volume', 'anthology', 'miscellany', 'biography', 'encyclopedia', 'dictionary', 'thesaurus'. (Here it must be mentioned that a thesaurus should be readily available for all children in their 'middle' years.)

### The topic web

From this start grew the plan of the topic in the form of a web. The teacher had already foreseen in her own mind the general pattern, and organized most of her resources, but she wanted her class to share in the final plan so that they had a complete overall picture and were able to contribute their own ideas. Fig. 9.1 shows the result, in a simplified form, which incorporated several suggestions from the children themselves that the teacher had originally overlooked.

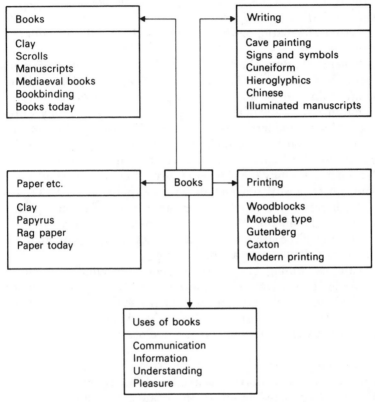

**Fig. 9.1** A plan of a topic in the form of a web

### The first three weeks

From this the children then selected their own special interests to follow up—one subject to be studied in a group, and one as individual research.

During the previous topic the teacher herself had arranged the composition of the groups, using a mixed-ability pattern with a chosen leader. By this time in the school year she knew her class well enough to be confident that no child was going to be spurned if she allowed them to form groups on a friendship or an interest basis. She was also aware that she had one child who, although a normal friendly youngster, preferred to work alone. So she allowed them all a free choice. If a teacher is going to follow this course she needs to be very aware of the social patterning within the room. Provided she has this knowledge, one of the bonuses of thematic work is that there is opportunity for increasing the type and range of group formation, which helps both social and linguistic development.

Several children then came together to study one particular aspect in some depth. The size of the groups varied from the one child (if one can be a group) who preferred to work alone, to six children. With each of the larger groups there was usually a break into pairs except for discussion of particular tasks or when decisions about the final form of their presentation had to be taken. The groups formed by the children were based mainly on friendships, but intervention by the teacher ensured that everyone had a place and a piece of work of which they were capable.

Each group was asked to investigate some practical aspect, for example, the making of papyrus, the making of paper from pulp, the testing of the strength of various types of paper, and finally the trying out of different ways of printing.

After examining forms of early 'books', the children made clay books for themselves. They had found photographs of Sumerian clay tablets complete with measurements, so the models were made to actual size and inscribed with a wedge-shaped stick. The idea of pressing to write, after our own method of scratching, seemed very strange to them.

Various writing tools were then considered and experiments carried out with natural materials, including, of course, quills. Despite their appreciation of the beauty of illuminated manuscripts, the slowness of writing everything by hand made them realize why printing was such a welcome invention.

### Further learning

Soon the necessity for further research using reference books became evident to the class, enabling the teacher to develop reading strategies, note-making skills, the development of flow-diagrams, and good, clear transactional writing.

### *Note-making*

Although a few children in this class were still very young, the teacher felt that it was not too early to introduce the skill of making very simple notes from references. There are a few teachers who still feel that every child must always write in full sentences: we would dispute this. Just as a child needs to recognize reading speeds and techniques, so he must be taught to appreciate the techniques that suit the purposes for which he is writing. There are times when only complete sentences are acceptable; but, for the making of notes for reference, short phrases or single words are all that are needed.

The easiest form of notes is of course, just a list, sorted and put into logical order; the simplest source for practice of this skill is possibly also a list, arranged non-sequentially. But note-making is such an important activity for almost all school learning that the sooner the children can master the art of extracting key words or phrases from continuous prose, the more command they will have over their acquisition of knowledge, and the sooner they will be freed of dependence upon the teacher.

(We are not referring to the copying of notes from the blackboard or work sheet, which has little educational value.)

## Using information gained

One of the criticisms levelled at topic work is that the child's final work often consists of material not understood. Unfortunately this is true of some of the studies we have seen: children have been allowed to look in one book for details that can be slightly altered and written out to fill up the pages of their own.

A method of overcoming this was devised by the teacher of this class. Once notes had been made the reference books had to be returned, and only then was the first draft of their written work started. The children were required to write out the information they had gleaned, in good functional English, using continuous sentences, with the aid of their notes. The poorer readers in the class were encouraged to limit themselves to one or two reference books only, but it is important that, as early as possible, good readers are emboldened to survey and skim several books, rejecting some and listing all those needed for further use, without feeling that they have to read every word. Therefore the abler readers in this class made notes from a number of source books, which also helped to obviate any danger of copying out great chunks of uncomprehended print.

The whole business of using books was put into a purposeful context in terms of reading and learning. This is inevitably tied up with classroom organization and approach. It is essential that what goes on in today's primary and middle schools is planned, significant, and directed towards a sound learning outcome. If this is the case, as it was with this topic, then the normal work pattern can provide all that is needed.

The chart in Fig. 9.2 shows those aspects of language that the teacher developed during this particular thematic study.

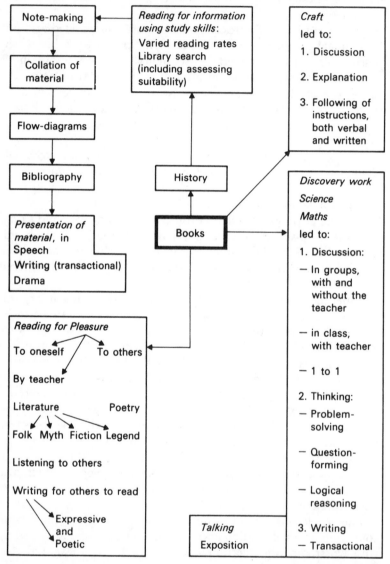

**Fig. 9.2** Showing these aspects of language developed during the thematic study

## Stimuli

The teacher used various other types of stimuli—film strips, outside visits, talks by people with expertise in the field—all of which ensured sustained interest and a desire to work both in breadth and depth. Yet she felt that the very best way to learn about books was to make them.

### *The making of a story-book*

Writing a long story for the entertainment of the children's friends provided the opportunity to produce real books. The first drafts were corrected, divided into chapters, illustrated, copied out, and the pages numbered. End papers were designed, publishing company, author, title, a short summary of the story (the blurb) and a contents list were added. Then the whole was stitched and bound into hardback covers made from scrap card. This was covered with old computer paper waste—disguised by being treated by marbling—and a dust jacket was made for the whole. On the back of the jacket many children also wrote the 'puff' of their next book.

## Method of final communication of findings

Much project work finishes with small groups of children knowing a great deal about one aspect, but having little idea of the work of other groups. To guard against this, the teacher decided to complete the term's work with a display of all written material, well mounted, and set off by attractive printed designs and models, together with a taped commentary synchronised with slides taken by herself and by the children during their research.

For this each member of the class had to consider their group's contribution most carefully, and an overall balance of factual information and creativity, using their writing as an art form, had to be achieved. The class interlaced their commentary with snippets of humour and re-enacted some of their experiments using natural dialogue. They were certainly gaining a sense of audience.

## An adult consideration of a balanced curriculum

To ensure a balance of learning the teacher drew up a further flow-diagram, shown in Fig. 9.3, which was meant not for the children but for her own guidance. It was then obvious which aspects of the curriculum were not being adequately covered by this thematic work. Some of these—mathematics and music, for instance—were therefore taken regularly as separate entities. For the rest she was able to plan her further topics for the year so that a just balance of subjects was ensured.

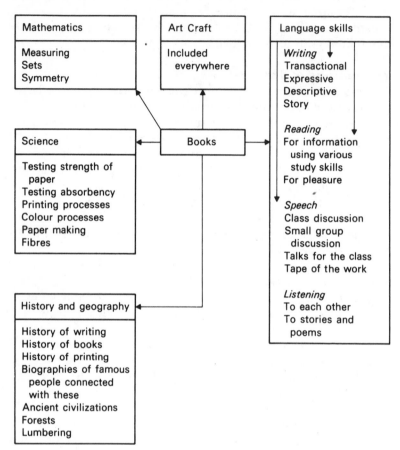

**Fig. 9.3** An adult consideration of a balanced curriculum

### 9.3 A year-based environmental study

Thematic work is not of necessity class-based; it can range from individual studies to projects that involve the whole school.

One two-form-entry junior school regularly organizes a week's stay at a field study centre for all its fourth-year children. It has become so accepted that no one opts out, and those children whose parents cannot afford to pay the cost are supported by funds raised locally.

This is not the place for a detailed survey of the whole venture—justice could not be done to it in a part of a chapter. Nevertheless, a great deal of work undertaken while away, and in the four-week follow-up period back in their own school, was directed towards literacy, and has much to offer.

Briefly the staff wished the children to study:

1. The habitat in the three different types of woodland surrounding the hostel and their effect on plant and animal life.
2. Mathematics—connected with the techniques of the above studies: scale drawing, use of quadrat frames and line transects, offset mapping, height finding by various methods, etc.
3. Man's use of the area, both historically and geographically.
4. The village in which they stayed, using an urban traverse to commence their close look at its development and its present life.

The area is rich in Roman associations, and for one part of their studies the children elected to examine this period of history in some depth. Whilst away they visited a Roman villa, and spent many hours in a museum specifically dealing with the Roman occupation of that part of the country.

Back at school they followed up this interest by research into books.

## Fiction

In any topic it must be remembered that a great deal of knowledge and many facts can be gleaned from reading good fiction connected with the subject. Not only factual information is the outcome, either; for literature can enhance and illumine a topic and heighten the awareness of the reader. In historical works, for example, the child can almost dwell in the period; in novels about other regions he can be transported. So, when the children were looking in detail at the Romans, a generous supply of relevant literature was provided.

## Non-fiction

The short span of memory in the child who is decoding print makes it well nigh impossible for him to gather knowledge from a book that is above his reading level.

Factual text used for research by children should be easily read and assimilated. Unfortunately, information books tend to be more densely written than fiction, to use more difficult vocabulary (not necessarily technical), and to write using sentence formation that is unfamiliar in speech.

Reading aloud to children is always important—the value of the shared experience of an exciting or moving story cannot be overestimated—but sometimes the choice should be non-fiction. Hearing the text read helps to familiarize children with technical vocabulary and with discourse organization of the more formal type.

A problem of supply and demand often arises here, too: good reference books are frequently expensive, and simple-to-read information books on topics suitable for older juniors are hard to find. Some organization is essential to help overcome this.

### Using reference books
The children grouped themselves according to various interests, and, with the assistance of all the flexible reading strategies they knew, selected relevant books. They were, of course, encouraged to discuss their choices as they made them.

Different groups chose to categorize these in different ways, all of them sensible and helpful for the final write-up of their findings, and suited to their own ability levels.

### Collating information
Obviously, the group's needs for specific books overlapped; and the school could not have provided sufficient material if all 70 children had been employed on the same task simultaneously. Many other related activities were taking place at the same time, so that no scramble was necessary. However, several groups *were* thus occupied, and the rules were, first, that the children were to search for several books for their own use using their surveying techniques; second, that as soon as they had rejected a book it was to be returned to the central store; and, third, when they had identified information that they needed and made a note of the title of the book and the relevant pages, this book was also to be returned to the central pool for use by other children, until it was again wanted by them for the making of more detailed notes. In this way books were more quickly released for general use.

The next task was to sequence the questions they had already been asking and put them into a framework that would help their subsequent paragraphing. (Figs. 9.4–9.8 show how the various groups organized this.) The children were then ready to make full notes from their chosen books—notes that would bring together information from several sources under the various headings that had been decided upon. On this occasion the groups were encouraged to share out the work among themselves, looking for very full answers to a few specific questions only, for they had important tasks ahead. Not only had their information to be accurate, and in depth; but the writing had to be of the right quality and in the right style to be recorded on tape for the use of a wider audience. Furthermore, they were to be asked questions that would help them to focus on wider implications of their new learning and the way it shed new light upon their concept of the world.

The teacher had organized a rich reading-aloud programme of fiction concerned with the period, knowing that the good style of many of the authors would influence her class. She also encouraged them to use material gleaned from the stories, to judge whether it was probably fact or merely the author's embellishment, and to weave this different information into their reports.

All the children were now ready for help in the marshalling of facts, so in a class lesson the children were taught how to sequence their information and to handle evidence objectively. Two groups had come across conflicting evidence in the books they were using—another useful teaching point, and an excellent reason for writing a letter of enquiry to a reliable source of information.

Most children in the upper junior years need quite detailed assistance when they have to cope with complicated argument or express more than one viewpoint. Earlier in their school experience children should have learnt to exclude their own opinions from the writing of factual evidence in reports. This should help in the new challenge. Detailed study should be made of an able writer's method of building up his data, noting the careful way he presents first one notion and its corroborative detail and the skill with which he then introduces opposing evidence. When the young writer starts out, a diagrammatic layout of key statements, together with their supporting detail, can help to clarify his thoughts, and form a framework for the first draft of his factual material.

All the children taking part in this study of the Romans were quite happy with the transactional mode of the writing of facts for their mounted display of work, but several felt that some more lively presentation was needed for the proposed recorded tape. Again a growth point was evident: the teacher suggested that one way of vivid portrayal of actuality was to write in the present tense as if one were really at the scene; another was to write dialogue and put information across by means of a short 'play for radio'.

So far we have looked only at the selection and recording of facts from various sources. These are important skills in themselves, but the *quality* of thought used by her class should always be in the forefront of a teacher's mind. Class or group discussion may be used to encourage the children to think about their topics and make informed judgements. In this particular case the teacher asked searching questions about the importance of the coming of the Romans in our country's development, about whether their way of life had had any influence upon our own; and she eventually asked the children to evaluate the importance of the Roman contribution to our own civilization as far as they could understand it. (Many teachers are skilled in asking questions about facts; everyone needs to make herself equally expert in questions about ideas and concepts.)

When their initial research and recording was well under way each group was given a specially prepared work card to lead their thinking into more demanding and complex tasks than that of literal recall. Some of these echoed and enlarged the questions above and some linked the historical research with both the geography of the area and the environmental studies in which all the children had been involved. Collation of material from such a variety of sources is not a simple matter, so it is best to allow very rough drafts, which can be discussed with the group and with the teacher to ensure that the sequencing is correct, the meaning clear, and the style flowing. Because these particular children were working on drafts from their notes rather than from their original sources, and because they were being asked to bring some thought of their own to the writing, the danger either of copying or of the style jerking from one sentence to another as the writer changed source books was obviated.

If, as in this instance, work is to be displayed, then there is a need for a fair copy, correct in all detail. But this must come only after his amended and worked-upon drafts have been evaluated by the writer in the light of his original purpose.

| Aspect | Book | Pages |
|---|---|---|
| Religion | *The Romans* | 34,35,48,49,104,108 |
| | *Ancient Rome* | 11,78,83–85,89 |
| | *Roman Britain* | 40 |
| Gods | *Roman Towns* | 8,10,11,25,27 |
| | *The Romans* | 43,49 |
| | *Ancient Rome* | 11 |
| Temples | *The Building of Ancient Rome* | 4–7 |
| A temple | *Roman Towns* | 42,43 |
| Death in a family | *Roman Family Life* | 55–61 |
| Sacrifices | *The Romans* | 48–9 |

**Fig. 9.4** Main topic: Romans (these aspects will be used as our chapter divisions)

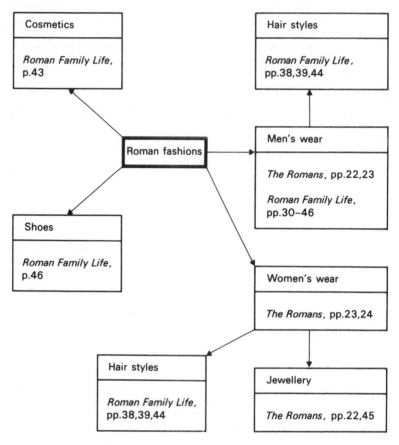

**Fig. 9.5** Main topic: Romans
Our topic: Roman fashions

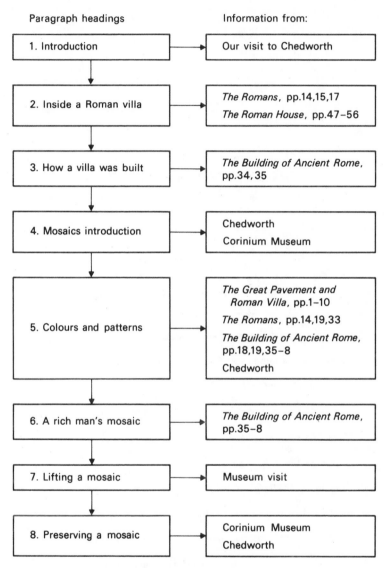

| Paragraph headings | Information from: |
|---|---|
| 1. Introduction | Our visit to Chedworth |
| 2. Inside a Roman villa | *The Romans*, pp.14,15,17<br>*The Roman House*, pp.47–56 |
| 3. How a villa was built | *The Building of Ancient Rome*, pp.34,35 |
| 4. Mosaics introduction | Chedworth<br>Corinium Museum |
| 5. Colours and patterns | *The Great Pavement and Roman Villa*, pp.1–10<br>*The Romans*, pp.14,19,33<br>*The Building of Ancient Rome*, pp.18,19,35–8<br>Chedworth |
| 6. A rich man's mosaic | *The Building of Ancient Rome*, pp.35–8 |
| 7. Lifting a mosaic | Museum visit |
| 8. Preserving a mosaic | Corinium Museum<br>Chedworth |

**Fig. 9.6** Main topic: Romans
Our topic: Villas and mosaics

Heating and water supply

Information: Chedworth

---

Baths

Information: *Roman Britain*, pp.27,32,34

*The Building of Ancient Rome*, pp.8,11,15,17,23–5,31,33–5

---

Lavatories

Information: The warden at Chedworth

The same pages from *The Building of Ancient Rome*

---

Our paragraphs will answer these questions:

1. Where did the Romans at Chedworth get their water from?

2. How was it stored and piped?

3. How does this compare with our water supply today?

4. What was water used for?

5. How were the baths heated?

6. How do we heat our rooms?

7. How did the Romans use the baths?

8. What were the lavatories like?

9. How does Roman hygiene compare with ours today?

**Fig. 9.7** Main topic: Romans
Our topic: Hygiene

| Subject | Source of information | Pages |
|---|---|---|
| The Roman kitchen | *Food and Cooking in Roman Britain* | All |
| The triclinium | *The Roman House* | 32–4 |
| The tablinum | *The Roman House* | 28,29 |
| The cubiculum | *The Roman House* | 37 |
| The garden room | *The Roman House* | 39 |
| The atrium | *The Roman House* | 23–6 |
| A Roman menu | *Food and Cooking in Roman Britain* | |

**Fig. 9.8** Main topic: Romans
Our topic: food
(This was carefully selected as a simple topic for a less able group.)

The questions these children had asked were:
1. What did the Romans eat?
2. Where did they prepare it?
3. How did they cook?
4. Where did they eat?
5. How did they eat?
(and, after discussion with the teacher)
6. Were there any special customs connected with food?
7. Is there anything that has influenced us today?

This resulted in a very-well-worked-out topic on the Roman day, with much model-making and cookery to illustrate their points. The children's pleasure at the Roman's introduction of now-common vegetables contrasted with the teacher's annoyance at the introduction of their popular medicinal plant—ground elder. Nothing, however, could induce the group to taste 'Roman snails', even though their descendants still abound in the area.

Notes made in the way suggested in Figs. 9.4 to 9.8 make the putting together of information collected from a number of sources a much simpler operation than trying to reorganize random jottings.

Not only does this method help with the collation of material, but there is a firm structure built in from the start, and the form of the final write-up takes shape as the children work. Particularly is this true of those who use the flow-diagram method. An added benefit is the ready-made bibliography.

**177**

After the final writing out there of course remains the map work, diagrams, illustrations, and general layout of the whole.

## 9.4 Expressive and poetic writing

Thematic work of this sort would be incomplete from a writing point of view if the only accounts to be included were of a transactional nature.

These children have been provided with a rich and stimulating experience and the chance to observe closely, but unless the teacher capitalizes on this it can be wasted.

Questionnaires are of doubtful value; we have seen children blind to the area all around them, blinkered by the obligation to answer specific questions. Rather, they should be encouraged to look, to feel, to wonder, to appreciate, and then to talk.

This might well be in preparation for written work, but a teacher sensitive to the needs of children may know that to write immediately might be to lose all joy.

Such feelings are frequently stored to be used later in different contexts.

A part of this study included a visit to an old mine working, an opportunity for the children to project themselves to some extent into the feelings of those unfortunate infants who slaved in the pits.

Some weeks later, one girl who had been very moved by the experience chose to write vividly, in the first person singular, employing a time-slip that had been almost real to her.

> I went in carefully, down, down, down, steeper and steeper, darker and darker.
> Cries of fear seemed to mumble in my brain from the slave-like child-miners of long ago.
> I looked at the rotting pit props, and saw the fool's gold glinting in the light of my nelly.
> At first I could see a distant square of light but that too disappeared.
> My back is sore with the weight of the billies of iron ore, the skin broken where gravel has been put under the sack to make me hurry.
> My limbs are tired, my arms aching with strain.
> The caves are weird and damp. I wonder why people have to grow up, the babies are lucky, they do not have to work.
> I stumble, slip and slide as I crawl through the slimy passages, I hear another cry of fear.
> It is cold and I feel the dampness on my hands.
> Coal, so soft it breaks easily, showers on my head.
> My friend is working in a seam above me. Now I know why he cried in fear, his notched pole has been hatefully knocked away leaving

him stranded on the ledge above, just to frighten him into harder
work. His pick is resting on his shivering shoulders.
I long for the bell to ring.

## Free verse

On the other hand, a child may wish to write immediately, like
Peter, who complained bitterly that their walk had been too long
and tiring.

> Squashy!
> Squishy!
> Swodgy!
>
> Mud slowly slithering down my wellies,
> How I hate the stuff.
> Hills, roads, fields in uncountable numbers,
> My legs ached,
> My feet didn't fit.
> My legs were lead,
> My feet had walked a lifetime.
>
> It's torture.
> A primrose, yellow in the sun,
> Crystalled dew upon its leaves
> Enjoying the day,
> Free in the Cotswold air.
>
> But me,
> I'm on a hike!

Certainly not great poetry, but these children had been encouraged to use this form when they were expressing sincere
feelings.

It is possible to make children feel at ease with this mode of
writing. First and foremost, they must have heard and enjoyed
poetry, poems not necessarily always about beauty and nature, but
about relations, grubby shirts, and dustbins, too. They should not
be asked to struggle after rhyme, for their vocabulary is not
extensive enough to protect them from reduction to banality.

Of course, they will plagiarize, using phrases and rhythms that
have been absorbed into their own repertoire. Here, for example, is
a Christmas carol written by Hugh, who had obviously enjoyed
'Hiawatha':

> On a snowy Christmas evening,
> On a Christmas Eve so frosty,
> From a stable shone a bright light,
> Shone the light so very brightly;

> There the Blessed Virgin Mary
> Laid her baby in a manger
> Bedded soft in straw and rushes
> There he lay a-slumbering deeply.

and so on, for three verses. It owes a lot to Longfellow, but something also to Hugh himself.

Teachers who give titles for poems to children, or who demand that they write about specific festivals, are asking for the well-nigh impossible. Even our Poets Laureate find the task difficult. (How about *On the Illness of the Prince of Wales*:

> Along the electric wire the message came.
> 'He is no better, he is much the same'?)

On the other hand, children *can* be inspired to attempt free verse, particularly when they are expressing deeply felt emotions.

## 9.5 Talking

Reading and writing are possibly the more obvious outcomes of this environmental study, but it would have been a very lopsided approach if it had neglected oral language. One spin-off from living with children in a hostel was the easy relationship that developed, enabling friendly informal talk to take place on most occasions.

Even though the teachers had hoped that this would happen, they felt that it was not enough. Small group discussions were an integral and planned part of the schedule, both during the week away and in the follow-up period—essential, they felt, if the children were to gain maximum benefit. This included:

1. A general discussion about the journey, the area, the buildings, the weather, homesickness—indeed, any subject at all—with the large party broken down into small groups usually accompanied by an adult.
2. Scientific discussion about the children's observations, hypotheses and conclusions; historical discussion, triggered by visits and artefacts; geographical discussion, after going round a farm, having a detailed look at topography and the present uses of the land; discussion, too, about map reading.
3. Mathematics, worked always in small groups of like ability, so that new approaches to practical work, like using a Silva compass or a clinometer, would be given at an appropriate level, and every child would be able to help solve the problems set for his group.

Back at school most work was done in small groups and the talk included:

1. Discussion of their findings from the reference books.
2. Discussion of the fiction connected with their topic.
3. Talk, in very small groups, when the children were asked to look critically at their reactions to their week away, and see if the experience had altered them in any way.

One boy said that it was his first time away from home and he had been very worried about being homesick: but he had not been, and will not worry in the future.

One said he had just not understood, before he went, what a warden was, and he had imagined a most unpleasant-policeman type. He thought in future he would ask more questions and not leap so readily to conclusions.

One girl reported, though the staff had not known, that she had been terrified at the thought of going away and facing a completely new situation. She now felt far less afraid of her forthcoming change of school and felt that she would be able to cope in the future with change and challenge.

All the children recounted incidents of friendships or quarrels and felt that they understood one another far better. Each and everyone commented that they felt more grown up.

Finally, talk brought together the whole experience, for the group produced a recorded verbal record on tape, to be played alongside the slides taken during the week. The children were shown all the photographs; from a wide range they selected those few that they wished to report upon. Then, by discussion, co-operation, and genuine hard work in making their contribution of a high enough standard, they produced an excellent recording.

An exhibition of all their work, their diaries, and their models was mounted in the school hall. Their parents, and the children of the third year together with *their* mothers and fathers, were invited to browse around, with the fourth-year children acting as guides, before seeing and hearing the tape/slide documentary.

## 9.6 Topics for thematic work

Suggestions for the central focus of thematic work are legion, but none are better than those selected by the children themselves guided by the able teacher.

They may stem from a literacy interest, perhaps based on one favourite work of fiction, or on a collection of stories and poems around a specific theme.

Perhaps one child's enthusiasm for his own hobby will lead his classmates into a topic, such as an excellent one we saw on railways.

Maybe, as in one school we know, a very young class had started a topic on the local church, and had found so much of interest that gradually all the school became involved. The outcome was a history of the building from its Saxon foundations to the present day presented in the form of unscripted drama and given as a 'Christmas present' to everyone, young and old, in the area.

Not everyone wishes to be so ambitious, of course, but it is always advisable to plan, at the outset, how one intends to conclude.

It is always a good idea to consider the mode of the presentation of the whole, and of the parts. Some information is best written; some comes over more vividly if a model is made; some can best be portrayed by sketches or diagrams; and many children can talk more freely and succinctly about their ideas and their research if they can put these prepared drawings on to acetate sheets for use with an overhead projector.

Teachers may wish to allow their children a wide choice or to select the type of final production themselves, perhaps from one of the following:

1. A verbal account, perhaps recorded, and maybe illustrated with slides on overhead projector transparencies prepared by the speakers.
2. A display of work.
3. A dramatic account.
4. A written account. There is a variety of choice—a wall book, magazine, newspaper, etc., or, of course, a book complete with index and bibliography, which may be an individual production or a co-operative effort.

Whatever theme is selected, and whichever way the final outcome is presented, the four aspects of language—reading, writing, listening, and speaking—can be seen to play an integral part.

### References

1. *A Language for Life* (the Bullock Report), HMSO, 1975.

# 10. The organization of the junior/middle school classroom

This chapter links directly with the discussion of classroom organization in the early years in Chapter 4. Its basic argument is that a classroom or base should be organized so that the following opportunities for talking, reading, and writing are readily available.

1. Opportunities for language that arise from first-hand experiences in the classroom or the neighbouring environment: these experiences need the support of well-organized materials in art and craft, science related to the environment, and mathematics, as well as those listed under 6 below.

2. Well-organized book and other printed materials: these provide opportunities through literature, reference, and information books in their own right, and act as back-up material for many of the activities listed under 1 above.

3. A range of suitable writing materials, especially those for the making of simple books: these will provide for the writing and recording activities arising under both 1 and 2 above.

4. The opportunities for developing a range of talking/thinking skills in small groups of up to five children or for individuals, as well as the more limited opportunities for dialogue that arise in class presentations and large groups or full class discussions. All pertinent audio-visual aids should be available.

5. The opportunities for planning and co-operation in a piece of work, which may be mainly written language, illustration, diagram and/or mathematical representation in its presentation, or a combination of more than one of these. There must also be opportunities to observe, compare, and generalize in the development of the theme.

6. Language opportunities arising from drama and music: these link properly with activities listed in 1, but because of their more specialized nature are not within the capabilities of all teachers.

7. Occasions for checking on children's weaknesses and arranging additional times for practice as near as possible to opportunities for use.

If the opportunities under 1 to 6 are exploited, then it follows that the provision for 7 should be incidental to much of the work being undertaken, and close to highly motivated activity which has a clear sense of audience, purpose, and presentation.

One of our arguments is that children's thinking and the language that formulates this thinking is frequently best achieved when the language/thinking process arises out of, and is supported by, first-hand experience. We are not implying that all talk and practice in reading and writing arises in this way, but that much of it does, and that, when this is so, it can be of a highly motivating nature. For many children there is a clear progression in which talk and written expression become steadily freer from reliance on the experiential and steadily more abstract in the relationships that can be understood and expressed. However, for some children this abstraction comes late or never, and their language skills need the impetus and actuality of direct experience throughout their school days.

## 10.1 Availability of materials

In many classrooms, much of this first-hand experience is already within the curriculum, if not always explicitly organized; but often the opportunities for language are not fully appreciated or developed. Certain valuable opportunities depend on materials being available or activities being organized, on the availability of books and other print materials, and on the size and organization of groups. Our emphasis is on flexible organization, with a wide range of materials available and groupings possible so that the teacher's repertoire of skills can be used to the full, and approaches and organizational needs can be easily met.

A further argument is that subject divisions are not normally helpful at this stage of a child's development, and that, for the development of the language/thinking skills outlined so far, broad curriculum divisions give richer opportunities. Thus science, geography, some history and some mathematics (in its applied form) can be subsumed under 'Study of the Environment', and art and craft materials used for observing, recording, and setting up experiments related to this work. The use of art and craft materials will both service other areas of the curriculum and act as opportunities for exploration, expression, and the acquisition of specific skills in their own right. Ideas and incidents from literature, history, religious education, or geography, as well as those arising from a purely dramatic or movement basis, can again link to other areas of the curriculum or be developed for their own sake.

Mathematics and music are subjects depending to a much

greater extent on sequential progression; they can link and enrich more general topics, but they need specific teaching and practice in addition. The Primary Survey carried out by Her Majesty's Inspectors and published in 1979 commented that tests showed the 'Efforts made to teach children to calculate are not rewarded by high scores in the examples concerned with the handling of everyday situations. Learning to operate with numbers may need to be more closely linked with learning to use them in a variety of situations than is now common.'[1]

It went on to comment more generally: 'The teaching of skills in isolation, whether in language or in mathematics, does not produce the best results.' Opportunities arising from broader curriculum groupings, then, need careful consideration.

For older children in the middle years, some subject divisions may be necessary, but there is a real danger of this happening too soon so that content and terminology override the development of general skills and competencies. We would argue that even exceptionally able children are best taught in this general way, with special advice and provision of books and materials with, on occasion, group work or individual assignments taken under specialist direction.

## 10.2 Organization of areas

In planning the organization of a classroom or unit the following areas of space need to be defined.

1. Art/craft/making area: close to water if possible and with easily cleanable surfaces; materials stored so that access is easy and a ready check on return of materials can be made.
2. Science/environmental study area: close to light with trays/drawers for containers and small equipment and working/display area for collections, experiments and presentation of findings.
3. Mathematics area, often linked to 2 but containing books, cards, measuring, and structural materials; easy borrowing and checking on return essential.
4. Book corner, containing reference, information, and fiction books with writing materials laid our or stored near by: this area should be as far as possible from doors and circulation space.
5. Graded reading materials, sometimes linked to 4, but organized differently and with a more limited range of purposes.
6. Other materials, such as those for music and drama, which may be included in the classroom or unit or kept elsewhere.

The division is a development from that outlined in Chapter 4. Further divisions into subject areas may be necessary in the upper middle school years. Where classes are grouped in units, often for year groups and usually with some shared space, some materials may be organized in the class bases, but this division needs careful thought. If we consider the range of materials we can make available under 1, 2, 3, and 6 above and the activities arising from them, we first notice that we have increased the range of naming words, whether of objects, materials, or actions, that are now within the children's direct experience. Even more significant is the possibility of developing the range of words to do with quality, the qualifiers, whether of colour, texture, shape, number, size, or pattern, or of quality and timing of actions. Much of this will be related to the 'reporting' use of language, but it will depend on sharpening capacities for observation and comparison, for seeing similarities and differences, and for making simple generalizations. All this language will be directly referable to objects seen, materials used, and tasks undertaken.

If we further consider the use of materials related to art and craft, to the study of the environment and simple science experiments arising from it, and to mathematics in its applied form, we can see opportunities for sequencing the parts of an activity, for explaining a process, recognizing relationships, and drawing conclusions.

Out of the activities of collecting, identifying, comparing, and recording we can see opportunities for the formulation of questions, the use of reference and information books, the seeking of explanations, the recall of past experiences, and the association of ideas.

On these occasions for the use of language, there are further opportunities for moving towards logical reasoning, for seeing alternatives, for setting up simple hypotheses, for anticipating what might be the outcome of an action, an experiment, or some exploration of materials, and for predicting the possible consequences. These opportunities are increasingly recognized in activities related to simple science, the study of the environment and mathematical activities, but are equally present, although not so readily recognized, in work with art and craft materials.

Every classroom could well have a set of wall pockets containing interesting language ploys, possibly duplicated on work sheets, which could be used by any child when he had completed his set work ahead of schedule. We have in mind such notions as sorting words into alphabetical order, crosswords, anagrams, comic strip sequences with large 'bubbles' for the insertion of suggested direct speech, simple instructions for suitable activities, searches—for articles and authors in encyclopaedias—simple sketch maps on which to draw specified routes, bus time-tables that accompany questions—indeed, any attractive occupations that reinforce current teaching points and stimulate language.

It is particularly important that adults working with children recognize the importance of such words as 'because', 'if', 'although', 'so that', 'unless', and 'either/or' when they are used in a way that indicates reasoning, and words such as 'if', 'might', 'could', 'should', 'probably' or 'perhaps', when they are used to show that the child is thinking ahead and attempting to anticipate or predict outcomes.

The formulating function of language is being utilized throughout such work; but, equally, opportunities for recall of past experience, for asking questions, and for using books as a constant source of comparison and additional information are implied in the discussion.

Other uses of language will arise incidentally from such organization, but many of these uses will have a more specific place in those aspects of organization discussed later in the chapter.

## 10.3 Organization of children

Having considered the organization of materials, we must now consider the organization of the children themselves. There are three major options before us: class teaching, working in small groups, and individual tuition. Each of these forms of organization is likely to be effective for certain limited objectives and is likely to achieve a considerable degree of success only for those particular objectives.

The whole class is economical and effective as a unit for learning where a general presentation to start a topic is the aim; where basic information or general instructions needed by all the children and within the understanding of all the children are being given, and where blackboard summaries, diagrams, or illustrations may be referred to; when the class is discussing the general progress and planning of some piece of work; where a short fifteen- to twenty-minute period of listening to a story, to poems, or other models of written language is needed; or where a general presentation of a completed piece of work is being made. It has distinct limitations in that the teacher often dominates to a degree where the language becomes a monologue for long stretches of time, and where involvement of the learners in any thinking or dialogue is minimal. Similarly, where instructions or the purveying of information is more than of a general nature, the span of attention and individual differences in children's capacity are frequently ignored. The expenditure of words may far outstretch individual capacity for absorption, and the organization of the class as a unit may become a barrier rather than an aid to effective learning.

Group work is likely to be most effective where numbers are kept small, from working in pairs to numbers of up to five or six, and where the task or assignment is planned with both the strengths and limitations of group-work in mind. There are two major types of grouping—by ability, and in mixed-ability groups. Ability groups should generally be used for those areas of knowledge and skill where the matter is highly sequential, as in aspects of mathematics, spelling, or advanced reference skills. The aim of such group work must be specific, and will be concerned with taking a group of children who are at a similar stage of knowledge or skill one step further.

The language is likely to be partly instructional and partly concerned with developing the children's thinking related to this new step and with ensuring that they can understand and formulate in their own words what they have learned.

The great strength of such small group work is that the instruction can be specific to the needs of the group and that, by means of discussion, the teacher can ensure that the work is understood and individual difficulties are explained. The real test lies in the teacher's skill in getting the children to explain what they have learned in the terms of their own experience. This method also enables the teacher to introduce what is to be learned in a way that encourages the children to think out some of the stages for themselves, developing their own powers of deduction and reasoning rather than merely memorizing the content or process.

Mixed-ability group work has a more general application and a rather different set of purposes. It enables children of varied ability to work together, planning and discussing their work and using their powers of observation and initiative. It is particularly valuable where the language has a practical basis, as in activities that include art and craft materials, a study of the environment, simple experiments, a dramatic outcome, or mathematical activities related to firsthand experience. It would seem to be particularly valuable where 'opportunities for discriminating, classifying and observing interrelations arise in connection with work', to use the words of the Primary Survey.

A possible pattern of the learning could be practical activity → discussion → consultation of books and other sources of additional information → further discussion → recording and final presentation with a clear idea of audience. The uses of language could be wide but specific and could include:

Planning together and discussing and collecting necessary material.

Naming, noting details, comparing.

Formulating questions.

Making simple generalizations.

Planning ahead and seeing alternatives and possibilities.

Anticipating what might happen and predicting consequences.

Explaining and justifying.

Using language of the imagination.

Much use of the formulating function of language and of recall of personal experience could be involved.

How can these language outcomes be ensured? First, the task must be clearly set out so the children have a specific set of objectives to work to. Second, the teacher must be free to intervene to extend the language/thinking and the practice in skills that is emerging and to give incidental help and guidance. The emphasis on organization of materials earlier in this chapter was to enable the children to have ready access to them and to enable the teacher to be free to move from group to group. As with ability grouping, the size of the group makes it possible for the teacher to join in a dialogue in which all the group can be involved in the thinking and formulation of ideas. This of course requires skill by the teacher in the use of questions and other cues, which (although the teacher gives any essential help) encourage the children to think through each step for themselves.

It can be argued that this approach would develop a highly observational and specific range of language skills which devalue imaginative language. But to start from the observational and factual seems to us one of the best foundations for language of the imagination. As we have said, in our view children should always be encouraged to use their own personal language to give form to the sensory impressions they receive, the relationships they notice, the detail they observe and the comparisons and generalizations that arise. This language moves easily into the language of the imagination. The language of the imagination is not the product of whimsy, though some of the tasks set for children in writing and art verge on the latter, for example some of the poetry or 'creative' writing and paintings such as 'imaginary animals'. The story is told that the young Leonardo da Vinci drew a fantastic and superbly realized dragon. It was a work of the imagination, but was fed by much drawing and observation of the lizards, snakes, and other animals of his environment from the earliest years of his childhood. It was this observational input that provided the material on which his imagination could work. Similarly, with language it is the observational base, the first-hand study, the opportunities to express these in various media and formulate them in words, as well as the hearing of examples from literature, that feed and give rise to language that will often be of the imagination.

Where group work is well organized and flexible, individual differences and needs will generally be met and much individual help can be given. Nevertheless, there may be a child at any point in the spectrum of ability who needs special individual attention. This may be a child who is capable of taking some interest or skill beyond the capability of the others, a child whose emotional problems make him require individual care to provide the stimulus to success and the capacity to work with others, or a child with learning problems where failure has become so deadening that only special attention can break his cycle of defeat. These pose special problems; and in the second and third examples, as Lawrence has shown,[2] the solution may be partly through language, the talking through of problems in a counselling relationship. The time needed for such children may be very great and not possible to provide if the demands of the rest of the children are to be met: it is here that the school needs a policy of special help and advice which may come from within the time of the head teacher or from other staff resources, from additional professional help, or the community.

Whatever the form of groupings, certain factors hold true.

1. Interaction with an adult who is sympathetic and knowledgeable in the possibilities of language is a potent factor in helping to increase a child's range of understanding and his capacity for thinking, and in extending his skills in using language for a wider range of purposes.
2. A child learns to use language by having opportunities to use it and not by passively listening, though listening will have highly specific uses in learning.
3. Increasing a child's range of uses of language through talk

provides the basis for increasing his range of uses of language in reading and writing.

We have discussed the organization of learning materials and ways of organizing children appropriate to different purposes in learning and teaching. Both of these have implications for the way we organize space within the classroom or unit, which teachers need to consider. We have suggested that the overriding need is for organization that is flexible and adaptable, and gives the teacher opportunities to work with the whole class (though for limited periods of time and with clear objectives), with different types of small groups, or with individuals. We have indicated the different opportunities for language development these forms of organization may give rise to.

One other organizational possibility needs to be mentioned. It is the use of older children to interact with and help younger children, the use of children to help each other, and the use of adults from the community to increase opportunities for language interaction. These sources sometimes provide sympathetic listeners, and sometimes provide motivators who give a fresh impetus. Some interesting work in Scotland used older, less able children to help younger children: the interesting effect was that the language skills of *both* groups increased considerably.

## 10.4 The use of exercises

We need to consider the use of exercises as a means of extending language skills, the most important consideration being that of transfer—do the skills acquired by largely mechanical exercises carry over into regular use? The evidence is consistent that, generally speaking, they do not. Yet exercises continue to be used extensively as a means of teaching language, increasingly so as one progresses through the junior and middle years and into the secondary school.

We consider that exercises do have a use, but a limited one. Where some facts, skills, or process are in use but not fully assimilated, and where, for the particular group or individual, there is a reasonable chance of their being successfully learned, exercises that are carefully and specifically selected can give the immediate practice needed to consolidate the instruction or step. This new knowledge then needs to be used immediately in some purposeful context. The key to successful learning is in selection and timing, and not in quantity or regularity.

Exercises frequently rely on reading in short bursts of one to fifteen seconds, the response being one of short-term recall or the selection or rearrangement of language already provided. Evidence that such exercises provide for any sort of intellectual development except for strictly limited purposes is lacking. Yet given these limited purposes, we can see the value of such practice for computation, spelling, or dictionary skills, always provided the child can see the future need. They can provide routine satisfaction in neatness and accuracy after livelier periods of activity, and can be used to occupy some children, leaving the teacher free to concentrate on a particular learning problem with others. The key is to use this very sparingly and with a clear intention of purpose, even though this purpose might be to fill a gap on a wet Friday afternoon.

## 10.5 Class discussion

A final and under-used means of extending the uses of language is in beginning the day with a short period of class discussion, going over the planning of the day and the specific tasks to be completed, reporting on progress of projects and group activities, considering class activities, and encouraging ideas, suggestions, and comments from the class.

Similarly, at the end of the day a listening time of 15 minutes for a story, poem, songs, and music from a group, accounts and presentation of work achieved, description of books read, and reminders for tomorrow provides a means of extending language skills as well as involving the children in planning and progress.

### References
1. *Primary Education in England, A Survey by HM Inspectors of Schools*, HMSO, 1978.
2. LAWRENCE, DENNIS, *Improving Reading Through Counselling*, Ward Lock Educational, 1973.

### Suggested reading
*Nuffield Junior Science Teachers' Guide 1*, Collins, 1967. This is the best manual on organizing for learning. It should be in every staff room library and act as a source book on classroom organization. Chapter 5 especially recommended.

BENNETT, L. and SIMMONS, J., *Children Making Books*, A & C Black, 1978. A good guide written by practitioners.

MELZI, KAY, *Art in the Primary School*, Blackwell, 1967. A very good basic book which gives a great deal of practical help.

ROBERTSON, SEONAID M., *Using Natural Materials*, Schools Council/Educational Publications, 1974. A good book for ideas in extending the range of materials which can be used with children. Excellent book list.

TOUGH, JOAN, *Talking and Learning*, Ward Lock Educational, 1977. Chapter 4 outlines the observed uses of language, and Chapter 5 lists and gives examples of the sort of questions and strategies teachers can use when conversing with children.

# 11. Recording progress in literacy

Teaching is, to a large extent, a matter of relationships; and depth of knowledge about a child and his background increase the teacher's ability to build up this rapport.

Her knowledge of her class as individuals can be improved by the keeping of thoughtful and carefully planned records, which should provide continuity throughout the years of education.

## 11.1 The need for record-keeping

Many teachers claim that they know every child in their class so well that they are able to judge intuitively the next stage of learning required and when this should take place. We do not believe that a teacher can hold in her head all the complexities of every individual child, his needs, and each necessary developmental process. It is obvious from the most recent research that many teachers are not good record-keepers. We do need to know and understand the children we teach, but if we are to be effective in the developmental process a systematic and detailed record of children's progress is essential to maintain full intellectual growth and learning.

> There is no substitute for first-hand knowledge of children and of the kind of learning situation in which they have been involved. But this should be supported by a full set of records which gives the receiving teacher information in several dimensions . . . records which accompany a child from the first or infant school are all too often inadequate.[1]

If we are to help the individual child achieve his maximum potential then progress must be monitored in a careful and systematic way—it cannot be left to the discretion or intuition of the individual teacher. Records should maintain continuity throughout a child's education. All too often this can be disrupted by the changes involved when moving from one class to another, let alone from school to school or district to district. Such changes can affect learning by retarding it for as much as six to twelve months. If education is to be seen as a whole and complete process, then clearly these transitional movements must be achieved as smoothly as possible.

Perhaps in the days when the curriculum was worked through a series of textbooks for each subject area, so-called 'progress' was easily maintained. With the introduction of the discovery approach to learning and the integration of subjects, however, the need for more detailed records has become evident. Certainly with this new freedom in teaching has come the complexity of monitoring children's progress. While children may be seen to be busy and actively involved in their 'project' work, it becomes necessary to question how teachers are able to judge whether or not an individual child is making satisfactory progress in all aspects of the curriculum.

Records are necessary not only for the monitoring of progress but also for the identification of the child's future needs, and teachers must question constantly which step should be taken next to meet the precise requirements of every child. Clearly, in the complex situation of the school where a flexible approach has been adopted, the teacher must know where each child is going and in which direction his interests should be channelled.

Thus, in the classroom where we are aiming to provide facilities that enable the individual child to attain his maximum potential, the keeping of carefully selected records will assist the teacher in the effective planning of learning experiences. Obviously, individual teacher's records will vary tremendously from school to school, and quite rightly; but we believe that there should be some form of unity at least throughout a school, especially in the major areas of numeracy and literacy, ensuring that certain basic skills are regularly observed and progress is sustained. It is this kind of monitoring that is fundamental to the child's total development.

Teachers need critical powers of observation and very clear methods of organization if they are indeed to cater for each individual child in the class. The combination of the intuitive with the more objective recording leads to greater skills in recognizing when the child is ready to go forward and will aid the sensitive awareness that is so necessary.

### The main purposes of record-keeping

1. Recording children's skill development and/or experience, and/or formation of concepts.
2. Maintaining progress and continuity in a child's education.
3. Assisting the teacher in diagnosing difficulties, and planning appropriate programmes.
4. Assisting the teacher in the organization of effective grouping of children for specific purposes.

## 11.2 Suggestions for main headings for an individual record

Doubtless each school will wish to amend and alter the categories we suggest and to elaborate in detail some of the items, but this must come after full debate in the staff room about the language policy.

### Prereading skills

The young child, when he talks, is communicating. He is using language when he converses with his teacher, or when he is in discussion with others; and the monitoring of his speech is, we believe, a vital activity for teachers. How else can we know when and how to intervene to help extend the child's range?

So first and foremost there comes talk.

1. Oral communication skills. It may well be that teachers will wish to break these down into the various uses suggested by Dr J. Tough and detailed in the Bullock Report. By this means they are more easily monitored.
2. Auditory skills.
3. Visual skills.
4. Ability to sequence.
5. Prereading book skills.
6. Oral comprehension skills.

### Early book skills

Children gain a great deal if they have been read to, especially if this is accompanied by a warm cuddle on the knee of a trusted and loved adult. In such circumstances they absorb many of the following facts:

1. Books must be held the right way up.
2. Pages are turned over one at a time from the front to the back.
3. Lines of print are read from left to right and from the top to the bottom of the page.
4. Print conveys an interesting message.
5. Pictures relate to the printed message.
6. Reading is an enjoyable activity.

Some preschool children will also be aware of the use of a contents table and an index, and through asking questions will 'crack the code' and teach themselves to read. However, many of the amusing 'howlers' of young children arise because they are apt to take literally the sayings of adults, and some intelligent children have been known to put an ear close to the page in an effort to hear what the letters *say*! In addition to the confusion arising from the inaccurate use of language by adults, some of the words we use to talk about reading have more than one meaning. 'Letter', 'sound', and 'line' are familiar to most children in very different contexts from that of reading.

It is important for teachers to be aware that children may make a slow start in learning to read if they have formed misconceptions about the reading process. The wise teacher will check, through observation, that each child has acquired the preparatory book skills before beginning his reading instruction.

### Later stages

As the child progresses through the school and develops skills in both reading and writing, these too must be recorded; nevertheless, attention to the oral skills listed above must not be neglected.

The recording of oral communication skills, for instance, can be extended to include such skills as the ability to hold an audience when telling a story, the ability to take part in reasoned argument, the ability to summarize and report, the ability to select the correct form for both material and audience, and the ability to hold a sustained conversation.

### Reading

The teacher's main long-term aims will, of course, be for each and every child to attain a fluency in reading, to use books to read for pleasure, and to turn to books willingly to seek for information. Her short-term objectives leading towards these goals, however, need to be clearly specified, showing carefully graded detail for each child.

1. Context cues.
2. Phonic skills. This needs to be broken down into its component parts in accord with the school's accepted phonic progression.
3. Study skills. Again, obviously, these must be detailed, and the information required for this can be found in Chapters 8 and 9.

### Writing

1. Motor skills for writing (itemized).
2. Written summaries, taken from a single source.
3. Combination of summaries from more than one source.
4. Written summary of an oral report given by someone else (note-taking).
5. Use of simple planning aids—lists, diagrams, webs, etc.

(It may well be felt that 2, 3, 4, and 5 above would sit more happily under the heading of 'study skills': it is in the nature of literacy that the strands are so closely woven and intertwined. It is up to the individual school to decide where best these fit for their own purposes, the important thing is that they are not overlooked.)

6. Written communication skills. It is possible to use the model referred to in Chapter 7:[2]

## transactional — expressive — poetic

Although it is important to give a great deal of practice in the expressive mode, clear records should be kept of a child's attempts to move along the continuum in either direction.

There is, we feel, no mystique about this, but a developing awareness by the teacher of how a child feels for the appropriate place upon the continuum to pitch his particular response. If this is noted, then help can be given in shaping the work so that his written forms can be extended.

The recent Primary School Survey found that:

> surprisingly, in only about a third of the classes were samples of children's written work regularly used to monitor their progress. In fewer than half the classes was children's own written work used as a basis for teaching spelling, syntax, sentence structure or style.[3]

Surely children's own work must create the very best record of progress that any teacher could keep, and the very best starting point for teaching.

Consideration here must be given to the amount of work (1) to be filed for the year and (2) to be passed on with other records. We would suggest that probably three typical pieces of work per term are enough to give the insight necessary.

### Format

Records must be simple to keep and easy to read; if they become too time-consuming they rob the children of valuable teaching time, so attention to format, storage, and key is essential.

Fig. 11.1 shows a suggested layout for an individual record card for the early years in school.

### Key

This can be so designed to show varying degrees of competence, the box being left blank for the child with no skill, and marked in an agreed progression as he moves through developing skills to a complete independence. (A diagonal line, a cross, a superimposed circle, and a completely blacked-in square is one suggestion; the use of colours is another.)

A record card marked in this way has a visual impact, and stages of progression and future needs are easily seen.

Key

☐ Shows no ability
◩ Has been taught
☒ Uses the skill at times
▨ Is completely competent

Writing skills

☐ Holds pencil correctly
☐ Can draw patterns left to right
☐ Knows the difference between
    upper and lower case letters
☐ Forms letters correctly
☐ Knows phonic sounds of letters
☐ Can sequence letter sounds

Visual skills

☐ Recognizes pictures
☐ Recognizes detail in pictures
☐ Can arrange a set of pictures in 'story order'
☐ Can sort and/or match pictures
☐ Can sort and/or match patterns
☐ Can sort and/or match letter shapes
☐ Can recognize letter shapes
☐ Can match letter shapes to sounds

(This can lead directly on to phonic skills)

Phonic skills

☐ Identifies initial letter sound
☐ Identifies final letter sound
☐ Identifies medial letter sounds
☐ Matches and names
    symbol/sound
☐ Consonants
☐ Short Vowels
☐ Initial consonant blends
☐ Final consonant blends
☐ Consonant digraphs
☐ Final 'e'
☐ Vowel digraphs
☐ Silent consonants

Book skills

☐ Handles books correctly
☐ Eye movements left to right
☐ Knows terms: 'letter'
☐     'word'
☐     'line'
☐     'sentence'
☐     'full stop'
☐ Can locate book by
    matching cover
☐ Can find relevant pictures
☐ Can find page numbers

(further suggestions in Fig.3.2)

Name _____  Date of birth _____

**Fig. 11.1** Suggested record card for early years (NB: Oral skills have been omitted from this record; they are of such major importance that we suggest the school draws up a separate ladder of progress with due regard to the specific needs of children in that school.)

## Storage

To be of maximum use the card must be readily available. A looseleaf folder with a ring binder is an obvious solution, particularly if one uses the type that allows the inserts to be 'stepped' down the file so that at least twelve names are visible at once.

These folders must be kept to hand—not locked in a filing cabinet, but on the desk or in the teacher's drawer, ready for easy and frequent reference.

Another useful retrieval system is formed by the provision of the type of file that consists of plastic envelopes welded into a hard-backed cover. Storage of children's work and notes on their development is then made simple.

## 11.3 Class records

A record card designed on the lines so far suggested will meet the first three purposes of record-keeping suggested on page 195 ideally, and, indeed, may be used for planning work for groups. It is better, however, when programming to use a matrix type of record in each area of skill development, on which every child's lesson is plotted. This will help the teacher to match activities to groups of pupils, leading to an economy in the use of teaching time and to a maintenance of appropriate balance between the didactic and exploratory approach to teaching. On this card we would suggest the use of a date; this will indicate not only the stage of development but also the rate of the child's progress through the skills recorded.

If this class record is well organized it should also indicate the general all-round progress in the development of skills within the class (see Fig. 11.2).

## Uses

To be effective records must be used by the teacher for the purpose of diagnosis, planning, and organization. Their use facilitates the efficient development of abilities through the wider curriculum, which is, in itself, a motivating force in the acquisition of basic skills.

Perhaps at the outset a school staff needs to decide, first, what is essential to record (this will then form the core for the school) and, second, what is desirable to record. In this way the individual teacher would have freedom to decide what is most appropriate for the stage and the abilities of the children in her own class.

| Skill to be taught | Name | Name | Name | etc. | | | |
|---|---|---|---|---|---|---|---|
| Uses contents table | 7.11 | 14.10 | 28.12 | 28.12 | | | |
| Uses index | 12.12 | 12.12 | 9.10 | | | | |
| Uses dictionary | 21.9 | 7.9 | 20.11 | | | | |
| Skims | 30.10 | | | | | | |
| Scans | | | | | | | |
| Makes notes | | | | | | | |
| etc. | | | | | | | |
| | | | | | | | |

**Fig. 11.2** Matrix record for study skills to be taught in Class 3x. The use of a date rather than a tick helps to indicate the rate of progress as well as the stage of development reached by individuals.

## 11.4 Children's recording

Allowing children to keep their own records of progress has advantages and disadvantages. The advantages are that it helps children to become involved in making judgements about their own progress; and, when they have become proficient at keeping their own records, the teacher's time is saved for teaching instead of recording. The disadvantages are that, if their introduction is not sensitively handled, they can lead to excessive competition between children and can also encourage youngsters to flit from one activity to another in order to obtain many ticks on their record.

If higher standards in basic skills are achieved through the wider curriculum, this will mean that teachers will need to provide a framework that will ensure that gaps are avoided in the children's development of skills and concepts. A record of a child's activities, which he can keep himself, will help to indicate areas that may have been neglected.

It is important that sound and sensible attitudes towards study skills are developed at infant level, and it is vital that children should develop the ability to plan the use of their own time. We believe that many teenagers who cannot cope with independent study at sixth-form and university level could have been helped by a suitable programme at the infant and junior stages. This programme should be planned to develop the ability to state long-term aims and short-term objectives by each child for his own development.

For example, although the concept of time is one of the latest to develop, infants can be helped towards sensible planning if given the right framework. Some teachers insist that children should undertake specific activities during the day but be allowed to decide when and in which order they will do them.

When the children become adept at making these decisions, the length of time for the child to plan can be extended over two days, then three, then four, so that eventually the children will be able to plan their own weekly programme. In order to ensure that a balanced curriculum is undertaken by each individual it will be necessary to have a *record of activities* for each child. One teacher of a reception class had a system for checking at the beginning of the afternoon and reminding each child about the activities he needed to do before hometime. The classroom was divided into work areas, and in each area she placed a hook on which coloured discs were hung. Along one side of the classroom she had a row of cuphooks with the name of a child and his picture symbol above each hook. When the child had undertaken an activity to the satisfaction of the teacher he took the appropriate disc, red for reading, white for writing, blue for maths, yellow for art and craft, etc., and hung it on his own hook. Although this was a transient record, it was well suited to very young children as it did not involve writing skills which are undeveloped in many children at this stage. A further development of this type of record can be provided by having a chart on which key activities or skills and concepts are listed. When the child has completed an activity, the appropriate rectangle can be coloured in. This system needs considerable teacher supervision in the early stages.

At junior level children can be encouraged to maintain a balanced programme of curriculum activities by the use of block graphs showing the subject areas of the curriculum and the skills used in integrated work. This can be further developed as a written chart at later stages in the junior school (see sample record of work done in connection with a newspaper topic: Fig. 11.3).

| Reading | Writing | Listening | Talking | Visits | Drawing, etc. | Measuring | Computing | Geography | History |
|---|---|---|---|---|---|---|---|---|---|
| *The Lumberjack* | Letter to mill | Tape 'Newspapers' | Commentary on slides taken at paper factory | Paper factory | Fashion picture for class newspaper | Sizes of paper; amount needed for making books | Cost of producing class books and newspaper | Location of wood for paper | History of printing |
| *Victorian Fashions* | Fashion article for class newspaper | | Report on interview | | Potato prints | Concepts of area | Graph to show favourite types of books | | The development of Fleet Street |
| | | | Discussion of factory visit | | | | Multiplication tables memorized to ease task of costing above | | Victorian fashions |

**Fig. 11.3** Record made as a result of a topic on 'Newspapers'

The method of record-keeping at different stages of a child's development should be discussed by the staff of each school and a common policy of progression for children's records should be developed. The effective use of these records will depend greatly on the teacher's ability to involve the child in discussion about his own progress, so that he competes against himself rather than against other children in the class. It is also useful to compare his record of work for the last term with his current term's work record so that he can see differences and appreciate the amount of progress he has made.

We suggested earlier that it would be useful to keep samples of three pieces of work each term in an individual folder for each child. If the pupil himself is involved in the choice of items for inclusion, it will help him to appreciate the difference in quality of his various efforts and also help him to make judgements about his own performance.

## 11.5 Flow-diagrams

When considering a project or thematic work a different type of record is required from that used in the identification of basic skill progress. In this connection flow-diagrams can help the teachers to organize the project, break it down into manageable units, and see possible lines of development. Flow-diagrams are an invaluable aid in the recording of project work, particularly when children have developed their own recording methods using simple versions. They are also extremely useful in helping to ascertain how each particular group in the class can be involved with a specific aspect of the topic.

It is important to remember that the open-endedness and flexibility of this type of work record should always be maintained.

Children's own flow-diagrams can also be valuable, not only in helping them to direct their own lines of enquiry and interests, but also in helping the teacher to identify their progress. Provided that children's own records are given status by the teacher and respected, these will often develop into more complex planning aids.

Diagrammatic plans of work help both children and adults to order their thoughts, to identify various aspects of the work under review, and to clarify lines of research.

If used to analyse the structure of a piece of writing, flow-diagrams can be a useful aid to comprehension and evaluation. Points of difference and similarity in two or more articles can be easily seen if each is expressed in flow-diagram form, and this makes comparison and decision-making more efficient. In addition, the flow-diagram is a useful *aide-memoire* for those who have a visual memory.

From all that we have said, it must be apparent that a systematic approach to record-keeping is essential and that, although teaching styles and children's needs will vary, there can be no doubt that progress in the many and complex stages of children's development must be effectively monitored if teachers are to be truly professional.

## References

1. *A Language for Life* (the Bullock Report), HMSO, 1975.
2. BRITTON, J. *et al.*, *The Development of Writing Abilities 11–18*, Schools Council Research Studies, Macmillan, 1975.
3. *Primary Education in England, A Survey by HM Inspectors of Schools*, HMSO, 1978.

## Suggested reading

FOSTER, J., *Recording Individual Progress*, Macmillan, 1971.

# 12. Drama

Drama is regarded by many teachers as a valuable aid to language development, and we support this view. It is important however to determine how it can be used most effectively in the classroom. Let us first of all consider a typical example of the kind of drama that is found regularly in the classroom; this needs careful analysis if we are to begin to understand the nature of drama as an aid to learning.

## 12.1 Directed drama
Example Lesson

> *Music*
> Record: 'Rodeo'; 'Billy the Kid' (Aaron Copeland).
> *Warm-up*
> Free movement by the children to the music of 'Rodeo'.
> *Relaxation*
> Children lie on the floor and relax, tensing and releasing muscles.
> *Story*
> Children divide into groups: frontier townspeople—shoppers, children, merchants, loungers, horsemen, etc. The scene is the main street in a Western American town in the latter half of the last century. Children are playing games; men and women are chatting, buying goods. A blacksmith shoes a horse, and outside the saloon lounging cowboys survey the street. A band of men ride into town, dismount and enter the bank. The Sheriff and his men conceal themselves near by and as the raiders emerge a gun battle rages. People take cover; some run away. The robbers are either killed or surrender and the townsfolk emerge and celebrate the victory with a joyful dance.
>
> The music of 'Billy the Kid' can be used to help the passage of the story and to set the mood for the action.

The example above is fiction and will not be foud in any drama manual or practical handbook, but similar suggestions for lessons can be found in many, so that it represents a fairly good example of what passes for drama in the eyes of many teachers. Certainly it would not be unusual to find such a lesson being conducted in primary and lower secondary schools.

In the above example, drama purports to offer a lesson structure, and yet it is impossible to discern what it sets out to teach. Also, like so many others of its kind, not only does it lack stated aims and objectives, but it also makes assumptions about the educational process that are alarming. It is little wonder that support for drama in schools has declined when such is the quality of its representation.

Yet if it is to be of value, criticism needs to be more precise and analysis more searching, to reveal not only why such an example is unacceptable, but also wherein lies good drama. Furthermore, some practical assistance for teachers to evaluate their work, some model that enables them to perceive purpose and direction, is essential. There is a genuine and desperate need for help, and too often the goods that flood the drama manual market have an immediate superficial attractiveness but prove to be of little value when put to the test. A straightforward questioning of the lesson example above might reveal issues that relate to drama teaching in general.

1. What is the reason for starting the lesson plan with music? Is it possible to discern the lesson's intended aims from the inclusion of this obviously important element?

Perhaps the music has been chosen to promote a sensitive reaction from the children, a creative response in free movement. Such an aim would be educative both in the physical and the aesthetic areas of the pupil's experience. To be done seriously, however, it would need to cover more than the brief period of warm-up.

Perhaps the use of a Western square dance introduction in this less heavily directed section of the lesson will serve as a taste of what is to come, the main feature. Certainly in practical terms it serves as a regulator, the controlling agent that the teacher does not wish to appear to be. The mood is created by the sounds, and the children's movement to it is predictable and easy to manipulate. Nor is any of this a bad thing as long as it is seen for what it is and not accorded some inflated justification. It also sets the mood of the lesson and determines what the expectations are going to be from this session—namely, that this will be essentially an auditory/physical experience, but with the 'physical' being the expressive mode in response to music cues, and not to those of speech: movement to music, not movement allied to speech.

2. What, then, is being warmed up, and why the period of relaxation? Perhaps the children are 'cold', meaning unresponsive or insensitive. This brief period is to get them moving and feeling. One might imagine that to get them thinking was also important, but maybe this exercise is being used as a corrective to intensive

classroom work. The relaxation is more difficult to explain, as true relaxation is a learned skill that takes time to operate. Perhaps this again is more of a control, a way of leading to the lesson's main attraction. To invite children to lie on the floor and to perform tasks the reason for which they are unsure is often to court disaster. Sometimes the main part of the lesson becomes for the children indistinguishable from the warm-up period, with the result that lesson control becomes difficult to maintain.

3. Why do we use the term 'story' for that part of a lesson that deals not in narrative but in drama? Does this story of the Western bank raid constitute the plot? Can the plot of any play exist apart from the dialogue that arises from the interaction of the characters? Is the plot of the play what the play is about?

In this example the story represents what is required by the teacher to be animated; the set of instructions, cued by music, which the children will obey through mime. If there is any freedom or creativity here, it lies in those details with which the child fills out the role. Yet because it lacks speech, the action must be very generalized so that the characters are, in fact, caricatures. The main street is not drawn to life but as a cartoon strip; the banal characters are predictable because they are drawn from the common pool of media stereotypes. At no time are the children able to influence the choice of theme, to comment upon it, to improve upon it. It has been decided who they are, where they are, what they should feel and do, and, worse, when they should feel and do it.

Nothing could be further from the nature of the creative arts; nothing could be further from a true educational concern. Nothing could more distort the face of drama, or reveal more clearly an immense confusion of aims—the blind teacher leading blind children down a road that leads nowhere.

4. What then are its underlying assumptions? These are two-fold, and may be thought of as the conscious and the unconscious, or the intentional and the unintentional. It was the conscious intention of the teacher to create an enjoyable experience, and it was her assumption that the class was eager to be involved in a drama lesson. She also wanted to share her own excitement invoked by the music, to harness it and to produce some creative and expressive work. It was her intention to get the class working together on a task which they would see accomplished with its attendant satisfaction. All were praiseworth intentions, and the assumption might have been correct, though none shoud take it for

granted that drama is preferable to mathematics or geography. Why was it, then, that the intentions were not realized, assuming the criticism to be valid?

The answer may lie in the unconscious belief that authority is the teacher's alone and that all things that happen in the classroom operate within that sanction. There is an assumption that the children know why they are doing what they are being asked to do, and have agreed to it. It assumes that the best ideas are the teacher's and that the lesson's success is demonstrated by the animation of them by the children, cued by music chosen and controlled by the teacher. It would be as though she dictated all their essays or as if the class painted by numbers she had prepared. The latter examples reveal how ludicrous such a situation would be, and yet in the name of drama it is perpetrated, and with wide spread incidence.

All work in the arts must acknowledge individual, creative need; must admit and foster the genuine expressive and communcative act. It must allow for real experience to be applied so that its significance may be discerned. So to ban talking from drama is like forbidding sounds in music or colours in art.

Fergusson, in *The Idea of a Theatre*, says, 'Drama eventuates in words'; the words spring from the act and promote a reaction. They reveal or conceal, admit or deny, extend or terminate, evade or express the feelings that exist between people.

Also, because drama is a social art that depends for its existence on consensus, language perpetually defines the limits within which the invention will operate. Words are a major part of the planning, the execution, and the reflection upon any piece of dramatic work undertaken in the classroom. Drama the perfect model of the social process, naturally employs language which is the major social, expressive, and communicative tool.

Drama is not merely oracy, however, and there is a danger that, in swinging from the movement-and-music approach, the pendulum may exaggerate the role of pupil–pupil, teacher–pupil talk to an extent that all that lies beyond words or between them gets lost and we have no longer 'an imitation of an action'. Everything can become too rational, too analytic, so that the dramatic conflict is regarded as potentially anarchic and is stifled at birth.

## 12.2 Drama as a means of learning

Drama represents a way of organizing experience by creating a heightened awareness through the play of language and gesture.

In this way it is possible to create a significant present in which the participant is able to develop both the perception and communication of social truths. The form works through action and reaction and is akin to other games that demand move and counter-move, startegies, and rules.

If there is a genuine child-based invention, then the 'story' or theme is only the outward, visible form of the inner concerns of the group. Thus a play about bank robbers explores the concepts of loyalty or compassion; a play about space travel questions the values that the invaders bring or those with which they are met by the indigenous population. The drama enables the subjective examination of such a topic as feudalism, the implications of the prodigal son, or the skill of Fagin's beguiling method of pickpocket training. This treatment assists the class not only to remember details of the story, but also to reflect beyond it.

Most teachers need to be clear about what they teach and why; the 'how' will always involve to a degree a measure of the intuitive, the immediate interaction of personalities. Nor is it any help to counsel the replacement of those teaching skills that have been acquired. Again, there is no prescription for how one should work, but there should be common understanding of why and to what end.

Having considered the reasons why we feel the example lesson is unsatisfactory, it is obviously important to turn now to a more constructive approach.

## 12.3 Stages in the drama lesson

To conduct a drama lesson is to conduct a way of learning, for it assists the development of perception–understanding, awareness, insight—and also expression, the ability to communicate insights in dramatic form. This process may be identified as happening in the course of a lesson or lessons, and its progress may be described as occurring within six broad stages: enquiry, decision, definition, committal, reflection, and appraisal. The process is represented in Fig. 12.1 which is a rocker model, that is, one that shows the action of perception and expression as a constant interaction and not a sequential experience; for it often happens that the expression of an idea clarifies it and sharpens the perception, which in turn assists better expression, and so on.

It may be of value to examine the model stage by stage, to expand upon the brief accompanying notes and to reflect upon the language content at each stage. But first it should be stressed that, while progression through all stages in one lesson is possible, it does

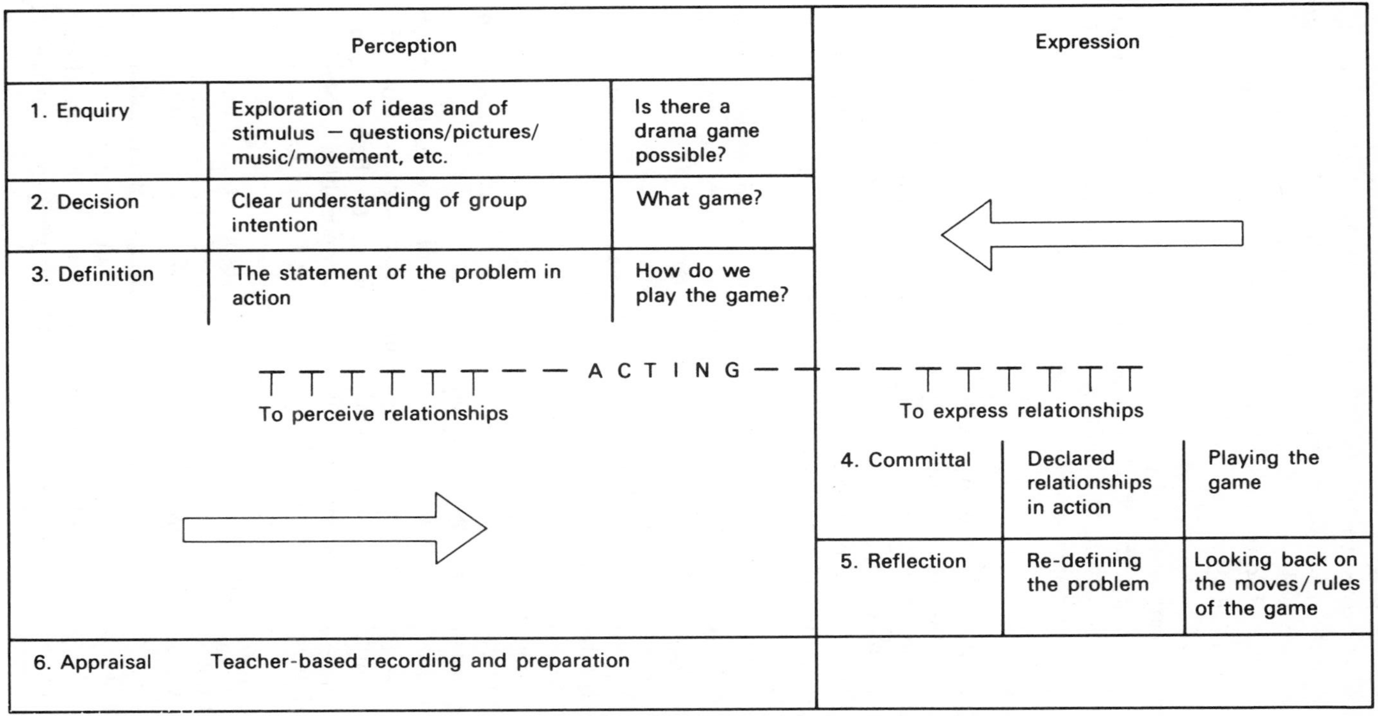

| | Perception | | Expression | |
|---|---|---|---|---|
| 1. Enquiry | Exploration of ideas and of stimulus — questions/pictures/music/movement, etc. | Is there a drama game possible? | | |
| 2. Decision | Clear understanding of group intention | What game? | | |
| 3. Definition | The statement of the problem in action | How do we play the game? | | |
| | — — — — — — A C T I N G — — — — — — | | | |
| | To perceive relationships | | To express relationships | |
| 4. Committal | | | Declared relationships in action | Playing the game |
| 5. Reflection | | | Re-defining the problem | Looking back on the moves/rules of the game |
| 6. Appraisal | Teacher-based recording and preparation | | | |

Fig. 12.1 Drama model for lesson analysis

not of itself constitute success. The class will reveal what stage they are at, and to attempt to rush them through work for which they are not ready is a waste of time. Frequently lessons do not get beyond the 'enquiry' stage, while the one in the example lesson above did not even get that far.

Like every other lesson, drama requires a start, a focus for the attention, interest, and potential involvement of the pupils. The difference lies in the degree of absorption and identification that it involves; for drama demands a willing suspension of disbelief, a commitment to play and to honour the rules of this particular game.

## Enquiry

The 'enquiry' period, whatever its stimulus—music, a picture, a piece of movement—must capture a genuine interest and not simply the coerced animation of the earlier example. Above all it should engage the teacher and the class in conversation. The teacher's questions should be designed to capture the pupil's deepening interest by causing him to feel and begin to explore his feelings in the safer medium of oral expression before he engages them in the dramatic medium. All those questioning skills already referred to in earlier chapters come into play to encourage reporting, imagining, reasoning, projecting:

1. What do you know about frontier towns?
2. Why would the townsfolk have gathered.
3. Why then would robbers have chosen that day to attack?
4. What do you think would happen to the robbers who surrendered?
5. What hopes do you think the robbers might have had of getting justice in a small prairie town?

This play is about not merely the act of robbery and murder, but about justice and mercy, the calculated assumption of the felon that if caught he can expect fair play. It hovers on the brink of one of the greatest questions, 'How is social order possible?' which is the constant reiterated question of the drama. It may be that in the 'enquiry' the answers to some of the questions may be explored in role play—prairie wives meeting after long isolation, the robbers planning the raid, the tip-off to the sheriff and by whom, the reaction of the townsfolk to the surrendered robbers. These are ways of living through an otherwise abstract examination, for drama is knowing by doing (just as many DIY manuals make sense only when one is acting upon the instructions as one reads them). They serve a distinct purpose: that of clarifying, of defining, of sharing experience, and, of course, of stimulating more direct talk. It is little wonder that tackling so complex a task may take up the whole lesson, but what does that matter if what has been done is of value and has been clearly appropriate to the class progress at that time? A tired class, a tired teacher, an excited class, an angry class, a timid class—all work fairly slowly; but an unco-operative class will not do anything at all, and persisting can be a waste of time.

We should however, beware of never looking beyond this stage, which is tempting, because, being often teacher-inspired, it is a very secure stage. We should be aware that for the drama lesson to become truly creative the onus must be laid upon the *class*, at the 'decision' stage.

### Decision

This stage of the lesson is marked by agreement to undertake a task; to explore some facet of human relationships, some aspect of human life. Often there will be an invitation 'to make a play', but this should not be thought of conforming to those literary models that are so familiar. What everyone has in common is that they examine an example of people who have a problem, i.e., human relationships under stress. But, as with the director assisting a cast to discover the play that lives hidden in the text, the teacher assists the class to be aware of the decision they are taking.

It can be that the challenge of making the decision is the 'enquiry'—sometimes from the earlier examination emerges that which the class wants to use as its play base. Let us suppose that the class has said it wishes to make a play about a dishonest teacher. The class is assisted by their teacher not merely to compose a story line, but to identify the problem. The class attempt to explain that children are more vulnerable: how can they accuse without proof? who is likely to be believed? and so on. The teacher probes their statements, may even play devil's advocate to test the commitment of all to this agreed topic.

The language here involves conversation between child and child, child and teacher. There are not only questions posed by the teacher but she offers opinions and challenges their statements—and they challenge hers. There can be a feeling of debate as the class argues for the teacher and themselves the dramatic potential of their choice. The teacher knows that their insights at this stage will be only partial, that the problem needs to be realized in action. But to pursue it in depth there must be that clarity of agreement, an understanding that everyone is playing the same game.

The danger lies in too much talk. We may exhaust the topic with the class orally and then invite exploration through drama when there is nothing left to explore. It is vital, therefore, that the teacher be aware of her contribution at this stage; that although the mood seems conversational, her object is clear—to assist the class to articulate an agreed intension.

### Definition

The 'definition' stage begins the examination in depth of the persons who make up the play. Through role play the class can establish necessary information about the dishonest teacher, the class, what articles have been stolen, and in what circumstances, why suspicion has fallen on the teacher, the dilemma of the students of how to accuse and to what authority.

Children adopt a borrowed personna; they recognize the rules of this invention because they are implicit in the social models that they are building. All this information is the raw material of the play. The teacher will encourage the class to chance its arm, to try out solutions no matter whether they succeed. The children's language will be planned speech as well as bursts of improvised dialogue. Sometimes the class needs to be stopped for a reminder or a redefinition of its decision; it needs to work always to a partially perceived end.

### Committal

The 'definition' and the 'committal' often merge imperceptibly. This occurs when the conscious planning stops, the teacher withdraws, the issues are being played out, and, though there is an agreed structure, the immediate, significant present is being created moment by moment. The children offer each other cues so that momentum is maintained, yet the piece is rich in invention. It is true improvisation, the freedom to invent and embellish, but always within the agreed structure.

The way the dilemma is presented and the degree to which it is resolved reflects the social maturity of the class. But it is their play, and their solutions must be accepted.

What is being described in the 'committal' stage is that creative use of language referred to in the Bullock Report, but less divorced from a total concept of drama. The experience may be likened to the process of rehearsal and performance in a theatre; the gaining of perceptions in the rehearsal stage, a definition of the characters, their language and their relationships, and the committal to the full invention with audience as a vital creative element. Unless we recognize this unity of drama we cannot hope to maintain and enhance our theatre. Already many people regard theatre as live television, and may have lost the skill and understanding to participate as an audience. In order to gain such appreciation a child should encounter in his education the opportunity for dramatic expression and should come to know it as a valid and dynamic force.

## Reflection

This conscious appreciation of the dramatic mode of expression is the purpose of the 'reflection' stage of the drama lesson.

This operation needs careful handling to avoid demanding an expression of what has already been said, but in another way.

Henry Moore was reputed to have declined to explain his sculptures, saying if he could have used words then he would not have expressed himself in three-dimensional figures. Equally, the teacher should come to terms with what is being expressed and should not always press for explanation.

From the children's point of view they have set themselves a task and are being invited to evaluate the measure of their success. 'Was this good?' is a less relevant question than, 'Did this work?'

The accomplishment of the group's purpose and the means by which this was done is a part of the educative process. It gives the class the power to use judgement based on their skills as craftsmen in play-making. It assists them to apply those values in the appreciation of both live theatre and dramatic literature.

Often there is an over-concentration upon using language to report events at this stage. Care should be taken to maintain the creative momentum by encouraging pupils to reason, project, and imagine around this situation they have created.

The lives of others have been truly entered into: it is not only their condition that will be discussed, but, more importantly, how they help to symbolize a general aspect of the human condition.

Again, the appreciation of the art of drama as performer or spectator demands an understanding of the purpose of the plot and its characters. Children must be brought to a confidence in their own artistic sensibilities, to a knowing that does not always spring from the rational. Nor should this confidence be applied only to an appreciation of things, but also to people; to the relationships that are the basis of all social activity.

## Appraisal

The last stage takes place away from the classroom and is the teacher's appraisal of the significance of what she has been shown by the class. This appraisal will extend not only to their progress in dramatic appreciation, but also to their social and emotional growth. For it is impossible to separate the arts from the reality that they both celebrate and challenge. A major reason for the use of drama in schools lies in its value as a social model. It allows pupils to develop a wide range of social roles with appropriate language in a number of simulated social situations. This enables them to define the situation in which they find themselves and to conduct themselves in a way that they find comfortable and satisfying. This happens at both the fictional and the literal levels at the same time. The child draws upon his past experience to conduct himself through make-believe situations and it is in this new context that the significance of these experiences is revealed to him. There is an important exchange of experience that is not merely verbal but is dynamically embodied in the make-believe. The teacher can be shown very clearly how easily or with what difficulty a child can cope with both situations. The child who finds it difficult to relate, to share, to tolerate in the classroom may well find the same problems in the world at large.

The teacher will use this knowledge, along with knowledge from many other situations, to help the child to integrate without losing his essential individuality. The passage of the drama requires and promotes a kinship that is more sensitive than the sports field but equally interactive. It provides a host of norms and values that offer a field of enquiry for the class—loyalty, bravery, guilt, shame, injustice, exploitation. The list of these abstracts is endless and their exploration is the pursuit for a lifetime. They genuinely offer a way of considering not only the life skills but social values in a world where myth-making can change values so quickly.

Finally, the teacher can observe the class and its use of language in many formal and informal situations. Few educational contexts can offer as much, and in an activity that is truly child-centred. The model assists the teacher to plan, to observe, and to reflect upon the progress of the class. It is analytic but also synthetic; it can help in knowing where to go as much as in where one has been. It can make it easier for teachers to accept the insecurity of less formal approaches by revealing that genuine work in drama is rule-regulated to an extreme. Above all, it should assist the teacher and the pupils to derive from the drama lesson the principal benefit—enjoyment.

# 13. Children's literature

## 13.1 Introduction

> Now what I want is Facts. Teach these boys and girls nothing but Facts. Facts alone are wanted in life. Plant nothing else, and root out everything else. You can only form the minds of reasoning animals upon Facts: nothing else will ever be of any service to them . . . . Stick to Facts, Sir!

As we said before, there have always been people like Dickens's Mr Gradgrind, ready to argue that the business of schools is the teaching and learning of facts. And some of the current debate in education, with its emphasis on preparing children for 'working life', is looking that way. Children now entering school at age five will not be going into the world of work for 15 years, however, and no one knows what work will be like then, or how much of it there will be. In any case, it is a very poor reason for including 'literature' in the work of the primary school.

What facts does literature teach? Sometimes, facts *can* be learned from stories. For example, through reading Phillipa Pearce's subtle story, 'Fresh',[1] a reader will learn that a freshwater snail can live only as long as a constant current of fresh water passes over it, and that it will die in an aquarium. But the justification for including 'literature' in primary school work must surely be sought elsewhere.

## 13.2 Literature as stories and poems

By 'literature', we mean stories and poems; and we mean those that children read for themselves, those we read to them as teachers and parents, and those that they make up for themselves and share with their friends. It should be recognized that, although people who write stories and poems are often thought of as beings apart from the rest of humanity, we *all* make up stories and poems. 'Nature, not art, makes us all storytellers . . . narrative imagination is a common human possession', as Barbara Hardy has said.[2]

Through the stories and poems to which children are introduced, it is possible to let them see their own stories as having an added importance. In this connection, we should like to see a greater emphasis in primary school work on stories and anecdotes *told* by children and teachers, as we think that the place of the oral story has been undervalued.

It is also our view that, at least in the early stages of literacy, the power that children feel stories have for them lies behind the actual business of learning to read. There are some children, but not many, who learn to read at five or earlier because they want to find out *information* from books; but for most, it is wanting to know what happens in stories that excites them into wanting to learn to read. If this is true, then schools should ask how they can justify giving to early readers the kind of books which do not contain genuine stories.

And, as children know very well, the shortest stories are jokes.

## 13.3 Literature in learning

One reason why stories and poems are so important is that they are a major means of learning about life, a person's emotions, and morality. In all areas of the primary school curriculum the mental 'operations' that children perform seem to be the same: they include representing, classifying and categorizing, generalizing, and hypothesizing. There are several languages available for doing this—the mathematical, the musical, and the visual. Word language has certain advantages over all of these, as we have already shown. People who write stories invite their readers to enter into another world, and they discuss with them what *might* happen there. They ask their readers to *suppose* along with them. And in responding to stories and poems, at whatever level, readers and listeners do their own supposing or hypothesizing. Two nine-year-old boys were talking about Daedalus and what he might be doing on the Island of Icaria after his son's body has been washed up at his feet.[3] They hypothesized that he might be sitting there praying or crying, or that he might have saved a life so that he could have his son's life back again, or that he might have eaten something and grown young again. Of course, the two boys were not conscious that they were making hypotheses: very few people are actually conscious that all of their learning depends on making and testing hypotheses, and then either accepting, modifying, or rejecting them.

In another example, a group of 10-year-old children were discussing *Stig of the Dump*,[4] since by the end of the first chapter they were still puzzled to know who Stig was and how he got into the dump. They hypothesized that Stig's parents might have been killed in a plane crash, and that because Stig never heard any adults speaking he could not learn to speak himself. (Linguists have written many learned books about such theories of language acquisition.) Later, we shall return to the question of children's responses to stories and poems, and how teachers can encourage this kind of learning through hypothesizing. But we would wish to note here that many of the oral group activities for reading development, such as a group prediction exercises and group cloze procedure—about which we mentioned our reservations earlier—are designed to encourage and make more explicit this activity of hypothesizing in relation to reading.

## 13.4 Literature for empathy

In experiencing stories and poems, children can project themselves into other people doing other deeds, and so they learn to understand other people and their characters and motives, and they learn to be more sympathetic. As children grow out of their egocentricity, they become more compassionate. The boys talking about Daedalus were learning about making hypotheses; and they were also learning about the human emotions of jealousy, about retribution and forgiveness—because they knew that Daedalus was being punished through the death of Icarus for the murder of his nephew Talos.

In Celia Berridge's *Runaway Danny*,[5] Danny runs out of the playground on his first morning at his new school because he is disappointed and unhappy and the other lads refuse to let him join in their game of football. Most boys can understand Danny's feelings. In *A Dog so Small* by Phillipa Pearce,[6] Ben was promised a dog by his grandparents as a birthday present, but the council forbade dogs, so they gave him a picture of a dog instead. The *fact* learned here is that a chihuahua is a Mexican miniature breed of dog; the *sympathetic understanding* learned is that, because Ben feels betrayed, he never wants to see his grandparents again.

These examples show children learning to feel empathy for the characters in stories. The great Russian folklorist Chukovsky pointed out that the goal of the storyteller is to 'awaken, nurture, and strengthen in the responsive soul of the child the invaluable ability to feel compassion for another's unhappiness and to share in another's happiness—without this a man is inhuman'.[7] It is not surprising that many stories for children are about animals: *The Tale of Peter Rabbit*[8] is a good example. This device takes human strengths and human weakness at a safe distance. And fairy tales tell the child exactly what Chukovsky asks of story—'to feel another's fate as one's own'. Thankfully, there is no such thing as a fascist fairy tale.

No one would suggest—and we certainly do not—that stories exist to solve readers' or listeners' personal problems. Yet it is true that to discover the characters in a story having the same fears and troubles and not dying of them is a comfort. Among other things, 'Hansel and Gretel'[9] tells a child that he may not be unique, and that others have been abandoned. Bernard Ashley's *Terry on the Fence*[10] is a story for older juniors. The hero Terry runs away from home because he is sick of being bossed about by his elder sister; he falls in with a gang who terrorize him into breaking into his own school and stealing transistor radios, and later is caught 'on the fence' about to carry out another raid. He is also on the fence morally, not knowing how to refuse doing what he knows is wrong as long as he is frightened of being bullied. Terry also discovers that he can feel sympathetic towards the leader of the gang, because he sees what made him into a bully. Terry's dilemma is one that most children will find recognizable.

A wise and informed choice of stories can be helpful, enabling children to 'sin at a safe distance'. Some teachers working with multi-racial groups have found that Rosemary Sutcliff's *The Eagle of the Ninth*[11] is a good way into the subject of slavery.

### 13.5 Literature as confirmation of personal experience

The stories and poems introduced to children will be recognizable to them in the face of their own experience, as they respond. We do not refer to the match between the material environment of the story and the child's, because this seems much less important than the experiences themselves. Why is it, for example, that *Where the Wild Things Are*[12] is so popular? It is adults, not children, who find the pictures uncomfortable. And the children recognize all the things happening in the story: Max being naughty and punished, Max running away, Max being so powerful that he can tame the wild things even though 'they roared their terrible roars and gnashed their terrible teeth and rolled their terrible eyes and showed their terrible claws' by simply 'staring into all their yellow eyes without blinking once'. And, as if this were not enough, there is Max who 'wants to be where someone loved him best of all', and Max who returns home, and Max who is forgiven. This story is a classic, in the proper sense of the word: there is a round journey, self-discovery in the process, and everything in it speaks directly to children.

There are many stories appropriate to all stages of a child's development that focus upon a central and recognizable experience. Many are about animals (as well as people) lost, or abandoned, or running away. There is 'Ping'[13] as well as *Mr Miacca*[14] at the earlier stage; there are the three robbers in Tomi Ungerer's book of that name[15] who are 'lost, betrayed and abandoned'; and later on there is Joan Robinson's *Charley*[16] and *From the Mixed-Up Files of Mrs Basil E. Frankweiler*[17] by E. L. Konigsburg, in which two children stake a claim for independence by camping out for a fortnight in the New York Metropolitan Museum of Art. This theme is seen, too, in adult literature, in the work of Joseph Conrad and Henry James.

Another theme immediately recognized by children is about size. The child has to discover how big he is in relation to the bigness of the world. And when he knows, he can change it, as Alice does. Giants and trolls, dwarfs and fairies abound in traditional stories. At one stage there is *The Giant Alexander*,[18] and at another, *The Shrinking of Treehorn*;[19] and the stories about Gulliver are outstanding examples for children of the shrink-story, although Swift's satire is certainly beyond most of them.

## 13.6 Literature for emotional experience

We think it is perilous for schools to ignore the education of children's emotions. We refer at several points in this book to the opportunities teachers should provide for children to express and to explore their emotions so that they learn to make constructive use of them. Primary school work includes, of course, many opportunities for this that are outside the field of a book about word language. Stories and poems are one way in which teachers can provide experiences of emotional weight, like this one, quoted in *Ways of Talking*.[20]

> Something tells me I am going to get licks
> I ent do nothing
> But I have a feeling
> Something will happen and I will get licks
> I think it because my left-eye jumping.
>
> Odette Thomas[21]

Many of Charles Keeping's picture books also illustrate the point we are making. In *Through the Window*,[22] Jacob has to watch events in the street outside from an upstairs window, and he sees an old woman's mangy dog run over by the brewers' dray horses. The people's faces are not shown and the text does not say what has happened, but the twisted lines of the shoulder's and the hands speak of the woman's tears and Mr Willett's attempts to comfort her. Alan Garner's *Elidor*[23] is another example, where children will be deeply affected by the closing scene in which the mortally wounded unicorn sings to save the world.

One of the devices that authors and poets used to give emotional weight to their writing is ambiguity. In books at the earlier stages, what happens in the stories is likely to be relatively unambiguous—there is no doubt about Jack and the Giant, for instance; and in *The Wolf and the Seven Little Kids*,[24] there can be no moral doubt that the big bad wolf suffers a deserved fate. But as children grow in maturity, so stories should become more ambiguous. Moral issues are not quite so clear-cut, and the meaning of a story not quite so simple. What kind of character is Long John Silver? He cannot be wholly good, because *Treasure Island* tells that he has done some wicked things in his time, but on the other hand he cannot be wholly bad, otherwise there would not have been such a quality to his relationship with young Jim Hawkins.

The quartet of books by Alan Garner that begins with *The Stone Book*[25] and ends with *Tom Fobble's Day* possesses a high degree of ambiguity which the responsive reader needs to tease out of the text. It is not always clear from the surface what is going on. Another remarkable example is the ending of Robert O'Brien's *Z for Zachariah*,[26] for the oldest juniors, perhaps. Poems like Charles Causley's[27] and many of the examples in *Junior Voices*[28] use the music of words to create powerful feelings in the listener, even when the ballad or the narrative is not in the least ambiguous.

## 13.7 Literature for pleasure

Perhaps we should have begun this chapter by saying that reading stories is for fun, not facts. Fun is undoubtedly a most important factor, and children delight in nonsense rhymes like:

> Algy met a bear
> A bear met Algy
> The bear was bulgy
> The bulge was Algy

Unfortunately, too many funny books written for children have an adult wit. Is the knickered humour of Spike Milligan something that children laugh at more or less than at Professor Branestawm?[29] Banana-skin humour and pomposity deflated—and every child knows that a naked king is hilarious—turn into a delight at puns, and the more atrocious the better. So, Norton Juster's *The Phantom Tollbooth*[30] is a book for the maturer reader (it coincidentally has an interesting definition of infinity).

There is also, in our view, a sheer pleasure in words to be encouraged through a good choice of stories and poems. For example, here is Ben Hazen's description of the sorcerer's laboratory before the apprentice receives his come-uppance:

> There stood the sorcerer's kiln, his cosmic oven, and the distillery where he made his secret chemical concoctions. And, there, too, were all the other tools of the sorcerer's trade: cauldrons and kettles, flagons and flasks, alantirs and ampulars, bubbling beakers and vapour-filled vessels—and piles of phosphorescent stones ready to be pulverised into magic powders and potions.[31]

Many language models can be demonstrated to children through the stories and poems chosen for reading aloud to them, and certain descriptions may well be savoured for a long time to come. *The Iron Man* has a special place for this reason among many. The language structures of the opening illustrate what we mean:

> The Iron Man came to the top of the cliff.
> How far had he walked? Nobody knows. Where had he come from? Nobody knows. How was he made? Nobody knows.
> Taller than a house, the Iron Man stood at the top of the cliff, on the very brink, in the darkness.
> The wind sang through his iron fingers.[32]

## 13.8 Literature for life

We have suggested that the knowledge children possess of stories and poems—those they have read, those they have had read to them, and those they have made themselves and perhaps told—benefits them in a variety of way. They gain:

1. An ability to make hypotheses in experiencing narrative and responding to it.
2. A growth of compassion.
3. An awareness of character and motive.
4. The opportunity of working through problems.
5. A growing tolerance of ambiguity.
6. The confirmation of personal experience.
7. The provision of emotional experience.
8. Enjoyment from reading/listening to stories.
9. A growing knowledge of vocabulary and language structures.

Examples have illustrated all of these points. We have also suggested that these gains are most likely to occur if the stories and poems are related to the cognitive, affective, and moral development of the children. This is one of the reasons why recommending books to other people is always such a chancy business, even though it is one of the important ways in which readers are made. The question of how children's choice is to be guided, if at all, and of what book provision should be made is taken up in the next chapter on the school's book policy. We would only point out here that sometimes the chief argument about what stories and poems to share with children hinges upon what the teaching programme dictates rather than on what is most relevant to the child. We think that it is a misuse of children's 'literature' to use it solely for what can be squeezed out of it into the topic on, say, volcanoes or the Vikings.

But we need now to take our argument deeper. The Bullock Report held that literature shapes the personality, refines the sensibility, and sharpens the critical intelligence; that literature is an instrument for the acquisition of empathy and values; that it is a personal resource reflecting a reader's fantasies and conflicts at any given moment; and that, responding to it, we refer it to our own experience and interpret, project, anticipate, and speculate.

While agreeing with these statements, we would wish to go even further.

Story and poem—in fact, all narrative forms—are about how to express feelings, about how to 'cleanse the doors of perception'; so that the child experiencing the narrative can find through it a harmony between in-here and out-there, between the things that are pressing inside him and the things outside him over which he has less control. Narratives are about a world that the child might like to have, and in that world he can practise the acts and emotions of the really-lived life. It is said that *The Hobbit*[33] was once banned in a public children's library on the grounds that escapist literature was not good for children. In answer to that, Ursula le Guin wrote: 'false realism is the escapist literature of our time'.

Narrative is a way of drawing up and testing out alternative models by which to live, as the examples quoted have clearly demonstrated. There is nothing to be gained or lost by drawing up and testing these models, because no one is required to go out and perform some immediate action after reading or hearing a story; no one need apply what the author has said. The reader or listener is a 'spectator' of the story and the characters and the events, a spectator of an idealized world. And because the spectator is freed from the necessity of taking any action as a result of the story, he is better able to make use of the narrative in order to find a harmony between his own inner necessities and the external demands laid upon him by the world in which he lives.

We would, therefore, agree that human beings may live 'more by fiction than by fact',1 as R. L. Gregory pointed out,[34] and that the place of literature in the work of the primary school is to foster this kind of living.

We also believe that there is great affective or emotional satisfaction to be gained from handling the images of stories and poems in 'play'; and that in this sense, too, all kinds of narrative enable the child to assimilate to his own experience and to accommodate to the world outside. This is simply another way, a Piagetian one this time, of looking at the harmony between outside and inside of which we have been speaking.

Our argument about the importance of 'literature' in the language work of the school has shifted from the specific gains with which we began to something more radical. We now say that stories and poems, made and received, are both natural and necessary to human experience and have a crucial bearing on how children see themselves, their world, and their part in it.

Perhaps by looking at 'literature for life' in this way, the idea of any elite of children's books or of a literary heritage can be avoided. Although we may not admire Enid Blyton's work, for example, we cannot deny that her books may have a place in a reader's development. Children may then be able to surprise every one with what they can bring to stories and poems of their own and with what they can take away from them. Their responses to *A Wizard of Earthsea*[35] and its two sequels, their discussion of the alternative forms of society depicted in *Mrs Frisby and the Rats of NIMH*[36] or of the nature of religious belief as put forward in *Shardik*[37] or of the kinds of dilema contained in *Grinny*,[38] may be much more apt than expected.

In Hans Andersen's story 'The Snow Queen'[39] (which is a private myth, not a fairy story), the boy Kay is frozen by a sliver of ice lodged in his heart. It is Gerda who rescues him from the Snow Queen's palace. We are here concenred that children denied a rich diet of appropriate stories and poems of all kinds may grow up like Kay—frozen—and taught to forget that the world ever gave them anything to sing about. The notion of the frozen child is Barbara Dockar-Drysdale's: 'all of us have unsung songs, unpainted pictures, unwritten pieces of music inside us.'[40]

In this area between the inner and the outer, children create their own imaginative and emotional inner worlds, populated by the secret and private things they need to make life tolerable. 'Literature' tells them that they are right to do so.

## 13.9 Response

It is beyond the bounds of possibility that the kinds of gains from stories and poems that have been discussed could be achieved by testing the children's 'comprehension'. It seems that the only way of helping children towards these kinds of gains is by the sort of open group discussion already described.

It is vital that teachers spend more time talking to children on equal terms about what they have been reading, and without always knowing all the answers in advance, and less time hearing children reading aloud. Reading aloud is one of the things children like least about reading; most of them wish that they were given more time for reading silently on their own. It is equally vital that children have more time for talking together among themselves about what they read; this is how adult readers go about it.

The children's discussion about *Stig of the Dump* has already been mentioned. Here is a short extract from the transcript.

| | |
|---|---|
| Jose | Yes, but how, how did he come to life, how did, what was he? |
| Mark | If he was a baby, he couldn't have survived. |
| Jose | And did he have any parents? |
| Mary | Well maybe in the plane crash. |
| Francesca | They died. |
| Mary | They died in the plane crash. |
| Mark | If there was a plane crash. |
| Mary | Well, there could be, and there . . . |
| Theo | We'll have to wait till . . . |
| Mark | It might not even tell you in, in the story itself. The story itself is really good because—some—usually stories start off like *The Hobbit*. Remember? It was all explaining, explaining who is who, Gandalf was this and Gandalf was that, but in this it goes straight on to what happened. Barney meets Stig and . . . |
| Theo | But there could be another book showing this. |
| Jose | Yes, like *The Witch and the Wardrobe* or something. |
| Theo | Like *Five on a Treasure Island*. |
| Jose | It could be a continuation. |
| Francesca | Like Clifford. There's many books about Clifford. |
| Mary | Clifford just goes on and on. |
| Jose | Yes, well, we're not discussing that. We're discussing about Stig and Barney, aren't we? Now, Stig and Barney, here, it says somewhere that he lived, he had everything made out of old rubbish and things. |

The teacher is not present and the children have had no experience of this kind of work. They do very well, taking it in turns to control the drift of the discussion. As they work towards a common understanding of the story so far, and its possibilities, they make comparisons with other stories that they know and make some quite mature judgements. They go on to remind each other of certain features of the story, and question how bracken can be growing on a chalk cliff and where the trees have come from. A discussion like this, ranging widely and producing such insights, would not have happened if the teacher had had preconceived notions about what should have taken place.

An important paragraph of the Bullock Report states that: 'to accept what is offered when we are told something, we have to have somewhere to put it . . . the framework of past knowledge and experience into which it must fit',[41] so that the new knowledge can be interpreted and apprehended. This same crucial point is made by Leo Lionni in *Fish is Fish*,[42] using pictures as well as text. The tadpole and the fish live together in the stream, but presently the tadpole becomes a frog and he goes travelling. When he returns to spawn, he explains to his fishy friend about the cows, but the fish sees them in his mind's eye with fins and tails. Similarly, in responding to stories and poems, children must begin by relating them to their own experience and what they already know. As the Rosens have pointed out, one way of talking about a story is 'to tell another one, or one like it'.[43] Here is Melanie, aged six, making up a story on request:

> Once upon a time there was a rabbit, and a daddy rabbit, and a mummy rabbit, and the queen rabbit, she, she was the best rabbit of all of them. One day, a witch rabbit came by, and, the witch took the princess rabbit, and the princess rabbit, when she made a ladder, and she climbed down from where she was staying, where the witch had put her, and, she went back to her mother, and one day when she was going out she met, a prince, and they got married.

It will be evident that this is 'Rapunzel'[44] rewritten for rabbits.

Sometimes the response will be a written one; and other forms of response than the spoken and the written are, of course, possible. The vocabulary and forms and style of the models shown to the children in the stories and poems they meet sometimes come back. Here is an 11-year-old writing:

> Loud shouts came from the court of King Arthur as they were having a Christmas Party. Then a tall green man rode in on a green

horse and so huge he must have been a giant. King Arthur said: 'What do ye want on this Christmas Day?' The giant said in a bold voice, 'I have come to ask one of King Arthur's knights to strike my head off and in a year's time to let me repay the blow.' He stopped. Not one of the knights answered to this for fear of losing his head. Then the giant said, 'If these are the knights of King Arthur's court, they're all as soft as putty. There is not one brave one amongst you.'

There is a satisfying balance here between the boy's originality and what he has derived from the telling he had heard.

We believe that children should not be forced into making permanent responses to stories and poems, although teachers do often feel constrained to provide visible proof of the work that has been done in class. We would not maintain that stories and poems are never starting points for further work—we know of instances where, for example, historical novels like *The Wool-Pack*[45] have started children off on exciting quests. We also know of a teacher who said provocatively: 'What do I do after reading *The House of Sixty Fathers*[46] to my children? Go down the hall and dramatize the bombing of Vietnam?' The warning sounded by the Rosens against the way 'literature' is sometimes killed dead in school is one that should be noted.

> It is as though there is a deep lack of confidence in the power of literature to do its work and a profound conviction that unless literature can be converted into the hard currency of familiar school learning it has not earned its keep. What will take the children more deeply into the experience of the book? This is the question we should be asking rather than, by what means can I use this book as a launching-pad into any one of a dozen endeavours, which leaves the book further and further behind, at best distant sound, at worst forgotten entirely?[43]

## 13.10 The read-aloud programme

It has already been suggested that a rich diet of story and poem is likely to lead to gains in the children's knowledge of vocabulary and language structure, in addition to all the other gains. But a good read-aloud programme is of importance for reasons not yet given.

Children at the initial stages of literacy are more likely to be motivated by an interest in fiction than fact. The read-aloud programme introduces them to the kind of language they will meet in books they read for themselves. However much book language and spoken language are the same, they are also different, and people do not generally speak like books. By reading widely to children, teachers can help them with their reading because they will then know that much more about the nature of the task, about the language of books, and how printed words work. And they will also know more about narrative structure. They will know, for example, about the rule of three in traditional stories, and after a time will be able to predict the pattern of events; they will also know that the simpleton is going to win, and that the poor man's son is better than the prince any day of the week. In addition, the read-aloud programme will introduce children to some books that are beyond their present reading grasp, giving them something for which to reach.

The story time is often, rightly, a special part of the school day, and we will be discussing its timing and setting in the next chapter.

## 13.11 Conclusion

The argument put forward in this chapter has been a simple one, and it ties together what was said earlier about literacy with what has been said here about 'literature'. If the power that motivates children in learning to read is fiction, then it makes sense that a rich read-aloud programme of fiction will enable children to read more readily and to continue developing as readers. Teachers begin with where the children are, if they are to be successful; and literature is where the children are. Furthermore, they deserve to have stories not only because they have to be taught about literature, but also because they are alive, and stories tell them what it is like to be alive.

There is a further aspect of this which has not yet been mentioned. Children are much more likely to become lasting readers if, as well as everything else that has been described, they meet adults who care *as adults* about reading. How often do children who are being taught and exhorted to read see their teachers reading, and responding to and discussing what they have read in a way to suggest that they themselves care for reading? It is our belief that schools need to find ways of demonstrating to children a spectacle of 'reading in action', as Edward Blishen once called it.

This point leads into a discussion of a school's book policy in the next chapter.

## References

Books marked with an asterisk are for teachers; all books not marked are for children and teachers.

1. PEARCE, PHILLIPA, 'Fresh', in *What the Neighbours Did,* Puffin, 1975.
*2. HARDY, BARBARA, *Tellers and Listeners,* Athlone Press, 1975.
3. SERRAILLIER, IAN, *Fall from the Sky,* Nelson, 1970.
4. KING, CLIVE, *Stig of the Dump,* Puffin, 1970.
5. BERRIDGE, CELIA, *Runaway Danny,* André Deutsch, 1975.
6. PEARCE, PHILLIPA, *A Dog so Small,* Puffin, 1970.
*7. CHUKOVSKY, KORNEI, *From Two to Five,* University of California Press, 1963.
8. POTTER, BEATRIX, *The Tale of Peter Rabbit,* Warne, 1902.
9. GRIMM BROTHERS, *'Hansel and Gretel',* Bodley Head, 1970.
10. ASHLEY, BERNARD, *Terry on the Fence,* Oxford University Press, 1975.
11. SUTCLIFF, ROSEMARY, *The Eagle of the Ninth,* Puffin, 1977.
12. SENDAK, MAURICE, *Where the Wild Things Are,* Puffin, 1970.
13. FLACK, MARJORIE, *The Story of Ping,* Bodley Head, 1935.
14. JACOBS, JOSEPH, *Mr Miacca,* Bodley Head, 1968
15. UNGERER, TOMI, *The Three Robbers,* Methuen, 1978.
16. ROBINSON, JOAN, *Charley,* Collins, Armada Lion, 1973.
17. KONIGSBURG, E. L., *From the Mixed-Up Files of Mrs Basil E. Frankweiler,* Puffin, 1974.
18. HERRMANN, FRANK, *The Giant Alexander,* Methuen, 1964.
19. HEIDE, F. P., *The Shrinking of Treehorn,* Puffin, 1975.
20. JACKSON, DAVID, *Ways of Talking,* Ward Lock, 1978.
21. THOMAS, ODETTE, 'A Sign', from *Rain Falling, Sun Shining,* Bogle L'Ouverture Publications, 1975.
22. KEEPING, CHARLES, *Through the Window,* Oxford University Press, 1970.
23. GARNER, ALAN, *Elidor,* Collins, Armada Lion, 1965.
24. HOFFMANN, FELIX, *The Wolf and the Seven Little Kids,* Oxford University Press, O/P.
25. GARNER, ALAN, *The Stone Book,* Collins, 1976.
26. O'BRIEN, ROBERT, *Z for Zachariah,* Collins, Armada Lion 1976.
27. CAUSLEY, CHARLES, *Collected Poems,* Macmillan, 1975.
28. SUMMERFIELD, GEOFFREY, *Junior Voices,* Puffin, 1970.
29. HUNTER, NORMAN, *Professor Branestawm,* Puffin, 1969.
30. JUSTER, NORTON, *The Phantom Tollbooth,* Collins, 1974.
31. HAZEN, B., *The Sorcerer's Apprentice,* Methuen, 1971.
32. HUGHES, TED, *The Iron Man,* Faber, 1968.

33. TOLKIEN, J. R. R., *The Hobbit*, Allen & Unwin, 1966.
*34. GREGORY, R. L., 'Psychology: towards a science of fiction', in *The Cool Web*, Bodley Head, 1977
35. LeGUIN, URSULA, *A Wizard of Earthsea*, Puffin, 1971.
36. O'BRIEN, ROBERT, *Mrs Frisby and the Rats of Nimh*, Puffin, 1975.
37. ADAMS, RICHARD, *Shardik*, Puffin, 1976.
38. FISK, NICHOLAS, *Grinny*, Puffin, 1975.
39. ANDERSEN, HANS, *The Snow Queen*, Bodley Head, 1975.
*40. DOCKAR-DRYSDALE, BARBARA, *Theraphy in Child Care*, Longman, 1968.
*41. *A Language for Life*, (the Bullock Report), HMSO, 1975.
42. LIONNI, LEO, *Fish is Fish*, Puffin, 1974.
*43. ROSEN, CONNIE and HAROLD, *The Language of Primary School Children*, Penguin, 1973.
44. HOFFMANN, FELIX, 'Rapunzel', Oxford University Press, O/P.
45. HARNETT, CYNTHIA, *The Wool-Pack*, Puffin, 1961.
46. DeJONG, MEINDERT, *The House of Sixty Fathers*, Puffin, 1971.

## Suggested Reading

COOK, E., *The Ordinary and the Fabulous*, 2nd ed., Cambridge University Press, 1977. As an introduction to myths, legends, and fairy stories, this is an invaluable guide in matters of choice and presentation.

FISHER, M., *Intent Upon Reading*, Brockhampton Press, 1946. It carries the subtitle, 'A Critical Appraisal of Modern Fiction for Children', and examines different kinds of children's stories in relation to their lives and their reading.

JONES, A. and BUTTREY, J., *Children and Stories*, Blackwell, 1970. A discussion of the importance of stories in children's lives, the kinds of response they might make, and the criteria for selection. It is a book full of practical ideas.

MEEK, M., WARLOW, A., and BARTON, G., *The Cool Web*, Bodley Head, 1977. A collection of papers by scholars, authors, and critics, arranged in five sections and all linked by explanatory inter-chapters. Many of these papers develop in greater detail the arguments put forward in this chapter.

TOWNSEND, J. R., *Written for Children*, Penguin, 1976. The revolution in children's book publishing over the last 30 years is amply demonstrated in this historical survey. Because of the lightness of touch it is a delight to read as well as being shrewd and thought-provoking.

# 14. Towards a school book policy

## 14.1 Introducing a Book Policy

The Bullock Report recommended that every primary school 'should have a book policy that reflects a set of objectives understood and accepted by the staff'.[1]

This book policy will be one of the major elements in a school's language policy and programme, and possibly a much more significant element than was realized when the Report was written.

The Bullock Report saw a book policy mainly in terms of a design for acquiring books so that stock does not 'grow by a process of random accretion'. The *proportions* between the different categories of books and their reading levels should be known, and further provision should be made in the light of the teachers' knowledge of the children. The older the children, the wider will be the spread of reading levels to be catered for; in a fourth-year junior class, for example, the range might be from reading level seven years to 14 years or more. And vertically grouped classes need special consideration, since the range may be even wider. But another question to be asked is whether the designed provision of books applies only to the 'library' books. Should it also take into account *all* the printed material that the children are likely to meet in school, from books for reading instruction to mathematics books and textbooks for social studies? How often are graded readers brought within the design of a school's book policy?

In most schools, one member of staff is responsible for the book policy. The Bullock Committee found that this teacher's task was often purely administrative, consisting of cataloguing, classifying, and administering the loan system. In addition, the recent Primary Survey[2] has pointed out that teachers with special responsibilities need the time and the standing to carry out their duties if they are to be effective. A school needs, therefore, to work out how responsibility for the book policy relates to other responsibilities, such as those for language development and mathematics.

In our opinion, the responsibility for formulating and carrying out the school's book policy must always remain a *collective* one, because every teacher is involved so closely with the teaching of literacy and the use of books. Although knowing about children's books and sources of information demands a constant effort to keep up to date, the selection of material is something that ought to concern every teacher. The person responsible for the book policy will no doubt be taking a lead in seeking out information, exchanging views, developing the reading curriculum, and also in developing children who are readers with personal tastes. But all of these functions are also the responsibility of every other member of staff.

Part of the book policy involves working out a procedure for the ordering of new books in which every member of staff can play a part. Some schools encourage children to bring books they think other children might like and which ought to be in the collection. This, like taking children to book exhibitions and bookshops and school library service points, is a way of involving them, too, in book selection.

Thought will also have to be given to the way in which books are fed into the school's system, so that children and teachers know what new books are available. As they are delivered, these new books can be made the subject of special displays and promotion. Holding a range of catalogues and review journals, visiting exhibitions, and browsing through bookshops are all ways of knowing what new books are being published, but they are not good enough substitutes for reading the books themselves.

In some schools, every member of staff undertakes to read one new children's book a month, and to introduce it briefly at a staff meeting later. During the course of a year, perhaps 100 new books might be discussed in this way—poetry, fiction, and information.

It will already be clear that a book policy means far more than simply the provision of books and their dispersal throughout the school. Although a book policy will almost certainly begin as a survey of the existing book stock, we would like to see it as something far more dynamic, as an instrument of the school's beliefs and purposes. And it must be, we feel, closely related to understanding such matters as reading process and how readers are made—the kinds of concern that have been expressed all through this book and that will be enshrined in the school's language policy as a whole.

It will be useful now to consider the book policy further under three headings:
1. Book provision and selection.
2. The organization and deployment of the books.
3. The purposes for which they are to be used.

## 14.2 Book provision and selection

The Bullock Report says that the classroom book collection should contain 'an encyclopaedia, a good dictionary, a good atlas, a collection of books ranging across the children's interests and touching all the major areas of the curriculum, a shelf of poetry and a range of fiction'.[3] Another of the Report's findings was that school book collections are often weighted towards information books to the neglect of fiction.

A school may well decide to list all the different categories of books that are to be provided and the proportions between them that are desirable. Information and reference books will include those for enquiry and the identification of specimens, more than one dictionary—some attend to derivations, others to alternative word meanings—and several atlases, which are notoriously difficult books for young children to comprehend. The encyclopaedias need to be chosen with great care: some children think these compendiums of information will answer all their needs for facts, but such books inevitably tend to deal in very generalized knowledge, and the arrangement of material does not follow a standard pattern. Of course, encyclopaedias are marvellous for browsing, and some consideration should be given to the amount of time allowed for browsing. Another reference book thumbed to death is the *Guinness Book of Records*,[4] a collection of fascinating superlatives which children like to possess in their memories like magpies are drawn to bright objects. Class book collections need more 'browsers' of this kind.

In framing a book policy, it may also be helpful to specify the *kinds* of fiction. Animal and family stories, mysteries, fantasy, adventure, stories about the here-and-now, those taking some account of the children's backgrounds, and stories about people of other times and in other places might all be included. Myths, legends, fairy stories, and folk tales are all traditional material, and essential. Examples of most of these categories were cited to support our argument for the importance of children's literature in the previous chapter. A popular argument in the world of children's books over the last few years has concerned the extent to which children wish to read about children like themselves. We have already made our position clear on this point.

The shelf of poetry will consist of action and nursery rhymes and nonsense verse. The selection will probably also consider the place of narrative and descriptive poetry, including ballad form and more introspective work; the range might be from material like

*London Bridge is Falling Down* [5] and Nicholas Tucker's collection, *Mother Goose Lost*, [6] to *The Pied Piper of Hamelin*. [7] The work of poets like Charles Causley [8] and Michael Rosen, [9] as well as anthologies such as Geoffrey Summerfield's *Junior Voices*, [10] should demonstrate to children that poetry need not be childish or precious, or always about fairies and flowers. Over the last year or two, an increasing number of anthologies has appeared in which poems and short prose stories are mixed: *Storyhouses* [11] is an outstanding example of this kind of book, showing a clear understanding of the art of narrative and the variety of its forms in the way the material is arranged and presented, interspersed with jokes, cartoons, drawings, and pictures in colour.

The provision will also include picture books, a category special enough to be considered separately. There will be paperbacks; and books written and made by children should certainly be a part of the collection. Most teachers would also want to include such ephemeral material as maps, guides, and magazines.

The other information books ranging across the children's interests and touching all the major areas of the curriculum are there to support the learning the teachers wish to have taking place, and to satisfy the children's own interests and enthusiasms.

There will almost certainly be a place for some adult books, which are often much more informative than those written for children, as well as the beautiful and expensive book about, say, brass rubbing. There will also be a need for material of purely local interest, especially as a support for environmental work going out into the school's neighbourhood.

Children's information books are not always examined critically enough, and we suggest that they might more often be looked at with some of these criteria in mind:

1. Is there a contents page, a list of illustrations, an index, a glossary, or a bibliography? Does the layout of the information help understanding and the location of a particular piece of information? The teaching of 'book skills' and how to find a required piece of information makes more sense if the books selected allow children to make use of these skills in their work.
2. Is the information general or specific? Is it in a logical sequence, and is the amount of detail appropriate?
   (The question of the readability of books will be taken up later (see page 246.)
3. Is the information accurate?
4. Is the vocabulary and language appropriate?

5. Are the illustrations linked to the text? Do they carry the required information, and are they captioned?

6. An increaing number of information books use captions as a second text parallel to the main one. Does it *look* different?

7. Is the book likely to involve the reader in making a response?

We think that too many information books written for children are treatments at second-hand so that their texts are dull and lifeless. It is always refreshing to find an author who writes about his subject with a kind of passion and who can communicate it to his child reader by speaking with a recognizable 'voice'. Richard Mabey's award-winning book *Street Flowers* is a notable example:

> Rosebay's seeds are a marvellous example of natural engineering. When the long pods are ripe, they unzip like bananas, and the downy seeds are gradually blown out by the wind. Each seed is fitted with a plume of about seventy silk hairs, which are nearly a centimetre long. But the seeds are so light it would take 1,000,000 to match the weight of one conker (the horse chestnut's seed).[12]

Some books transmit hidden messages of which their readers are not always aware (and perhaps not always their writers, either). For example, what is deduced from a book that depicts all Germans as beer-drinking, Volkswagen-driving, and sausage-eating folk? The sexist stereotype has been well and truly exposed by now, so that no one can be unaware of it. Just as pernicious as the stereotype is the book that fails to distinguish fact from opinion: the size and bone structure of dinosaurs are proven fact, but the colour of their skins and the reasons for their extinction are matters for speculation. Even such a title as *All About . . .* may be easily misunderstood, for no book can tell *all* there is to know about a subject; knowledge is infinite.

Knowing the contents of the book in the collection and being ready to discuss these prejudices with children are the only ways of avoiding the kind of pitfall we have been describing.

## 14.3 The organization and deployment of books

In the world of school libraries, the oldest argument has been between those who favour central libraries and those who want classroom collections. It is a pointless argument. The books simply need to be accessible to children wherever they are working and as often as possible, and each school will work out its form of organization accordingly. In some places, this may mean a reservoir of books, mainly reference material, held in some central place; it may be a designated room, a corridor, or a remodelled cloakroom. And if the pool of information books is kept in such a place where children can conveniently work from them, some help will need to be given, perhaps in the form of a subject wall index, so that children can find the books they want.

But we are firmly of the opinion that a school's book policy should require classroom collections of books and book corners wherever it is feasible. If the books are where the children are, answering both their planned and spontaneous needs for reading and for information, then there will probably need to be a central organization of the school's total book stock in order to bring this about. Basic classroom collections are then drawn from this more or less permanently, and this is augmented for as long as required by shorter-term borrowing from the central pool and from such outside sources as schools' and public library services. In any event, no book policy can afford not to establish close links with these services. The Bullock Report says that 'the ebb and flow of books into and out of the collection will be a continuous process',[13] since a collection that never changes from week to week or from term to term is unlikely to keep the children excited about books. Too little change is as bad as too much, and the classroom collection should change since it reflects the changing needs and interests of the children.

However, there may also be a need for a core of books in every classroom collection which is known by the teacher quite intimately, and perhaps by the children, too. This known collection enables connections to be made between children's experience and the books, and between books and other books. For example, when a child brings to school a skull he has found, the teacher will be able to point him to *The Clue Book of Bones*[14] as well as, say, *Hedgehogs*,[15] and then perhaps lead him further to *Mary Anning's Treasure*,[16] one of Gerald Durrell's books, or an account of bone discoveries in an adult book.

Some schools have highly organized libraries in specially designated rooms with complex systems for borrowing books— 'charging', as it is called in public libraries. We are not generally in favour of any system that makes it harder rather than easier for children to get at the books, any more than we are of library 'periods', which, if they are the only times provided, impose limits on children's access to books. Loan systems are meant to cut down losses and enable books to be traced; yet few primary schools are so large that the teacher with overall responsibility for the book policy does not know where most reference books are; and where a policy of free access to books applies without cards and loan tickets, it has been found that losses are negligible.

It is essential, however, that there is a clear organization understood by both teachers and children, so that everyone knows how the books are arranged and dispersed.

Flexibility of organization also raises the question of classifying, cataloguing, and colour-coding. There are at least three ways of colour-coding: by subject, by difficulty, or by the type of material (e.g., book, chart, film, or slide). It does seem sensible to classify books in some way, so that when reference material is returned to the central pool it has a place, and particular books can be found again. The broad subject areas can be colour-coded to help this happen; or a simple number classification such as simplified Dewey can be used, which is consistent with what children will find in public and secondary school libraries. Whatever system is adopted, the children will need to be shown how it works, and it must be simple enough to be understood. Colour-coding books by difficulty is another matter, and will be discussed under the heading of readability.

Colour-coding according to the nature of the material will be unnecessary unless the school has set up a 'resource centre'. The arguments about resource-based learning have already been weighed. There are schools that have developed this kind of work in an imaginative way, but sometimes it can mean that children are left on their own to struggle through 'topic work' that is arid and divorced from any other experiences or activities. It is not then surprising when these children fall back on copying from information books without understanding what they are doing, and under the mistaken impression that they are learning. But if the school has decided to develop its way of working along resource-based lines, then guidance should be sought from advisory staff or publications such as those from the School Library Association.

In good primary schools, teachers have found ways of working in which children are closely involved in genuine enquiries which are rooted in direct experience; they are engaged with the materials, and the information books. Work of this kind has already been described in detail.

We know of a class in which a group of children were studying the trees in the school grounds. They were making and binding their own books, which contained drawings and paintings, many of them careful and detailed and noting changes over a period of time; they had identified the trees and written accounts of their structure, the yearly cycle, and the different properties of the timber and the uses to which it was put.

In the same class, other enquiries were going on at the same time: one group was looking at birds, and because the gulls never stayed still for long enough in the playground, the teacher obtained a stuffed one from the museum and a lively argument occurred about which kind of gull it was, backed up by information books. If the books are organized in the way we have been suggesting, being available at the point of use, this kind of work is more likely to be taking place, with information books being used in a vital way as an integral part of the learning experience.

Unfortunately, some of the work that some children do demands a use of books divorced from anything else, so that the books become a substitute for real experience. Both fiction and information books can constitute real experience if the learning is set up in the right way. An extreme case of the artificiality of book work is quoted by Russell Stauffer:

> A friend of mine, visiting a school, was asked to examine a young class in geography. Glancing at the book she said, 'Suppose you should dig a hole in the ground, hundreds of feet deep, how should you find it at the bottom—warmer or colder than at the top?' None of the class replying, the teacher said, 'I'm sure they know, but you don't ask the question quite rightly. Let me try.' So, taking the book, she asked, 'In what condition is the interior of the globe?' and received the immediate answer from half the class at once, 'The interior of the globe is in a condition of igneous fusion.'[17]

Many teachers group the books about seashells around the collection of shells, the books about fish by the aquarium, and the books about castles next to the children's models and paintings and their photographs of the ones visited. In this way, the children are not placed in the position of possessing information from books that they do not understand. For example, the child who knew that a rodent is 'a small mammal with its front teeth specially adapted for gnawing' may have been working at the level of verbalism, because it later turned out that she could not recognize a rodent when she saw one. Making an attractive display of the books around the classroom and in the book corner, full-frontal as often as possible also helps children to see and follow the kinds of links between books and real knowledge that we have been describing.

**239**

## 14.4 The use of books

It has turned out, of course, that it is impossible to talk about the provision, selection, organization, and deployment of books without saying something at the same time about their use. We have spoken of forging links between books and real things and real experiences, about careful selection of books across all categories, and about bringing books to children in as wide a way as possible, organizing them flexibly so that children have easy access to them at all times.

Children will not learn to find their way about books and to discover what they want to know unless they are shown. The book policy should take account of the fact that book skills will need to be taught. By 'book skills' is meant an understanding of alphabetical ordering; the use of index, contents page, the list of illustrations, the glossary, and bibliography, and the ability to assess whether the contents of a given book will answer the purposes. There are skills that are specific to the use of atlases, such as coordinates for reference, which will probably have been taught during the course of the mathematics programme. Many of these search skills, or study skills, have been discussed in an earlier chapter, and ways in which they can be developed were suggested. They are best learnt in the service of the kind of work described above: children will learn how to use an index because they need to know something, not because they have been given an exercise in it, in the same way that a child learns to ride a bicycle because he wants to get somewhere. The Primary Survey was very clear on this point: 'The teaching of skills in isolation, whether in language or in mathematics, does not produce the best results.'[18]

One important 'study' skill is in using more than one book about a given subject. In the previous chapter there was the example of children comparing *Stig of the Dump* with other stories, particularly *The Hobbit*. By a wise provision, the same activity can be encouraged with information books. A child studying fungi, for example, should have access to more than one book for identification and giving further information. By comparing the books, he may discover that there is disagreement about which ones are edible and which are poisonous. This is an actual example of how fallible books can sometimes be! If the school's book policy lays it down as a principle that books should be used in this way, then the development of comparative and critical reading is encouraged, children will begin to ask their own questions about what they are reading, and they will be able to make the important discovery that books and print are not always right. In other words, they will learn to recognize error and propaganda.

Although books were separated from each other into various categories for the purpose of examining the provision of them, it is probably undesirable that children should be taught to make the same distinctions too soon. It is unfortunate when they categorize fact and fiction too early and too rigidly, usually to the disadvantage of the latter. As we remarked at the beginning of the previous chapter, fact is not the chief business of fiction; but facts can be learned from fiction none the less. For example, an interest in spiders or rabbits would become something wider and more sensitive if a child read *Charlotte's Web*[19] or *Watership Down*.[20] And a study of, say, the Great Fire of 1666 would take on a different perspective if Hester Burton's story of imprisoned Quakers, *Through the Fire*,[21] were to be read. Story seems to give solidity to facts in a remarkable way, 'contextualizing' information and giving it personality so that it becomes something more like knowledge. It is noticeable that during the last two or three years an increasing number of new information books have appeared written in the narrative form.

An earlier chapter has distinguished between three levels of reading— the independent level, the instructional level, and the frustration level—and an indication was given of what these levels actually mean for a reader, and the number of his errors. From the point of view of the book policy, it is now useful to make another three-way distinction—between residual reading, actual reading, and potential reading, an idea first suggested by Jenkinson.[22] The 'residual' has to do with out-grown stages of reading, and these books are the old favourites, comforting like a baby's blanket; the 'actual' derives from the situation in which the child is now, and reflects present abilities, interests, and needs; and the 'potential' is a level of reading that 'suggests what the child is growing into'— say, a slowly awakening interest in polar exploration and Captain Scott's diaries. The child who read Enid Blyton, Asterix, *A Dog So Small*[23] and *Watership Down* all in the same week was reading at all three levels, as readers, in the true sense of the word, must do. The school book policy should accept this fact and allow children to read in this way. Nothing has done more damage to the cause of literacy than the notion that there is a threshold to reading, and that to have passed across this threshold is to have become fully literate, knowing all there is to know about reading. Reading is not like hurdling to the finishing line. As I. A. Richards said in his book, *How to Read a Page*, 'We are all of us learning to read all the time.'[24] If it is true, as we think it is, that adult readers read at a variety of levels and for different purposes and according to mood, then we think the book policy should allow children to do the same. This is one of the ways in which 'a spectacle of reading in action', as Edward Blishen called it, is demonstrated.

It is because of our wish to see reading of these kinds encouraged that we have reservations about the colour-coding of books according to their difficulty, and about programming children through the reading curriculum rung by rung. It may well suggest to children that they should always read a book at the next level of difficulty.

Furthermore, the greater number of 'bands' or levels of difficulty, the narrower each band inevitably becomes, restricting the opportunities for reading widely. This problem of the 'tramline' effect is not avoided even by mixing into each band books from higher and lower bands, but marking all the same code. It still does not allow the developing reader enough scope to make his own choices and to read backwards to *Where the Wild Things Are*[25] and forwards to *The Lord of the Rings*.[26]

There is evidence to suggest that, as children grow older, they spend less time in school reading. It is a sad comment that, after all the effort given to reading instruction, the amount of voluntary reading should decline like this. The importance of browsing and silent reading has probably been underrated in recent years, and the school's book policy will need to recommend practice on both these points.

In a growing number of schools, silent reading is now timetabled and *everyone* reads, not just the children—an old idea writ new. It is not sufficient, in our opinion, that voluntary reading should take place only 'when you have finished your work'; this simply tells children that this is a low-status activity.

The stratification of reading material that colour-coding tends to produce is, then, in our view, undesirable. But it is of paramount importance for the *teacher* to know which books are at what level. One teacher had a card index system on which all the books she used for 'directed' reading were coded according to their difficulty. If she wished to guide a particular child, she would write the titles of some half-a-dozen appropriate books on his book-mark. Of course, the child was also free to read as he pleased. Another school is experimenting with the idea of placing a cloze text inside the cover of its books, drawn from passages within them; the child knows that if he can make sense of the cloze text the book will be within his grasp.

## 14.5 Reading aloud

The importance of reading aloud to children has already been emphasized; the reasons why stories should be read to and by children at the three levels of the residual, the actual, and the potential were fully given in the previous chapter. It introduces them to vocabulary and sentence structures they may not already know, as well as to the language of books and the way stories work—for example, the rule of three, which is ubiquitous in traditional stories. This 'read-aloud' programme also makes accessible to children the books they cannot yet read for themselves. We think that a school's book policy should have something to say on the frequency, timing, and setting of those occasions when stories and poems are read out loud.

In the same way that children seem to read less voluntarily as they grow older, so they seem to be read to less as well. In at least one primary school, however, children of all ages are read to at least *four* times a day, including during assembly times. In other cases, story-time may be one of the few points in the day when the children all come together as a unified group to share in an activity. We think that a class should be read to at least daily, irrespective of age. Traditionally, story-time has always been at the end of the afternoon. There are, of course, good reasons for this: it is a quiet time when everybody comes together at the end of the school day, 'unwinding' before going home. However, it sometimes ends up as a homeward scramble which spoils the occasion; besides, there is a hidden message about the importance given to story if always it comes at the end of the day when everybody is tired. Why is it not at the beginning of the day sometimes, when children and teachers are fresh? In some schools it is always first on the afternoon's programme. Reading poems and stories to children could more often be a group activity, in which the teacher or another adult reads to a group because it happens to be appropriate at that particular moment in their work. In some schools, staff make themselves available in the book corner at certain times of the day, reading aloud books chosen by the children.

Reading aloud to children requires just as much care and preparation as any other classroom activity. The way the reading is to be introduced needs thinking out, as well as how the children are to be grouped. Many teachers like to gather their children

**243**

round them in an informal way so that the setting is a relaxed one. The art of the story-teller and story-reader deserves some study: the use of gesture, intonation, and other voice qualities are significant in effective presentation. It is easier if the reader already knows the story, so that he can look at the audience as well as the book. Generally, we think that teachers should not read stories and poems for their children to which they themselves do not feel committed, because the sharing may not then be a genuine one.

It is often taken for granted, as we have tended to do, that reading aloud to children means reading stories and poems. But there is a powerful case for reading extracts from good information books, and for many of the same reasons. Here is a passage from Leslie Jackman's *The Beach*:

> Suddenly the sea exploded with a jillion silver sparks and I saw why the heron had been fishing there—a living stream of sand eels eddied to and fro, occasionally erupting into a cascade above the surface.
>
> So many were there that the inshore edge of the vast shoal was moving like tinsel on to the beach. For several metres inshore the sand was alive with the movement of their bodies, for sand eels are equally at home wriggling through the sand or swimming freely in the sea.
>
> Perhaps this was a mating assembly, but whatever it was their numbers were out of this world. Maybe a million, maybe three million. . . .
>
> After a while I moved on; my last sight of them was a wave, clogged with silver.[27]

Quite apart from the language and the facts of natural science here, there is an important discussion point about the numbers required for the survival of a species.

Sometimes reading aloud means reading an extract for a special reason, because the teacher wants to give the children a taster or to leave the story at a cliff-hanging point. It may, of course, be a short story from an anthology. But it would be quite wrong if the children never heard the whole of, say, *The Lion, the Witch and the Wardrobe*;[28] books should not *always* be left unfinished.

## 14.6 Picture books

Picture books are a special category of book calling for some special consideration. Many of the more noted picture books invite child and adult to share and to explore an experience in terms of word language and visual imagery, and the teacher therefore has an important part to play in 'mediating' picture books to children.

Not only do children learn to 'read' the pictures; for some, these books are their first sight of how stories are put together and shaped inside books.

Wanda Gag's *Millions of Cats*[29] is an example of a picture book in which text and illustrations flow continuously together; the pictures have a refrain, the gnomish old man wandering along winding roads and followed by a growing procession of cats, which is matched by the refrain in the text of 'millions and billions and trillions of cats'. A book like *How a House Happens* by Jan Adkins[30] is quite different; here, clear pictures and simple statements are closely interwoven. Other books also take care to be authentic, like Edward Ardizzone's pictures for *Dick Whittington*,[31] or Barbara Cooney's *The Little Juggler*,[32] which captures the style of the illuminated manuscript. Traditional folk art is adapted in other books, such as McDermott's *Maui and the Big Fish*,[33] while still others have pictures with a strong tactile quality—Carol Barker's *King Midas*[34] is an outstanding example.

Picture books offer to many children their first experience of quality art, and they can provide special satisfaction in terms of visual stimulus, response to texture, the power of the story itself, and the emotional life of the child. The point we wish to make here, as forcefully as we can, is that children should not be given the idea that picture books are only for younger children, and that by the age of nine they should have outgrown them. Some children, of course, use information books like Bernard Brett's *Captain Cook*[35] or the textless *The Story of an English Village*[36] as they would a picture book.

One reason why children may come to give up picture books is that they have been given them too early and have failed to understand them. The work of Charles Keeping was mentioned in the previous chapter: his books are powerful experiences, and may not best be met at the age of five, or six or even seven. The picture books by Pat Hutchins, although many of them are now Picture Puffins, are also quite complicated: *Clocks and More Clocks* and *Tom and Sam*[37] are examples where the concepts are not as simple as might be expected, and so these are books that need talking about.

It is therefore our view that older children need picture books no less than the younger ones, and that the teacher should ensure they do not grow out of them. What is the right age, for example, for meeting the Lowry-like pictures of Helen Bradley's *And Miss Carter Wore Pink*,[38] an evocation of an Edwardian childhood?

## 14.7 Poetry

We may have appeared to have neglected poetry more than we should, although the provision of appropriate poetry books was discussed earlier. We are certainly anxious that the book policy should provide poetry of all kinds and find ways of encouraging the reading of it. We think that much of this work will be oral; because poetry, above all else, demands to be shared through reading aloud. Many children have a natural ability to write poetry, and what they write themselves ought to find a place in the reading of it, too.

Once, school timetables included a poetry period. The Bullock Report argued succinctly that poetry works best when it is needed, not when the timetable decrees it. As the authors of *Reading Matters* say, 'The problem is how to present poetry in a relaxed, confident and pleasurable manner so that it is neither intellectually frightening nor emotionally sloppy.'[39] The work of poets like Michael Rosen should certainly dispel these fears:

> I'm the youngest in our house
> so it goes like this:
> My brother comes in and says:
> 'Tell him to clear the fluff
> out from under his bed.'
> Mum says,
> 'Clear the fluff out
> from under your bed.'
> Father says,
> 'You heard what your mother said.'
> 'What?' I say,
> 'The fluff,' he says.
> 'Clear the fluff out from under your bed.'[40]

## 14.8 Readability

Readability has to do with matching children and books. By using various formulae, which usually measure length of words and length of sentences, an assessment of reading level can be made. It must be clear, however, that formulae can measure only a small part of all those factors governing readability. Eric Carle's *The Very Hungry Caterpillar*[41] and Alan Garner's *The Stone Book*[42] both have the same readability levels, as measured by a graph; but no one could suppose that these two books are of equal difficulty.

The unmeasurable factors within the text include such matters as print, layout (line-breaks in early readers sometimes come in quite the wrong places), language structures, and concepts.

Anthologies are expecially difficult to assess because the readability levels are not constant throughout. Then there are the factors within the reader that are unknown to the formula, such as motivation, previous knowledge, and perseverance.

Because readability formulae measure word and sentence length, it is sometimes supposed that, by shortening the words and the sentences, the text can be made easier to read. But this is not always so. Simplifying a text may reduce the amount of 'redundancy' so that the reader cannot predict so much, with the result that the text becomes harder to read. That is to say, by simplifying a text there are fewer words a reader does not have to recognize; so he has to pay much closer attention to the words that are there, and those words have to carry the full load of information.

Enough is now understood about the process of reading to make it clear that reading a text whose meaning is compressed into as few words as possible is a hard task, and that reading as if every word is crucial to meaning is inefficient reading. Of course, it has always been known that reading a 'dense' text is harder than reading a light one. Furthermore, simplifying a text may mean making the information more general and less specific, in which case the conceptual level may rise. A simplified explanation may not even be the right one. Teachers need to be on their guard and to look carefully at any modified text to see that it is not distorted so as to be either ambiguous or downright misleading.

It has been found that teachers' subjective assessments of the readability levels of books are usually fairly accurate. If these intuitive judgements are backed up by a close knowledge of the books in the collection and a similarly close knowledge of the children, then there seems no good reason for using readability formulae except as an occasional check. The simplest way of finding out if a book is within a certain child's grasp is to see if he can read it. If a child of known reading ability can read a given book, then that book should lie within the reach of children with a similar reading ability.

Matching children and books by using readability measures also requires knowing the children's reading age. Enough has already been said on this topic (see page 35) to show that this is also very hard to quantify. It seems unjust, therefore, to direct children's reading on such crude evidence as reading age and readability levels. Some schools have used children's own book reviews as a guide, although writing these reviews should never become a penance. In other cases, a sheet is fixed inside the back cover of the books, and readers are invited to make brief comments to help later readers.

## 14.9 Ownership of books

Owning books is tightly related to reading them, and it is an aspect of the provision a school makes. Shops where children's books of quality can be seen and purchased are not always easily reached, and many schools have therefore set up book clubs and shops themselves. One of the disadvantages of some book clubs is that the books cannot be seen and handled before ordering for purchase. School bookshops are of two kinds: the sale that takes place at certain times, termly or annually, such as parents' meetings or before Christmas; and the shop that is open on a regular basis during school time and perhaps outside normal school hours for whole family visits. Staff take time and trouble to talk with children and parents about the books on sale and, perhaps, to recommend likely ones. This seems to be yet another demonstration of 'a spectacle of reading in action' to which we referred previously. The School Bookshop Association, in addition to its own journal featuring children's books and articles about them, offers advice on setting up school bookshops and how to obtain a licence.

Where a major effort of this kind has been made, teachers have noticed that children's attitudes towards books and reading have undergone a change for the better.

We are not suggesting that simply exposing children to books will make them 'catch reading' like a kind of measles. The school must, of course, cause more positive things to happen— introducing the actual books to children; reading books to them and discussing books with them; according a high status to reading for pleasure as well as for instruction throughout the work of the school; guiding children's choice of reading material; and teaching them how to make optimum use of books.

Another decision within the school book policy relates to home borrowing: are children allowed to take books home? We think the policy should declare in favour of this. Some teachers have been worried about damage to books or the loss of them; others feel that whoever keeps a book must want it, and therefore the book must be doing some good. If children are to use books freely, then loss and damage is a part of the price. Some schools have set up special collections, sometimes of paperbacks, for home borrowing; and these books are not just those cast out of the school's main collection because they have seen better days.

## 14.10 Staff collection

Many of the ideas we have suggested in relation to school book collections for children—the provision, selection, organization, deployment and use of the books—will also apply to the collection for the staff. Sometimes, the process by which these collections have grown is even more markedly one of random accretion.

There should be a selection of books about primary work in general and about all areas of primary curriculum in particular, including the manuals of any reading schemes used in the school. The collection ought to include official reports on education and surveys such as Plowden and Bullock Reports and *Primary Education in England*; and books that act as resources for ideas in all areas of the curriculum, such as *Science 5–13* and the Nuffield Guides. There will almost certainly be links between the policy documents worked out for all areas of the curriculum and the books in the staff room collection.

However, teachers do not always know what books are in their collection. Within the field of the book policy, such steps as directed reading by staff and reporting back at staff meetings will probably have to be taken, in order to make sure that new books introduced into the collection are known and the existing stock reviewed from time to time as staff change.

## 14.11 Conclusion

It has been our contention in this chapter that, in framing its book policy, a school needs to consider the provision and the organization of *all* kinds of books throughout, and the uses of them that are to be encouraged. If this takes place along the lines suggested, we believe that teachers' aspirations for their children— that reading should become a pleasure and a resource for life—will become a reality.

## References

Books marked with an asterisk are for teachers; books not marked are for children and teachers.

*1. *A Language for Life* (the Bullock Report), HMSO, 1975.
2. *Primary Education in England, A Survey by HM Inspectors of Schools*, HMSO, 1978.
*3. The Bullock Report.
4. *The Guinness Book of Records*, Guinness Superlatives, 1977.
5. SPIERS, PETER, *London Bridge is Falling Down*, World's Work, 1968.
6. TUCKER, NICHOLAS, *Mother Goose Lost*, Puffin, 1974.

7. BROWNING, ROBERT, *The Pied Piper of Hamelin,* Warne, 1889.

8. CAUSLEY, CHARLES, *Collected Poems,* Macmillan, 1975.

9. ROSEN, MICHAEL, *Mind Your Own Business,* Collins, Armada Lion, 1975.

10. SUMMERFIELD, GEOFFREY, *Junior Voices,* Puffin, 1970.

11. JACKSON, DAVID and PEPPER, DENNIS, *Storyhouses,* Oxford University Press, 1976.

12. MABEY, RICHARD, *Street Flowers,* Kestrel, 1976.

*13. The Bullock Report.

14. GWEN, A. and DENSLOW, J., *The Clue Book of Bones,* Oxford University Press, 1968.

15. WHITLOCK, RALPH, *Hedgehogs,* Priory Press, 1974.

16. BUSH, HELEN, *Mary Anning's Treasure,* Gollancz, 1969.

*17. STAUFFER, RUSSELL, *Teaching Reading as a Thinking Process,* Harper & Row, 1969.

*18. *Primary Education in England.*

19. WHITE, E. B., *Charlotte's Web,* Puffin, 1969.

20. ADAMS, RICHARD, *Watership Down,* Puffin, 1973.

21. BURTON, HESTER, *Through the Fire,* Hamish Hamilton, 1969.

*22. JENKINSON, A., *What Do Boys and Girls Read?,* Methuen, 1940 (O/P).

23. PEARCE, PHILLIPA, *A Dog So Small,* Puffin, 1970.

*24. RICHARDS, I. A., *How to Read a Page,* Routledge & Kegan Paul, 1943 (O/P).

25. SENDAK, MAURICE, *Where the Wild Things Are,* Puffin, 1970.

26. TOLKIEN, J. R. R., *The Lord of the Rings,* Allen & Unwin, 1969.

27. JACKMAN, LESLIE, *The Beach,* Evans Brothers, 1975.

28. LEWIS, C. S., *The Lion, the Witch and the Wardrobe,* Puffin, 1970.

29. GAG, WANDA, *Millions of Cats,* Faber, 1929.

30. ADKINS, JAN, *How a House Happens,* Walker, New York.

31. LINES, K., *Dick Whittington,* Bodley Head, 1970

32. COONEY, BARBARA, *The Little Juggler,* Constable, 1964.

33. MCDERMOTT, K., *Maui and the Big Fish,* Hamish Hamilton.

34. BARKER, CAROL, *King Midas,* Watts, 1972.

35. BRETT, BERNARD, *Captain Cook,* Macmillan, 1970.

35. BRETT, BERNARD, *Captain Cook,* Macmillan, 0000.

36. GOODALL, JOHN, *The Story of an English Village,* Macmillan, 1978.

37. HUTCHINS, PAT, *Clocks and More Clocks; Tom and Sam,* Bodley Head, 1970.

38. BRADLEY, HELEN, *And Miss Carter Wore Pink,* Jonathan Cape, 1971.

*39. MCKENZIE, MOIRA and WARLOW, AIDAN, *Reading Matters,* Hodder & Stoughton, 1977.
40. ROSEN, MICHAEL, *Wouldn't You Like to Know,* André Deutsch, 1977.
41. CARLE, ERIC, *The Very Hungry Caterpillar,* Puffin, 1974.
42. GARNER, ALAN, *The Stone Book,* Collins, 1976.

## Suggested reading and sources of information

CHAMBERS, A., *Introducing Books to Children,* Heinemann, 1973. A common-sense view of story-telling and story-reading; how to use the library; and how to set up a school bookshop (see below). This answers the problems of how to get children hooked on books and how to keep them that way by letting them read hungrily.

MCKENZIE, M. and WARLOW, A., *Reading Matters,* Hodder & Stoughton, 1977. An immensely practical account of how to select and use books in primary school classroom collections, with many children's books cited to support the arguments. Particular sections cover picture books, fiction, poetry, non-fiction, and other materials. There is no better account of the considerations that lie behind a school book policy.

National Book League, Book House, West Hill Road, Wandsworth, London S.W.18. The NBL has an information service, permanent and travelling exhibitions, and publish many annotated booklists. The children's book officer offers advice and information.

School Bookshop Association, 1 Effingham Road, Lee, London, SE12 8N2. The school bookshop officer will supply information about the Association, including which local booksellers will be willing to help. The Association has a travelling exhibition and issues its own journal, *School Bookshop News.*

School Library Association, Victoria House, 29–31 George Street, Oxford OX1 2AY. As well as local groups holding meetings to discuss common concerns, the Association's journal, the *School Librarian,* carries a large and respected review section. Annotated booklists are published, as well as other publications about school resource centres.

*Recent Children's Fiction,* County of Avon Education Department, (ASA/1GB), PO Box 57, Avon House North, St James, Barton, Bristol BS99 7EB.

# 15. Building a school language policy

A language policy means, ultimately, looking at how language affects learning throughout the curriculum. It embraces speaking, listening, reading, and writing; the sort of stimuli teachers provide and the sort of questions they ask; the books available and how they are organized; the style of handwriting; how spelling is taught; and so on. A language policy must contain a reading policy and a book policy, and must look at the range of writing children are given to do. It is concerned with much more than language itself and extends to the way language develops a child's capacity to think, to reason, and to express his meanings clearly and appropriately.

Chapter 1 of this book gives the basis for the thinking that lies behind the subsequent chapters, which are concerned to give examples of good practice based on wide experience and knowledge. These chapters do not present prescriptions for easy success, and they are in no sense packages to be copied. They are intended to illustrate thinking on different aspects of the organization of language and literacy in the pre-secondary years. They are also intended to provide starting points and comparisons which will generate ideas in the minds of the readers of this book. These ideas will be effective only if each teacher makes them relevant to his or her own individual circumstances and own special environment.

Each school's policy will arise from that school's own particular needs, decided by its catchment area, its size, the outlook and insights of its staff, the attitudes of the parents, and the interests of its head teacher. The policy will grow out of discussion among the staff and will develop and change as individual teachers increase their ability to observe children's language, try out and extend their skills of developing language, collect for themselves examples of language for discussion and comparison, and experiment with organization, materials, and methods.

The policy will need to be written down, in sections, following careful discussion and after a certain measure of agreement has been reached. It is advisable to set any conclusions down in looseleaf form so that they can be easily revised as corporate wisdom develops. A policy will be different in detail from that of neighbouring schools and will involve a great deal of thought, exchange of views, pooling of good practice, and greater awareness of what is happening inside the school between each teacher and the children in his or her care.

Like many all-embracing things, a language policy has to be subdivided and its parts considered separately as well as each part being firmly related to the whole. It is at this point that priorities establish themselves. The basic mode of language is the spoken form. It can be argued that this is so important to the development of all other modes that, unless attention is given to it, none of the others, whether reading, writing, or listening, is likely to develop in depth; that the key to quality and effectiveness in both learning and the formal language skills lies in attention being given to the development of spoken language.

The spoken form is a convenient starting point because it is the form to which the greatest lip-service is given and where the gap between pretension and practice is most marked. It is the form that is least understood and most neglected in the classroom. We can see why this is so and sympathize with teachers in their neglect of it. Given the size of most classes, spoken language is difficult to control, difficult to measure, and difficult to organize, and there is no visible product to demonstrate that teaching and learning have been effected. When only one adult is available and there are 30 or more children, any difficulties are compounded. Yet a serious attempt to come to terms with this issue is an essential part of any language policy.

A reading and writing policy derives from a policy for developing spoken language; the most important resource in implementing these policies is the professional skill of the teacher, yet the effectiveness of that professional skill is likely to be diminished unless all three policies are underpinned by the carefully planned provision and availability of books and other print material.

Below we set out a series of headings that present a structure for discussions leading to such a language policy.

## 15.1 A checklist to help in planning

1. A policy for developing talking and listening (see Chapters 2, 5, and 6). Consider:
   (a) Opportunities for talk/discussion in those areas of the curriculum strong in first-hand experience, e.g., science/exploration of the environment, art and craft, use of materials, music and drama/movement.
   (b) Opportunities for talk/discussion arising from literature, poetry, history, religious education, geography.

(c) Special opportunities for presenting language, e.g., daily reading to the class, assemblies, listening times, presentations at the end of a project; or for practising language, e.g., poetry, rhymes, songs and jingles, using tape-recorders, drama.

(d) The teacher's understanding of the notion of functions of language and the formulation of a simple checklist of the more obvious functions as a guide to observation and analysis (see Chapters 2 and 11).

(e) Strategies teachers could use, for instance different types of questions (see Chapter 2).

2. A statement, carefully discussed and agreed, on the links between spoken language and reading/writing, showing the school's view regarding the use of children's talk and early writing as a basis for beginning reading and listing published materials that help to bridge any gaps (see Chapter 3).

3. A policy for reading, which would lead from 2 above to consider:

(a) alternative approaches to suit differing individual needs;

(b) the provision and organization of materials to provide for these alternative approaches;

(c) the advice and help available for those children whose needs are not met by planning under (a) and (b);

(d) the development and extension of reading, e.g.,
   (i) use of information books;
   (ii) use of dictionaries and encyclopedias;
   (iii) use of indexes, contents pages;
   (iv) how to summarize and make notes;
   (v) skimming/scanning/etc.

(See chapters 8 and 9 for a more complete list).

4. A policy for developing children's written language (see Chapters 6 and 7).

This last item must include recognition that writing and speech are so closely interwoven that without good spoken language development the school cannot expect fluency in writing. The richer the child's oral language contribution and development, the richer and more interesting his writing should be.

Handwriting is a skill that does require specific teaching, and suggestions and ideas could be included in the policy document as well as statements that draw attention to the dependence on a degree of co-ordination and motor control, and the frustration caused if a child is expected to master this skill too early.

Attention should be drawn to the quality of objectivity in writing, for it can be reviewed, returned to, and refined at leisure after the event. It helps children to form concepts and ideas, and this is its heuristic function. It is also a social activity and is therefore rooted in a desire to express the self.

If it is to have meaning and be effective children must see a specific purpose for the activity. All too often we find children are expected to write about something completely outside their experience—'A day in the life of a film star', for instance—and it must be stressed that this kind of exercise will lead to shallow, expressionless stuff. The Primary Survey says: 'The extent to which children were required to produce work set by teachers but not arising from other work or personal interests suggests that much less writing arose from pupils' own choice than is sometimes supposed.'[1]

It is vital that we should allow children to use language for their own purposes. In writing, the child is generally sharing his experience with an imaginary listener. The ebb and flow of personal experience is caught in the process of writing and helps a child to bring order into his world

5. Margaret Clarke, in her book *Young Fluent Readers*,[2] found that the book provision for children who could already read well when they started school at five was often inadequate. The work of both Frank Whitehead *et al.*, in *Childrens' Reading Interests*,[3] and James Maxwell, in *Reading Progress from 8 to 15*,[4] indicated a correlation between the availability of books and the amount of reading undertaken. James Maxwell's survey also showed a strong relationship between school activities and the stimulus to out-of-school reading. The carefully planned provision of books is an essential underpinning to all the steps so far suggested as part of a language policy. Chapters 13 and 14 above, as well as the books of Frank Whitehead and James Maxwell, give much background information for the successful planning of such provision, which requires a carefully thought out policy for the selection, buying, and organization of books.

6. There must be a policy for involving parents practically in the school language programme. We must consider how they can be encouraged to use talk more effectively in the home, to provide a richer background for reading, and to take a greater interest in their children's reading and writing. Has the school used the interest and skill already there in the children's homes? How can parents and other members of the community be used to help to extend the children's language skills?

The above headings and questions provide an overall structure and pattern for our thinking within which further aspects of language can be considered. When these have been thoroughly explored each individual must ask herself which are the most appropriate steps to be considered next. A further list could cover the school's policy for handwriting (see Chapter 7), and for the teaching of spelling (see Chapter 7); how visits are organized and what specific value they have for language development; whether there is a written 'guide' to help children in their projects (see Chapter 8); how children's written work is presented and given value and appreciation (see Chapter 7); how tape-recorders are used and whether their value in extending opportunities for spoken language is exploited; and whether assemblies and 'listening times' are used to extend language opportunities.

In developing a language policy we should make sure that we can walk before we try to run. Its development is likely to be a slow process, and one headmistress whose school already had a reputation for its well-thought-out work in language found that it took her three years before she could produce a considered statement arising from careful discussion with her staff which approximated to the main headings suggested in this chapter. To these she added a section on continuity with the stages of education both below and above.

The danger of a *reading* policy becoming a substitute for a *language* policy is a real one and implies a lack of understanding of the place of language in intellectual development. It remains crucial to a good language policy however, that reading is thoroughly and systematically considered. The following checklist, as with the headings set out on pages 253–55 for a language policy, is designed to give a structure for discussion and to encourage the asking of the right questions, even though the answers may be difficult to find.

## 15.2 A checklist leading towards a reading policy for a school

Five preliminary points need to be made:

1. There is no one way of teaching reading: different groups of children or different individuals need different pathways. The teacher's knowledge and his/her repertoire of approaches and skills needs to be wide and the materials available need to be both plentiful and varied.
2. The best language for beginning reading is language near the

child's own natural speech patterns: thus he is able to use two sets of clues—those from the decoding skills of shape/sound recognition, and those from his knowledge of context and sequence.

3. For the child in difficulties the reading process is a very complex one. In the past it has generally been taught as a mechanical process when it is predominantly a thinking process. Chapter 6 of the Bullock Report sets out to show its complexity and to point to the dangers of having a simplistic view, for example in the teaching of phonics

4. Evidence shows that planning and system in the teaching of reading are important. However, the structure of this planning does not come from adherence to a narrow scheme. It comes first from the teacher's *knowledge* of the process and *understanding* of the alternative pathways to success, second from records of individual progress and the occasional use of checklists which ensure that a child's weaknesses are noted and attention given to them, and third from the broad sequencing of the materials available.

5. For most children the teaching of reading stops at seven years when they reach the end of the first school reading schemes: thereafter they are taught reading only if they find themselves in a remedial group. The post-initial skills of reading, which are closely linked to study skills, need to be developed as a high priority, especially in the junior and middle years.

### Early reading

1. Has the school a language policy? (Bullock: Principal Recommendation 4). What range of spoken language does it encourage? What activities are planned to encourage a wide range of language use, and do these include the use of play in the early years?

2. What materials, collections, and displays are available, and what range of activities is offered that will provide the basis for a rich vocabulary and range of use?

3. Has the school considered involving the parents, e.g., by lending them books for reading to the children at home, or by advising parents of preschool children about what to read to them?

4. Is any use made of the children's own spoken/written language in the teaching of reading?

5. Is the fact that there is no *one* way of teaching reading reflected in the reading materials available? Is there one scheme or a variety of schemes? Are only the best parts of some schemes incorporated? Are the schemes/parts of schemes coded to get comparability of levels?

   A very experienced group of teachers may be able to dispense with formal schemes by devising their own progressions through the use of 'real' books and their children's own writing.

6. If language near a child's own natural speech patterns is some of the easiest material on which to learn, does the early written material available satisfy this requirement?

7. Many children never understand that 'print' means 'message'. What opportunities do the children have for establishing this principle—in their homes? in school? Do we use the signs, notices, advertisements, and posters that surround them? Is a range of interesting 'real' books as opposed to readers, primers, and supplementaries available in each classroom? Are the children read to from these and other sources daily?

8. How are letter shapes introduced? Is care taken that the position in space of each letter is made clear, for instance by marking the base? Do children know the letter names, and is there a school policy with regard to this?

9. The Bullock Report (Chapter 6) emphasizes both the importance of phonics and the danger of a simplistic view of the relationship between shape and sound. How are phonics to be taught context? Have sounds any meaning if they *are* taught out of context? Is there a school policy on the place of phonics?

### Reading beyond early years

1. A school needs to pursue its policy for continuing reading after children have left the infants or first school stage. Chapter 3 suggests that, as well as the early skills of decoding and simple reading for meaning, the more complex skills need considering from the early years. Chapter 8 suggests that these skills must be developed and extended throughout the junior and middle years.

2. How can reading be treated as a thinking process? A school must consider how children tackle different reading tasks, for example looking for facts in an information book compared with reading instructions or reading a narrative. Are children encouraged to use the various contextual clues in a text?

3. Frequent opportunities for using reference material are often given to children in the junior and middle school years. However, the skills they need to make full use of these opportunities are often neither analysed nor taught. Chapters 8 and 9 consider these skills in detail.

4. It is often assumed that the making of systematic notes develops naturally from opportunities to collect information from books. In our view this is an incorrect assumption. Children need 'on-the-job' instruction in making notes from different sources and discussion on how these notes can be synthesized into a final statement.

5. Different subject areas make different demands on reading skills. The demands of mathematics need consideration from the early years. In the middle years, where the use of textbooks becomes more frequent, readability levels need special consideration.

### The reading environment

1. We need to make a survey of the availability as well as the range of books in our schools. What sorts of books are available in each classroom? Which are more appropriate for shared spaces? We need to look very carefully at the *actual* availability of books kept in a central collection and consider how many children use them, how often, and for how long.

2. In many classrooms or shared spaces teachers have made great efforts to ensure that a good range of information books is available, but often fail to provide much fiction and poetry. Chapters 13 and 14 give information that should help to get this balance right.

3. In what ways does the school demonstrate that it values reading? Is there a permanent, easily accessible, display of books? Are there short-term displays? Are displays of books related to projects and/or topical events? Is reading part of assemblies? Are older children encouraged to read to younger children? Are special occasions set aside for children to talk about books they have read? Are there books clubs?

Is the public library visited, and are children encouraged to become members? Is the librarian invited to the school?

The Bullock Report made this statement: 'If there is one general summarising conclusion we offer it is that there is nothing to equal in importance the quality and achievement of the individual teacher to whom most of our suggestions are addressed.'[5] The recent study, *Fifteen Thousand Hours,* by Michael Rutter and others,[6] which looked at the factors making for success in a group of inner-city secondary schools, gave further evidence that more than buildings, equipment, or systems— or even class size—in the end, there is no substitute for a good teacher. It is the teacher's own knowledge of language and repertoire of skills and approaches combined with her knowledge of children, attitudes to individuals, and willingness to consider her teaching in depth, that is fundamental to the success of any language policy.

A teacher needs to know how to listen and what to listen for, and to develop greater skills in dialogue with individuals and small groups so that children's ability to think things through is developed. These are new skills which traditionally have not been required. A teacher also needs to find opportunities for widening the range of uses of language, whether in talk, reading, or writing, which a child has at his command, and to extend and develop a child's language without destroying his confidence or rejecting the language he has already acquired. Making reading a process with a real sense of purpose and widening range of uses, developing a child's capacity to organize and present information, and acquiring a knowledge of literature that will stimulate and extend her children's understanding are other aspects of a teacher's growing personal resource.

All teachers, and not just those with generalist responsibilities, need some understanding of how language works, both at an individual level and as a means of communication in the home, classroom, or society. This is true also of subject specialists where specialist vocabulary and assumptions in using language may seriously hinder possibilities of learning.

If a teacher's personal knowlege and professional competence are to be nourished, then the nature of the responsibility for language within the school has to be considered. The Bullock Report recommended that every school should have a suitably qualified teacher with responsibility for advising and supporting her colleagues in language and the teaching of reading. This teacher may also guide her colleagues by keeping them well informed about courses that are currently available, worth while, and suitable. She needs to keep up to date about books, resources, and materials, and in so doing will need the assistance of other members of staff, for the task is almost impossible alone. The organization of help for reprographics, whether through the school system or by parents; the development of storage and retrieval systems; and the distribution of equipment and visual aids may also be areas where she could play an influential role.

On a possibly more important level she ought to have some overall responsibility for purchase of books, for grading and interlinking reading schemes and text books, and for ensuring that a just balance of reference books and good fiction is readily available. A large school might well have a librarian; if so, her task is lessened, if not, then this area, too, falls within the jurisdiction of the teacher with the language responsibility post. And, of course, she must draw up the first draft of a working document – the school's language policy.

But we need to go further than this. There must be real authority behind the language policy if it is to be effective; this means the authority of the head teacher in a small school, or the head or deputy in a larger school, backing and giving force to the policy as a whole and strengthening those who have specific responsibilities for making it effective.

This authority should ensure opportunities for considering language, some of which might be: meetings of staff to discuss language matters; organization to enable staff to pool knowledge and encourage the sharing of good practice; staff of different year groups or upper and lower parts of the school meeting separately to consider common problems and the best use of common resources; staff who have undertaken in-service training being given support and opportunities to use their additional knowledge.

The following questions need to be asked:

1. Has the school considered the use of an 'occasional day' holiday for having an in-service conference for all staff free from everyday pressures to consider together aspects of language?
2. Is a teachers' centre, residential centre, college of education, or some other suitable place available for such a conference?
3. If not, is it possible to organize such a conference more modestly in the school?
4. Will the LEA give help for such in-service training?
5. Can the local college of education provide resources and help free of charge for such a venture?

In one school the head teacher taped spoken language between groups of children and these were used for analysis and group discussion. In another a 'language file' was put in the staff room and teachers wrote up interesting examples of language and described topics or activities that seemed to have produced opportunities for good language. The file was used as a basis for staff discussion as well as a useful source of comparison and ideas. In another school, discussion led to a concentrated look at what was actually happening in school: what sort of reading was actually taking place in the juniors; what opportunities there were for sustained reading (or whether most reading was in response to questions and instructions and of a very brief duration); and whether the extension skills, discussed in Chapters 8 and 9, were being developed. The school then went on to consider how much reading was encouraged out of school, how much time the class teacher had to listen to reading aloud, whether ouside help could be brought in to act as a sympathetic audience, whether good models were read to the children, and how much literature and poetry was introduced in the course of a term. From such starting points a much wider awareness of language possibilities arose.

There has been much discussion nationally about the core curriculum, and some of this discussion has been curiously backward-looking, as if our response to the demands and stresses of an increasingly technological society was a return to the safety of curriculum and content rather than an attempt to define and develop those processes which may be of equal, if not greater, significance. One of these core processes of education and a central thread of the curriculum is language; but language as it relates to experience, and used both transactionally and expressively in a wide variety of ways. In one sense it does not matter which areas of the curriculum provide the main impulse and motivation for this language: the important thing is the thinking and reasoning skills that are developed and the opportunities for formulation and expressive use that are provided.

This takes us back to the arguments outlined in Chapter 1 and developed throughout this book. It is not in a balanced curriculum, in the sense of doing a bit of everything, that real development lies, but in opportunities for children to formulate their impressions, to observe detail, to compare and generalize from first hand experience, to perceive relationships, to see alternatives and probabilities and predict what might happen, to enter imaginatively into another person's point of view, and to create small worlds in the imagination.

At any one time in the classroom the major experience underpinning this development may be based on an exploration of the environment in a way that is both scientific in its approach, observation, and analysis, and expressive in the work it gives rise to. At another time, the major experience may arise from the use of materials in art and craft or the use of literature or drama or from the exploration of an historical or geographical topic.

Two classrooms illustrate this emphasis. One was at the top end of a small infant school, near the pit stacks of the old West Riding, where the combination of materials used and an exploration of the environment gave magnificently realized opportunities for the development of language in a way that was both vividly expressive and observationally acute. In the other class, a curriculum based on natural history closely observed and recorded in drawing, painting, and stitching, from which the children's capacities were extended through the use of books and developed through talk, led into a wide range of observational and imaginative language/thinking skills with a high degree of intellectual sophistication.

In both cases the curriculum was not strictly speaking a balanced one, in the formal sense, but the areas providing the chief motivation for learning gave all that was needed for a striking quality of intellectual development in children. In most schools an approximate overall balance in the curriculum can be achieved by arranging for a teacher with one set of enthusiasms and a bias of knowledge to be followed by a teacher with different abilities and interests in a subsequent year.

A school needs to remember that it cannot do everything well or put resources and energies equally into all curriculum areas. Priorities are essential, and the advantage of language, as we have interpreted it, being seen as the first priority is that the curriculum strengths of a teaching staff can be used to the full to provide the basic experience from which language can emerge.

In so doing, it will develop and heighten children's capacity to respond both to the imaginative possibilities of living and to the day-to-day transactions that are part of life in a technological age where instructions, interpretation, information, forms, and figures, as well as the blandishments of the media, form part of an increasingly exacting environment.

Language thus acts as the mediator of intellectual and social development and as the basis of those formal skills of communication, reading, and writing that are essential to competence in living in a sophisticated society. It also acts as the basis for developing those social skills of ease of communication which make for emotional satisfaction.

In our view, all children have a potential for using language, which can best be developed through talk arising from the children's own experiences. It follows that a classroom should be organized to provide experiences that give wide and stimulating opportunities for such talk.

An essential part of this development of language lies in interaction with an understanding adult who has the skill of involving children in a dialogue that extends the children's way of thinking, and in interaction with other children about topics and problems that challenge them intellectually. The child's established basis of talk then acts as a foundation that underpins and supports the skills of reading and writing. We emphasize this relationship because it seems to us such an important one.

Much of this book is concerned with sources of knowledge and examples of practice which will enable a teacher to plan and intervene effectively in the development of reading and writing skills. We believe that the potential of children in these skills is, far too frequently, left unexplored and undeveloped, either because the place of dialogue and the development of talk is misunderstood or because it is assumed that schemes, packages, and exercises, in whatever disguised form, will provide the necessary stimulus and depth.

Our view is based on observation of children and is concerned with the development of their potential as individuals. Education based on extending first hand experience, which is channelled into intellectual and social development through the systematic use of language in a way that is both highly exploratory but at the same time carefully structured by the teacher's knowledge of possibilities and organization of opportunities, has been tried only modestly in the past. Much of the knowledge and some of the skills and insights teachers need for such teaching are comparatively new.

We have tried to provide access to this knowledge and to these skills and insights in the hope that, through them, children may be educated, in some small measure, with greater understanding.

## References

1. *Primary Education in England, A Survey by HM Inspectors of Schools*, HMSO, 1979.
2. CLARKE, MARGARET, *Young Fluent Readers*, Heinemann Educational, 1976, p. 4, no. 5.
3. WHITEHEAD, FRANK, CAPEY, A. C., and MADDREN, WENDY, *Children's Reading Interests*, Evans/Methuen Educational, 1975.
4. MAXWELL JAMES, *Reading Progress from 8 to 15*, NFER, 1977.
5. *A Language for Life* (the Bullock Report), HMSO, 1975.
6. RUTTER, M., MAUGHAN, B., MORTIMORE, P., and OUSTON, J., *Fifteen Thousand Hours*, Open Books, 1979.

# Index

# INDEX

Printed and bound in Great Britain by
Hartnoll Ltd Bodmin Cornwall